Erdoğan's Civil Death Project

Persecution of the Hizmet Movement in Türkiye

James C. Harrington & Coşkun Yorulmaz

28 27 26 25 1 2 3 4

Published by Blue Dome Press
335 Clifton Ave.
Clifton, NJ, 07011, USA
www.bluedomepress.com

ISBN
Paperback: 978-1-68206-045-2
Ebook: 978-1-68206-542-6

Library of Congress Cataloging-in-Publication Data

Names: Harrington, James C., 1946- author | Yorulmaz, Coşkun author
Title: Erdoğan's civil death project : persecution of the Hizmet movement in Türkiye / James C. Harrington & Coşkun Yorulmaz.
Description: Clifton, NJ, USA : Blue Dome, [2025] | Includes index.
Identifiers: LCCN 2025034734 | ISBN 9781682060452 paperback | ISBN 9781682065426 ebook
Subjects: LCSH: Gülen Hizmet Movement | Erdoğan, Recep Tayyip--Political and social views | Gülen, Fethullah--Political and social views | Crimes against humanity--Turkey--21st century | Genocide--Turkey--21st century | Protest movements--Turkey--History--21st century | Turkey--Politics and government--21st century
Classification: LCC DR603 .H377 2025
LC record available at https://lccn.loc.gov/2025034734

"An outstanding book describing the devastating effect Erdoğan's attack on the Gülen Movement has had not only on the innocent victims of his 'hate campaign' but also on the freedom, democracy and prosperity he promised in his early years. The book exposes how Erdoğan has used religion to demonize many of the most educated and patriotic Turkish citizens, a step backward for this country that aspires to be a regional power."
—***Andrea Barron****, International human rights observer and advocate for torture survivors, Washington, D.C.*

"This volume's insightful brilliance and careful thoroughness together offer a key instrument with which the outside world can better understand the simple and complex horrors associated with Erdoğan's despotic regime—in defiance of the stream of falsities emanating from Türkiye and typically swallowed whole as truthful by the mainstream Western media."
—***Ori Z Soltes****, PhD, Georgetown University. Author of* Between Thought and Action: An Intellectual Biography of Fethullah Gülen

"... a harrowing and meticulously documented analysis of President Erdoğan's campaign to eradicate the Hizmet movement. Through mass purges, emergency decrees, the bending of the judiciary, torture, hate speech, and the criminalization of dissent, they reveal how an entire segment of Turkish civil society was driven toward "civil death."
—***Johan Heymans****, Managing Partner at Van Steenbrugge Advocaten;* ***Johan Vande Lanotte****, Former Deputy Prime Minister in federal governments in Belgium (from the "Afterword")*

Contents

Extended Contents

Chapter 8
THE SYCOPHANT OPPOSITION 141

Chapter 9
DETENTION CENTERS AND PRISONS 147

Chapter 10
SUICIDE VICTIMS AND PSYCHOLOGICAL PRESSURE 167

Chapter 11
WHOLESALE UNDOING OF LEGAL RIGHTS 173

Chapter 12
ABDUCTIONS AND VIOLENCE IN FOREIGN LANDS 187

Chapter 13
CONTINUING OPPRESSION OF HIZMET 193

Chapter 14
SHIFTING DAILY DISCOURSE AGAINST HIZMET 215

Chapter 15
INFLICTING HATE ON THE GÜLEN FAMILY 227

Chapter 16
HATE SPEECH AND POLITICIDE 235

If you kill the intellect, morals also die.
When intellect and morals die, the nation becomes divided.
The day you can buy the judge, justice dies.
The day you kill justice, the state also dies.[1]
Mehmed II

A nation whose judicial power is not independent
cannot be accepted as a state.[2]
Mustafa Kemal Atatürk

Freedom is never more than one generation away from extinction.
It has to be fought for and defended by each generation.[3]
Ronald Reagan

1 Rıdvan Karadöngel, *İnsan Portresi* (Kitapyurdu Doğrudan Yayıncılık, 2017) (Kitapyurdu Direct Publishing, 2017), p.333. *See also* Ahmet Şimşirgil, *Adalet Ustaları* (Kitapyurdu Doğrudan Yayıncılık, 2017) (Kitapyurdu Direct Publishing, 2017), p.111.

2 Republic of Turkey, Ministry of Justice, General Directorate of International Law and Foreign Relations, "The Judicial System of Turkey and Organisation of the Ministry of Justice," Diş İlişkiler Ve Avrupa Birliği Genel Müdürlüğü (Foreign Relations and The European Union General Directorate), https://diabgm.adalet.gov.tr/Resimler/SayfaDokuman/2492019170148THE_JUDICIAL_SYSTEM_OF_TURKEY_AND_ORGANISATION_OF_THE_MINISTRY_OF_JUSTICE.pdf, p.3.

3 Ronald Reagan, "Remarks at the Annual Convention of Kiwanis International," Ronald Reagan Presidential Foundation & Institute (July 6, 1987), https://www.reaganfoundation.org/ronald-reagan/reagan-quotes-speeches/remarks-at-the-annual-convention-of-kiwanis-international/?srsltid=AfmBOopQppFb1tmu95T-3BqU7oon9OEVM66C2hio8JgErMw29ZV4yJYu7.

Foreword

Two reasons motivated me to help author this book about the hate-driven campaign of Türkiye's President Recep Tayyip Erdoğan to eradicate the Gülen Movement, also known as Hizmet.

One is my unwavering commitment to international human rights. This is no fleeting interest. Over the years, I have participated in human rights missions to Chile, Guatemala, Ecuador, Israel, and the Palestinian territories and helped author a book on femicides in Ciudad Juárez, Mexico. My long legal practice and teaching career in the United States (for nearly fifty years) was dedicated to human rights.

The other motive is my long association and friendship with many people within Hizmet and my admiration for their worldwide efforts to shore up civil society.

My journey with Hizmet began by chance during an interfaith trip to Türkiye in Fall 2008 that eventually inspired me to write about Fethullah Gülen, the movement's spiritual teacher, who passed away in October 2024, and his acquittal of conspiracy charges, also in 2008, related to allegedly plotting to overthrow the secular government and create a religious-based state. The irony is not lost on me that what Erdoğan is now doing is what the Turkish courts acquitted Gülen of doing. Gülen was innocent; Erdoğan is not.

Dozens of journeys across Türkiye, Europe, North America, and beyond have led me to interact with the people of Hizmet and develop deep respect for them. Before Erdoğan became who he is now, I talked with judges, entrepreneurs, educators, attorneys, journalists, academics, and everyday common folk in Türkiye who, while not part of Hizmet, respect it. They, too, are at risk for even the slightest perceived association with Hizmet. Some with whom I shared *çay tea* are now imprisoned in Türkiye, while others have had to flee their homes. For their safety, I have not dared to contact them in recent years. The danger to them is too great. I worry about them.

As a long-time observer of Turkish politics and Erdoğan's broken relationship with Hizmet, I have found that relying on U.S. media alone paints an incomplete picture. Only in helping prepare this book did I fully grasp the depths of depravity in Erdoğan's unprincipled battle against Hizmet and his disdain for civil society, let alone justice. Equally disturbing is his readiness to deploy hate speech so recklessly and malevolently for his self-aggrandizement and that of his cohorts for power and wealth, without regard for the long-term damage to the nation's halting efforts at democracy.

The extent of Erdoğan's deep-seated hatred is unfathomable. He shatters so many innocent lives in his wake. The stories are numerous and tragic. One of the more deplorable is his willingness to target and harm even the relatives of Fethullah Gülen, some of them quite elderly.

The following chapters examine how Erdoğan has weaponized three critical props of the state—the judiciary, the religious establishment, and the media—to serve his agenda, a calculated effort, years in the making, to wage war on Hizmet.

This book is a collaborative effort with Coşkun Yorulmaz, a distinguished Turkish attorney and human rights defender now in exile from his native country. I am fortunate to have been one of the collaborators with him and with others, who offered suggested text, comments, advice, and help with navigating the contours of the Turkish government's persecution of Hizmet. My thanks to Dr. Yorulmaz and to everyone who was part of this joint endeavor.

The courage of those who have withstood Erdoğan's virulent campaign and suffered for it and the bravery and persistence of those who continue the struggle for justice and a better future for Türkiye are impressive and poignant. Also inspiring is the continuing work of the people of Hizmet to serve the international community in the face of so much adversity and pain. To them all, I dedicate the work that was my honor to contribute to this book.

James C. Harrington

Introduction

Toward the end of the last century, after years of organizing, the Hizmet Movement emerged in Turkish society as a major proponent of civil society. "Hizmet" (roughly translated as "service" in the world), also known as the Gülen Movement after its spiritual teacher Fethullah Gülen, achieved prominent recognition for its educational and multicultural work in Türkiye and elsewhere in the world.

Hizmet emphasizes dialogue, tolerance, and notably embraces a contemporary and moderate interpretation of Islam. Hizmet was also unique in being a movement that reached out of Türkiye to benefit the world community. *Time Magazine* in 2013 named Gülen as one of the world's one hundred most influential people.

After collaborating with Hizmet for a decade or so in the early 2000s to move Türkiye closer to the European Union, Erdoğan and his Justice and Development Party (AKP) that he co-founded shifted away from the shared goal of developing Türkiye's democracy and veered toward nationalism, political Islam, authoritarianism, xenophobia, and corruption. Hizmet rejected those values and began to part ways.

Hizmet, with its broad spiritual base, entrepreneurial prowess, moral compass, savvy media use, community service (schools, hospitals, and humanitarian work), and global reach, took on a different and dissenting voice. It posed a political and social challenge to the regime's growing autocracy and evermore evident corruption. Erdoğan came to view Hizmet as his nemesis that roadblocked his march toward authoritarian rule.

Because Hizmet called into question their unethical values and antidemocratic maneuvers, Erdoğan and AKP moved to isolate, denigrate, marginalize, dismantle, and suppress Hizmet. This included oppressing anyone opposing the government as associated with the "Movement," even if they were not, as a way of being rid of them, too. This book makes the case for a regime politicide project against Hizmet in violation of both international law and Turkish law.

The 2013 Gezi Park protests and Erdoğan's brutal suppression of that environmental effort suddenly turned Türkiye's direction. When the December 2013 corruption investigations broke onto the scene a few months later, implicating Erdoğan's family, friends, and officials, he moved to blame the Gülen Movement and make it the target of a merciless hate speech campaign, transforming people who had political disagreements with him and AKP into enemies of the country.

Erdoğan had already begun his anti-Hizmet campaign after the Gezi Park uprising, but it was nowhere as intense and concentrated as it would become. When the December 2013 corruption investigation came about, he accused the police officers, prosecutors, and judges involved in it as part of Hizmet's arm in the judiciary and the police and retaliated against them.

Then came the shadowy 2016 coup attempt, and the government radically escalated its systemic oppression with mass arrests and detentions against opposition groups, especially targeting Hizmet. Within hours of the coup event unravelling, Erdoğan accused Hizmet of being behind it, an accusation he knew to be false. He blocked any meaningful domestic or international investigation of who indeed was responsible. That alone should raise questions about the coup's origins and how the government addressed it internally. And the larger question: was the regime complicit in any way?

Erdoğan used the event to strengthen his "strongman" direction. He initiated a lawless process that suppressed fundamental human rights like freedom, security, and the right to a fair trial as state policy, sidelining international law and Türkiye's internal law. Erdoğan targeted Hizmet for obliteration because it was a bulwark in building civil society, contrary to his visceral political ambition.

Overnight, he engineered the largest public employee expulsion recorded in world history. He purged hundreds of thousands of good and decent professional individuals from gainful employment, preventing them from earning a living and supporting their families. He unlawfully incarcerated thousands and subjected many to torture. The agenda was politicide, a political version of genocide.

His purge included judges, including members of the county's highest courts, many of whom were detained, arrested, jailed, and even tortured. The purge encompassed one-fifth of the judiciary. This went hand-in-hand with Erdoğan invoking state of emergency powers for two years so he could rule by decree. He also revamped the criminal justice system to make it less protective of people's rights.

Erdoğan used Hizmet as the scapegoat for his power grab. One of the arrows he and AKP pulled from their quiver was hate speech. For them and the elites whom they represent this was a necessary step toward expanding and consolidating political power. Regardless of legality or morality, they would crush any dissent or opposition, real or imagined, by whatever means possible. Erdoğan unleashed the most intensive and extensive hate-driven campaign in modern Turkish history.

This hate-fueled campaign of political annihilation violates international human rights norms, undermines democratic self-governance, and has rendered Türkiye's judicial system into a sham. Hate speech, the hostile expression directed at individuals or groups based on attributes like race or personal beliefs, ostracizes segments of society, propagates intolerance, justifies discrimination, and instigates violence, all which international law prohibits.[1]

Erdoğan hoodwinked the country and induced his traditional political opponents to join his hate campaign to undermine civil society and constitutional order. His religious and nationalist allies quickly jumped on board. Those complicit in Erdoğan's authoritarian scheme, at the expense of Hizmet, might do well to remember President John F. Kennedy's admonition in his 1961 inaugural address: "Those who foolishly sought power by riding the back of the tiger ended up inside."

Hate speech often emerges during pivotal political-social transitions. In Türkiye, individuals and groups have been targets of hate speech, repression, and denial of fundamental rights during distinct epochs. In the Turkish historical narrative, various minority groups such as Kurds, Alevis, Romani, Armenians, Christians, Jews, and immigrant refugees have all found themselves on the receiving end, at one time or another.[2]

The absence of a mature democratic societal fabric in Türkiye in terms of understanding and protecting civil liberties has fostered a public social climate rife with practices that undermine democracy. The hate speech campaign found resonance within society, promoted by incessant government propaganda and lies, compounded by autocratic ploys.

Rather than engaging with Hizmet politically and letting the country decide its options, the government weaponized hate speech. While Hizmet supporters are direct victims, the people of Türkiye at large will suffer damage long into the future. Any national repressive hate campaign of the ilk that Erdoğan has engineered and unleashed coarsens the culture of the country, undermines civil society, and divides the nation.

The persecution has been unrelenting. Its goal: impose civil death on anyone associated with Hizmet. Politicide, political genocide. The regime's campaign involved serious violence, threats, assaults, and harassment in prisons, detention centers, and in civilian life. Civilians, prompted by hardline government policy, also perpetrated similar actions. The judicial authorities acquiesced, sanctioning rampant injustice and illegality. The hate campaign has not lessened.

Erdoğan and AKP have ruthlessly bent, and continue to bend, any semblance of legal order against those who oppose them and methodically demonize their opponents and bash their critics so pervasively that much of the country accepts the unlawful actions and human rights violations as legitimate or fears challenging the underlining hate-perpetrated philosophy lest they also get slapped down.[3]

Erdoğan's crusade to destroy the Hizmet Movement is a linchpin of his war on dissent generally, which is alarmingly ego-driven. He will plough under anyone in his way. He cares not one iota about the damage he causes to individuals or the country. It is about his agenda, not the nation's.

Erdoğan fashioned his attack on the Gülen Movement as a way of diminishing legal and constitutional protections for the entire country as he became increasingly autocratic. His two years of emergency decrees, many of which the AKP-dominated parliament made permanent, have radically undermined Türkiye's civil and criminal law system.

The state of emergency rule by decree, originally invoked for three months, was renewed sequentially every three months for two years until public opinion and international pressure finally pushed an end to it. There was no national security reason for a two-year state of emergency. Whatever breach of public order occurred with the odd and fumbling coup was restored within days by the government's admission and braggadocio. Erdoğan devised the two-year emergency rule so that he and company could accumulate power and quash dissent.

It bears repeating a hundred times over that, by 2024, eight years after unilaterally declaring Hizmet an armed terrorist organization, even though challenged to do so, Erdoğan has not produced an ounce of proof or single fact to remotely support his assertion. There is no evidence and never was. He launched a gratuitous witch hunt, peppered with hate speech and crimes. He wantonly besmirched people's loyalty and patriotism and upended their lives.

The Gülen Movement was a sharp thorn in his side, which pierced deeper and deeper every year into his ambition for power and wealth, which was at complete odds with Hizmet's ideals of democracy, the rule of law, and civil society.

Even when Fethullah Gülen died in late October 2024, Erdoğan could not restrain his vituperative hate speech or show a modicum of civility. He publicly said Gülen had suffered a "dishonorable death" and likened him to a "demon in human form." Nor did he even try to hide his politicide agenda to eradicate Hizmet, pledging the movement would be "completely eliminated."[4]

Türkiye's impressive political progress toward democracy between 2000-2010 is long gone. So too has perished the dream of joining the European Union.[5] This regression will adversely affect Türkiye for untold decades. Erdoğan has sabotaged the legal rights and protections that the country had painstakingly built up in recent years. Türkiye, a nation of eighty-seven million people, is backsliding in parliamentary democracy under despotic governance.

A human rights report in May 2015 by one of this book's authors, "Turkey: Democracy in Peril," tracked how Erdoğan had begun his quest for power at the expense of the Gülen Movement and set out on his path undermining the country's democracy.[6] Unfortunately, the report was prescient of what was to come.

An overview of human rights issues in Türkiye as of 2020 is available in a series of twenty essays, *Human Rights in Turkey: Assaults on Human Dignity,* addressing a variety of subjects, including some presented by this book. It provides important background.[7]

The list is long of international reports and court decisions (close to one hundred) that have carefully chartered Erdoğan's totalitarian trajectory and warned about its danger to Türkiye's democracy. Those reports and decisions amply buttress this book and appear as references throughout, all of which cry out for international condemnation.

One of the most recent is Stichting Justice Square's 2024 careful study on hate policies that have contributed to crimes against humanity in Türkiye. It documents how hate crimes are not just individual rights violations but systematic government policy. The report presents the societal repercussions alongside case examples,[8] which, while anecdotal, reflect a larger reality. This book encompasses that study and myriad other reports and resources.

This book offers an overview of the horrendous persecution of Hizmet, which Erdoğan has propelled for more than a decade, through an organized campaign that is violative of international norms. This book does not provide a day-by-day chronology of the persecution. That information is painstakingly documented and available from other sources. To include a chronology of that specificity would make the book unmanageably long and require more than a single volume. This book is more of a synopsis than a catalog.

The drive to eradicate Hizmet continues unabated, even as the reader turns these pages, years after the state of emergency officially ended in 2018. In the first five months of 2024, the regime detained or arrested 1,877 people for Hizmet connections. During his first year as Interior Minister (June 2023 – May 2024), Ali Yerlikaya oversaw operations that detained or arrested 9,251 Hizmet-affiliated individuals, about 771 persons per month, and bragged about it.[9]

The politicide continues unchecked and is filled with daily manifestations, many of which occurred during the writing of the book, such as jailing and prosecuting young people, teenagers, for Hizmet association because of the way that they talk or interact with each other.[10] The absurdities reflect real pain and show how firmly entrenched is the effort to be rid of Hizmet.

In July 2024, for instance, the government arrested 128 people for Hizmet connections. Two months before, in early May, they arrested thirty-eight high school and primary school students, including fourteen students younger than age fifteen.[11]

Another police operation two weeks later detained 544 people. The accusation was providing educational coaching assistance to children of imprisoned Hizmet parents, thereby supporting miscreant families. The police detained high school and university students, most of whom were girls, along with their mothers. The authorities held sixteen children under age eighteen separate from their mothers at the police station and subjected to psychological abuse.[12]

The never-ending crackdown has swept up people whose only charge was providing food or assistance to victims of the government's non-stop "witch hunt," to use Erdoğan's phrase.[13]

In May 2025, the government detained 320 people across the country for questioning, mostly university students and recent graduates, many who had travelled abroad. The interrogations were about their relationship with the Gülen movement and involved questions over constitutionally protected and otherwise lawful activities. Particular interest was paid to where students travelled and with whom they had met, that is, Hizmet people outside the country.

Turkish authorities continue to ignore rulings by the European Court of Human Rights against detaining and arresting people on vague charges, which encompass legally protected freedoms. No charges involve actual conduct to overthrow the public order.

Erdoğan has gone so far as to strike at the heart of democracy: elections. On March 19, 2025, Istanbul mayor and prospective presidential candidate Ekrem İmamoğlu of the opposition Republican People's Party was arrested and then jailed on allegations of corruption, extortion, bribery, money laundering, and supporting terrorism. This came just days before his party was set to nominate him.

That İmamoğlu was widely believed to likely be a successful presidential candidate in upcoming elections was not lost on the country's people. Few were the doubters that this was not a raw political move by Erdoğan. If there was any doubt of its political machinations, the government buried that doubt by summarily stripping İmamoğlu of his college diploma, a requisite for presidential candidates, on the day before his arrest. His party still nominated him, an act of defiance.[14]

Widespread protests involving hundreds of thousands of people took place across Türkiye. The government responded as Erdoğan typically responds: suppression, retribution, and punitive measures. The regime arrested more than 2,000 people and levied suppressive measures against social media and the regular media that reported the repression.[15]

There is no foreseeable end or winding down the persecution of Hizmet. After outlining Erdoğan and AKP's history and current pathway to render the Gülen Movement unto annihilation, the book concludes with an analysis of whether Erdoğan and Türkiye should be liable to an international tribunal and whether they are guilty of violations of fundamental human rights and crimes against humanity, making them culpable under the various international conventions to which Türkiye has bound itself as well as its own "crimes against humanity" legislation.

The fact that so much was going on at the same time by different actors makes it difficult to divide this book neatly into a strict chronological sequence or stand-alone chapters. The purging of the judiciary, the hate speech campaign, taming of the media, and the state of emergency all interplay with each other, for example, but not necessarily sequentially. Keeping the interplay in mind is helpful in reading the book. There are many balls in the air at the same time.

There is a subtext running through the book: the incremental march toward authoritarian rule around the world, including in the United States and Europe, the gradual bending and coopting of civil society institutions to serve an autocrat's agenda. Erdoğan gives us a lesson from the playbook of despotic governance that we dare not ignore.

The final question is how should the international community respond? And with what actions, and with what immediacy? The cry for justice is loud.

The politicide rages on. Only the international community and their governments, acting together, can halt it.

Endnotes

1 António Guterres, "United Nations Strategy and Plan of Action on Hate Speech," United Nations (May 2019), https://www.un.org/en/genocideprevention/documents/UN%20Strategy%20and%20Plan%20of%20Action%20on%20Hate%20Speech%2018%20June%20SYNOPSIS.pdf, ("…. keeping hate speech from escalating into more something more dangerous, particularly incitement to discrimination, hostility, and violence, which is prohibited under international law.").

2 *See* Hasan Aydin and Winston Langley, "Introducing Human Rights in Turkey" and Ercan Balcioglu, "Human Rights in Turkey: Past, Present and Future," in Hasan Aydin and Winston Langley (eds), *Human Rights in Turkey: Assaults on Human Dignity* (New York: Springer, 2021), pp.3-22, https://doi.org/10.1007/978-3-030-, pp. 23-48, https://doi.org/10.1007/978-3-030-57476-5_2.

3 *See* Mehmet Efe Caman, "Authoritarianization and Human Rights in Turkey: How the AKP Legitimizes Human Rights Violations," *Human Rights in Turkey: Assaults on Human Dignity.id.*, pp. 179-197, https://doi.org/10.1007/978-3-030-57476-5_9.

4 Michael Rubinkam, "Thousands mourn Fethullah Gülen, a Turkish spiritual leader who died in the US," Associated Press (Oct. 24, 2024), https://apnews.com/article/fethullah-gulen-turkey-dead-funeral-burial-69336b5a23988b0c-2c350a4799ff6c51.

5 *See* Gülsüm Alan, "Turkey's Accession to the European Union in Context of Its Human Rights Violations: Observations of a Journalist from Brussels," in Hasan Aydin and Winston Langley (eds), *Human Rights in Turkey: Assaults on Human Dignity* (New York: Springer, 2021), pp. 451-471, https://doi.org/10.1007/978-3-030-57476-5_20.

6 James C. Harrington, "Turkey: Democracy in Peril" Hizmet Movement News Archive (May 2015), https://hizmetnews.com/sds/wp-content/uploads/2017/10/Turkey-Democracy-in-Peril-JC-Harrington.pdf.

7 *Supra* n.2, *Human Rights in Turkey: Assaults on Human Dignity*. See also "General Country of Origin Information Report on Türkiye (August 2023)," Ministry of Foreign Affairs, Government of the Netherlands, https://www.government.nl/ documents/reports/2023/08/31/general-country-of-origin-information-report-on-turkiye-august-2023.

8 "Hate Crimes Against the Gülen Movement in Turkey," Justice Square (29 Feb. 2024), https://justicesquare.org/wp-content/uploads/2024/03/STATEMENT-HATE-CRIMES-AGAINST-GULEN-MOVEMENT-IN-TURKEY.pdf.

9 Mustafa Özmen, "Immigratie-en Naturalisatiedienst: The recent wave of mass arrests that have taken place in Turkey between 6 and 30 May 2024 (including minors and students - for providing support to families of detainees)," Justice Square (June 05, 2024), https://justicesquare.org/wp-content/uploads/2024/06/IND-MAY-NOTIFICATION_2.pdf. *See also* "The Crackdown on Humanitarian Aid in Turkey," Advocates of Silenced Turkey (May 2024), https://silencedturkey.org/wp-content/uploads/2024/05/THE-CRACKDOWN-ON-HUMANITARIAN-AID-IN-TURKEY-Web.pdf.

10 "The Teenage Girls Case: A Call for Justice," Advocates of Silenced Turkey (Dec. 8, 2024), https://silencedturkey.org/the-teenage-girls-case-a-call-for-justice.dero.

11 *See* Turkey's Crackdown on Students and Women: Criminalising Ordinary Life, "The Arrested Lawyers Initiative (22 Sept. 2024), https://arrestedlawyers.org/2024/09/22/turkeys-crackdown-on-students-and-women-criminalising-ordinary-life/.

12 "Appeal to United Nations High Commissioner for Human Rights," Justice Square (May 16, 2024), https://justicesquare.org/wp-content/uploads/2024/05/Urgent-Appeal_-Mr.-Volker-Turk-1.pdf.

13 *Supra* n.5, "The Crackdown on Humanitarian Aid in Turkey."

14 For an overview and summary, see "Arrest of Ekrem İmamoğlu," Wikipedia, https://en.wikipedia.org/wiki/Arrest_of_Ekrem_%C4%B0mamo%C4%9Flu; and see "The peculiar Turkish corruption issue behind Istanbul mayor's arrest – and how it became a tool of political oppression," The Conversation (March 24, 2025), https://theconversation.com/the-peculiar-turkish-corruption-issue-behind-istanbul-mayors-arrest-and-how-it-became-a-tool-of-political-oppression-252933.

15 For an overview and summary, see "2025 Turkish protests," Wikipedia, https://en.wikipedia.org/wiki/2025_Turkish_protests.

Chapter 1

Hizmet and Erdoğan's Oppression: An Overview

The Hizmet Movement

The Gülen or Hizmet Movement is a global civil society undertaking inspired by Fethullah Gülen, who died in October 2024, and guided by his teachings. The movement is known for its educational, cultural, and humanitarian initiatives.

The movement grounded itself in dialogue, tolerance, and a progressive interpretation of Islam. Its goal is to foster coexistence through promoting universal human values. The movement views itself as a contemporary social initiative, mirroring civil society movements within secular democratic states that foster civil society and are governed by the rule of law.[1]

Gülen had come to believe that promoting tolerance, compassion, communication, education, and cooperation was the way to combat the root causes of societal violence, terrorism, and conflicts. This underpinning supports Hizmet's commitment to worldly and spiritual well-being while abjuring violence, extremism, or divisive sectarianism.[2] Hizmet volunteers collaborate with diverse individuals and organizations for the multinational advancement of civil society.

Hizmet, for example, has sponsored a signature youth International Festival of Language and Culture for twenty-one years, held yearly around the globe, drawing more than 15,000 performer participants in 550 events in 160 countries, "...to celebrate our world's cultural diversity and create opportunities for international friendship-building around shared human values."[3]

Central to Hizmet's philosophy is the crucial role of education in driving social, economic, and political progress. A robust educational system is critical to sustaining the rule of law, social justice, and protecting people's rights in a pluralist society.[4] Originally beginning with preparatory courses for university entrance exams in Türkiye, Hizmet expanded its educational reach to operate 2,000 schools in 140 countries, serving hundreds of thousands of students worldwide.

The movement seeks to help serve as a unifying force in regions marked by ethnic and religious divisions by promoting peace-building activities, fostering civil society engagement, and facilitating dialogue.[5] In Türkiye, this occurred with the Kurdish and Alevi communities.

The movement gained global prominence in the mid-1990s through its interfaith and intercultural dialogue efforts. Gülen's 1998 meeting with Pope John Paul II at the Vatican highlighted those steps. This meeting, however, drew disdain from the country's religious establishment, as did Gülen's outreach to the Jewish community.

Despite international praise for its progressive interpretation of Islam, Hizmet has faced resistance from various factions within Türkiye, including Islamists, secularists, and nationalists.[6] An ironic twist is that, before becoming hostile to Hizmet, many of its current enemies and their children benefited from Hizmet educational opportunities, including Erdoğan's daughter.

Politicide: The Regime Goal of Annihilating the Gülen Movement

The Political Instability Task Force, sponsored by the U.S. government, distinguishes between genocides and politicides. In genocides, victimized groups are defined primarily in terms of communal characteristics (i.e., ethnicity, religion, race, or nationality). In politicides, the victim groups are defined principally in terms of political dissent or opposition to the regime and dominant groups. Genocides and politicides are consequences of state failure, such as economic distress or lack of solid democratic structures.[7]

In Türkiye's case, people associated with Hizmet became subjected to a legal structure grounded on discrimination against them for "political or other opinion" reasons. Erdoğan built a discriminatory edifice for the collective elimination of Hizmet, punishing its members and sympathizers, purging them from the public and private sectors, generating societal hatred and prejudice against them, isolating them from society, devaluing them, portraying them as criminals, and physically and psychologically punishing them. Civil death, politicide, was, and remains, the objective, in violation of both international law and Turkish law.

Erdoğan sought to (and eventually did) realize his objective through incremental stages of the hate speech toward Hizmet. He began by targeting Hizmet as a suspect organization, using false and fabricated generalizations. He then associated Hizmet with terrorism, which led to his linking Hizmet with the 2016 coup fiasco. The Gülen Movement became a scapegoat for the country's societal, economic, and political adversities. And finally, he equated the movement with violence despite Hizmet not being involved in any violent actions and being philosophically non-violent. Erdoğan's hate language escalated incrementally and steadily.

Evolution of Hate Language Toward Violence and Politicide

Hate speech knows no boundaries in its manifestations. Hate speech aims at inciting violence of some kind, whether physical, psychological, economic aggression, or demeaning and sexualized behavior. Verbal assaults and hostility can encompass mocking, degrading name-calling, destructive criticisms, false accusations, coercion, and threats. Psychological violence entails threatening, pressuring, intimidating, ignoring, or ostracizing an individual.

Systematic and policy-directed hate speech has driven grotesque crimes against humanity, from the Jewish Holocaust to genocides in Bosnia, Rwanda, Uganda, and Myanmar, among some tragic examples.

Between December 2013 and May 2017, Erdoğan publicly invoked hate with at least 240 terms or phrases against Hizmet or Fethullah Gülen himself, using vile names and phrases, some of which included the following and variations thereof:

> Grave robbers. Body snatchers. Characterized by lies, deceit, subterfuge, dissension, conspiracy, and slander. Treacherous terrorist organization. They have no morality! They have no decency! They have no love for their homeland, nation, or flag! They are slanderous!

> So lowly, so treacherous. Traitors. Terrorists. We will boil them down to their molecules. Perverted. Evil virus. Vampires. Spies. "FETÖ." Coup plotters. Assassins. Parallel structure.... Gang. Agents, puppets, pawns of foreign powers. Murderous. Pseudo-saints. Brainwashed. What an impostor he [Gülen] is! Blood-sucking leech. Charlatan. False prophet.[8]

The number 240 does not encompass how many thousand times the media and others repeated and adopted the words and phrases. Nor does the number account for how often those words and phrases have been uttered or shouted in speeches since May 2017. Erdoğan orchestrated an incessant drumbeat of hate speech. This vocabulary became the government's everyday language and that of the media it controlled.

"Congregationist," "parallelist," and "community" ("cemaat"), which Erdoğan and colleagues seized upon, are neutral terms in English, but they have twisted them with negative connotations and incorporated them into their hate speech lexicon.

The International Journal for Crime, Justice and Social Democracy published a 2020 report of surveys and interviews of hate crime victims since 2013, which found that participants' victimization experiences increased significantly in tandem with rising anti-Hizmet rhetoric. This was particularly prevalent after the December 2013 corruption probes and following the so-called attempted coup. The victims' responses suggested that the perpetrators were motivated by the regime's Hizmet denouncements. The rising hate speech and hate crimes against Hizmet had devastating effects on participants' daily life and social interactions.[9]

Hate speech in the form of state propaganda takes on its own life and insidiously creates its own reality. The more it is incessantly pounded into the general population, the more people believe it. It is a critical tool for authoritarian regimes seeking to consolidate power.[10] It is how they manipulate their nation's history in search of power at any cost. They reshape their countries, cover over their corruption, and create an alternate "legality" that upends the rule of law to protect themselves and oppress their real or would-be opponents. And they do so by drawing on a playbook used by disreputable figures like Benito Mussolini and Adolf Hitler, among many others.

Erdoğan's narrative after the December 2013 scandal included terms like "parallel structure" and later "FETÖ." Before the scandal, he began with softer phrases like "dirty schemes" or "games of dark circles" but transitioned to harsher rhetoric like "proxy organizations cloaked in religious attire" or "foreign-rooted, domestic betrayal cliques." In retrospect, that gradual rhetoric build-up worked well over the years until he attained the level of harshness he wanted and needed for his agenda. This strategic propaganda evolved into a social politicide hammer against Hizmet.

The term "FETÖ" (Fethullahist Terror Organization) became the primary Erdoğan moniker to stigmatize Hizmet members and affiliated individuals as objects of hatred. The acronym degrades, humiliates, and insults them while creating an atmosphere of enmity, prejudice, and even violence. This term became the handle to legitimize unlawful practices such as arrests, unfair trials, illegal dismissals from employment, unlawful detentions, ill-treatment, and even torture. It communicates the message that would justify criminal activity against the "guilty" parties lest they go unpunished.

The government-endorsed, anti-Hizmet hate speech project became a vehicle to legitimize human rights violations against members of Hizmet, sanctioning mistreatment and torture by state officials within detention centers or prisons. This also created a climate of assumed immunity in which public officials, as well as ordinary citizens, believe they can engage in insults, threats, and physical harm toward Hizmet without repercussions, undermining the rule of law and making justice impossible to attain.

Fabricated false information consistently paints members of Hizmet as traitors, leading to their absolute condemnation. Being a traitor is one of the most odious civic crimes possible in the eyes of fellow citizens.

Given how Erdoğan has restructured Türkiye's legal system, it is impossible to rectify or halt false, misleading, or hate-filled news published in written, visual, or social media against a Hizmet supporter or Hizmet itself. The courts reject lawsuits against such slanderous statements under the guise of freedom of expression and press but not the other way around.

The term "FETÖ" became weaponized to ostracize and target individuals in Türkiye. This label, used by both the government and opposition against anyone associated with Hizmet, has become a tool for defamation, aiming to strip individuals of their professional positions and institutional affiliations. Türkiye's ultimate step was to declare Hizmet to be a terrorist organization. No Western country recognizes Hizmet as a terrorist organization.

Türkiye's Constitutional Court ruled that the term "FETÖ" itself was not slanderous but did concede it could be used in a libelous manner.[11] The court essentially issued its imprimatur on a term that Erdoğan introduced into the country's vocabulary with slanderous intent but which, the judges said, had since taken on a non-slanderous meaning *per se*. That was quite a dance by the court, inartful but not unexpected. After all, a third of their colleagues had abruptly lost their jobs, even at the highest level, because the regime perceived them as too close to Hizmet. Some judiciary members were confined to detention or prison and received cruel treatment there.

The Data

The relentless persecution of individuals affiliated with Hizmet, driven by hate speech and a systematic "witch hunt" jumpstarted by Erdoğan, continues to have devastating consequences years after the 2016 flopped coup attempt. The scope and severity of this campaign are evident from the staggering numbers of people investigated, arrested, convicted, and sentenced, as well as the widespread human rights abuses that they endured.

The statistics vary according to source and operative dates. No matter which data set one consults, the numbers are stunning and almost surreal in their magnitude. One striking figure to keep in mind is that the government suddenly labeled more than two million people as terrorists.[12]

High-ranking government officials, such as former Vice-President Fuat Oktay and Minister of Justice Bekir Bozdağ, perpetuated the spread of hate speech by labeling those with alleged ties to Hizmet as "terrorists," as they laid out the numbers for the public.

In July 2021, five years after the slipshod coup attempt, Oktay said, "...the number of terrorists expelled since July 15, disguised as judges and public prosecutors, is 3,968..."[13] The persecution never ended but continued unabated.

At a November 2023 press conference, Bozdağ described the alarming scale of the crackdown, with hundreds of thousands of individuals prosecuted, convicted, or subjected to judicial control measures for alleged coup involvement and links to Hizmet:

> Looking at the statistics of actual coup cases, there are 289 files, and within these, 8,725 individuals have been prosecuted. Among them, 1,634 received aggravated life sentences, 1,366 life sentences, and a total of 4,891 people received sentences, 1,891 of them being with a specific duration. 2,870 people were acquitted, and decisions were made for 964 people that there would be no sentences.
>
> There are also memberships to the organization [Hizmet]... Regarding membership to the organization, there are 203,511 files that have been so far concluded. Currently, there are 64,058 files related to FETÖ under detention. There have been decisions for 107,492 individuals in cases under detention. Currently, 1,299 individuals are in detention, 22,636 individuals under judicial control, and 29,093 individuals for whom arrest warrants have been issued. There are 12,909 convicted people, and 3,303 whose sentences have been postponed. Thus, if we count those convicted, we see there are 16,212 individuals. There are 161,282 individuals under judicial control...."[14]

Between 2016 and 2018, the regime discharged 129,411 public officials from employment through fifteen emergency decrees. Among those dismissed, 107,138 were men and 22,273 were women. Even after the state of emergency ended in 2018, thousands more were dismissed by administrative decisions.[15] As of 2021, this figure was at 134,258.[16]

The government dismissed of 4,261 judges and prosecutors through the Supreme Board of Judges and Prosecutors, of which 3,392 were men and 904 were women. Including military judges, rapporteurs of the Constitutional Court, auditors of the Court of Accounts, and ongoing dismissals, the number exceeds 5,000.[17]

Additionally, the government shuttered thirty-five healthcare institutions, 934 schools, 109 student dormitories, 104 foundations, 1,125 associations, fifteen universities, and nineteen unions and confiscated their assets on allegations of being linked to Hizmet.[18]

Government and non-government sources paint an unnerving picture of the breadth of Erdoğan's "witch hunt" against Hizmet. These data are astonishing in themselves but underrepresent reality. Respected outside sources widely accept that, for several factors, the actual figures are higher than those reported. Nor do the cold numbers on paper even start to capture the deep underlying pain, misery, and suffering of the people and their families whose lives these numbers represent but do not describe.

The regime's shutdown of Kimse Yok Mu ("Is Anybody There?") in 2016 is representative of this. As a partner humanitarian organization with the U.N. High Commissioner for Refugees (UNHCR), Kimse Yok Mu had been active since 1999 in delivering emergency relief in disaster zones, providing health care in poor countries, and rebuilding infrastructure in 113 countries, including Türkiye.[19] The Hizmet-related relief group became an official NGO in 2004 and, at the time of its closure, was renowned for building wells in small, outlying rural African communities.

Not only did Kimse Yok Mu staff suffer, but so did countless poor people around the globe. Children of impoverished communities in Africa lost medical care and nutrition support. Kimse Yok Mu would no longer be on hand to respond to natural disasters around the world, such as earthquakes and tsunamis. What was the point of terminating Hizmet's international humanitarian work? It was the work of a person devoid of any compassion. This is but one example of the far-reaching personal damage inflicted by Erdoğan's war on Hizmet institutions.

Mustafa Yeneroğlu, a Turkish parliament member from the Democracy and Progress Party (DEVA), released a report, "Normalization of Lawlessness: Cases of Members in Armed Terrorist Organizations," which revealed that, between 2016 and 2020, the government initiated criminal investigations of at least 1,576,566 individuals for alleged membership or association with an "armed terror organization," most of whom were associated with Hizmet.[20] Not surprisingly, the number of

Turkish asylum applications to European countries exceeded 17,000 in the three years following the aborted coup attempt.

The Solidarity with Others in-depth report in 2023, "Hate Speech of the Erdoğan Regime: 'Feto (!) [sic]'" presented fuller, staggering data[21]:

- 2,217,572 individuals processed by prosecutors
- 561,388 persons against whom prosecutors filed public lawsuits
- 374,056 people convicted by courts
- 154,970 individuals sentenced to imprisonment by courts
- 129,410 persons terminated from public service through emergency decrees
- 50,000 public officials dismissed from employment by administrative decisions
- 4,383 judges and prosecutors summarily discharged from employment
- 5,990 academics dismissed from employment at universities
- More than 1,500 lawyers detained
- More than 300 journalists arrested
- 302 pregnant mothers / mothers with babies detained / arrested
- 157 ill persons detained / arrested
- 44 people with disabilities detained / arrested
- 132 individuals who died in prisons
- 8 deaths of people in law enforcement custody
- 1 person who died in court
- 36 deaths of individuals while fleeing the country
- 92 suicides among individuals processed
- 9,232 human rights violations in prisons
- 57 average daily detentions of people
- More than 3,000 individuals held in solitary confinement cells
- 1,410 closed or seized associations
- 19 closed or seized unions
- 19 closed or seized federations
- 4 closed or seized confederations
- 15 closed or seized universities
- 1,034 closed or seized private schools
- 853 closed or seized dormitories

- 301 closed or seized prep schools
- 10 closed or seized foundations
- 29 closed or seized publishing houses
- 20 closed or seized magazines
- 53 closed or seized newspapers
- 6 closed or seized news agencies
- 19 closed or seized TV channels
- 22 closed or seized radio stations
- 47 closed or seized healthcare institutions
- 6,565 seized properties
- 213,696 properties subjected to precautionary measures
- 1,075 closed businesses
- 1,251 businesses placed under trusteeship
- More than 234,410 canceled passports
- More than 300,000 destroyed books
- 28 individuals abducted within Türkiye through illegal means; and
- 98 individuals abducted from outside Türkiye through illegal means

The U.S. Secretary of State's Türkiye Human Rights Reports for 2021 and 2023 underscored the ongoing human rights abuses targeting individuals accused of links to Hizmet, including enforced disappearances, torture, arbitrary detentions, and infringements on freedom of expression and the media.

The 2021 human rights report by the U.S. Secretary announced that, since the coup attempt, Türkiye had detained 312,121 individuals and arrested 99,123 people on alleged Hizmet links.[22] Between July 2020 and July 2021 alone, the regime detained 29,331 individuals and arrested 4,148 for Hizmet affiliation.[23]

Two years later, the U.S. Secretary's 2023 Human Rights Report continued to highlight a broad spectrum of human rights abuses in Türkiye, including enforced disappearances, torture, arbitrary detentions, and significant infringements on freedom of expression and the media, particularly targeting journalists and government critics.[24]

The report's focal point of rights abuse in Türkiye in 2023 was still persons accused of Hizmet links, with 15,539 individuals imprisoned as of July 2023 and many subjected to mistreatment and denied due process. The report pointed to a broader pattern of Türkiye's transnational repression and misuse of international law enforcement tools against Hizmet members (Interpol, for example, as discussed later).

Besides the damning reports by the U.S. Secretary of State, other governmental entities and respected non-governmental organizations, such as Amnesty International,[25] Human Rights Watch, and the Stockholm Center for Freedom,[26] have published detailed reports on distinct aspects of human rights violations in Türkiye. There are upwards of a hundred reports.[27] One of the more recent is Finland's,[28] and Stichting Justice Square' mid-2024 update.[29]

The systematic and planned nature of Erdoğan's policy is evident from the consistent hate speech and ruthless oppression directed at Hizmet, as documented in the many human rights reports. Nor does a one-time arrest suffice for the government. People who manage to win release or are acquitted by a court are then re-arrested for a similar charge under the absurd guise of "reorganization"[30] or whatever an official can conjure up.

This amounts to unlawful double jeopardy. Apart from doubly afflicting an individual, the detentions and re-arrests of individuals serve as a tactical strategy to perpetuate the societal perception of criminality and stoke ongoing hatred.

Collateral Damage: Disastrous Impact on the Nation's Health

With such a data barrage, the numbing figures may divert us from reflecting on the day-to-day anguish represented by the individuals behind the numbers. A multitude of people, who had no relation with Hizmet other than benefiting from the generosity of its associates, also bore the heavy brunt of the regime's hatred for Hizmet.

A look at the impact of the country's healthcare system, which was already severely inadequate, helps fill in the picture of the wanton callousness of state of emergency decrees that adversely affected not only Hizmet-associated medical staff but their other compatriots whose well-being was dependent on them.

As to healthcare professionals, with the combined figures of those dismissed from the civil service and those who lost their jobs after the government shut down their institutions, the number of discharged doctors, academics, nurses, midwives, and hospital staff reached more than 21,000 as of March 2019.[31]

Of those, 5,261 were medical doctors and academics (675 academics taught medical sciences), who lost their jobs after the closure of Hizmet-linked universities; 1,200 doctors in the private sector abruptly became unemployed when the government shut down Hizmet-related hospitals, medical centers and health clinics and purged 1,684 physicians from the Ministry of Health.

In 2016 alone, government decrees summarily shuttered fourteen hospitals and thirty-six medical centers for their ties to Hizmet. On a similar pretext, four hundred pharmacies across Türkiye suddenly lost access to the electronic prescription system of the Social Security Institution, an act meant to force these pharmacies into bankruptcy overnight. In addition, Turkish media report that nearly 1,500 pharmacies came under investigation.

Patients were left distraught as multiple medical centers and hospitals shut down. Given the shortage of hospitals and staff members, many patients could not receive medical help. In addition, the Turkish government violated adequate access to healthcare and medical treatment for imprisoned patients. The situation was aggravated for those in solitary confinement, contrary to the European Prison Rules.[32]

How can a government justify disastrous, calibrated actions that undermine the nation's health, morally or in terms of basic human rights?

Postscript: Erdoğan Tolerates No Language Against Him as He Uses Against Others

Erdoğan knows full well the power of words and what he is doing with his use of hate speech. In Türkiye, it has long been a crime under Article 299 of the Turkish Penal Code to "insult the president," but the law was little enforced. Since Erdoğan became president in 2014, however, that figure has jumped to 160,000 prosecutions in two years. Nearly 39,000 people have stood trial for insulting Erdoğan,[33] whatever "insulting" meant.

There have been court sentences in 13,000 cases. Judges sentenced 3,600 defendants to prison and acquitted 5,500 people. The remainder were fined but not imprisoned. One hundred of the defendants were not yet eighteen-year-olds when they were sentenced (twenty-four were between the ages twelve and fourteen when they committed the alleged crime).

Nobody is safe from Erdoğan's flex of his Article 299 muscle: Politicians, artists, scientists, schoolchildren, housewives, athletes, street vendors, entrepreneurs, singers, or journalists—anybody can be (and has been) accused of insulting the president, whatever that vague term means, which is whatever the government and the judges say it means. Derya Büyükuncu, the six-time Olympian from Türkiye, was the subject of six arrest warrants for "insulting" Erdoğan and banned from the country's swim teams.

The anomaly is that Erdoğan can speak vicious and vile words of hate against Turkish citizens, but those who refer to him in greatly milder and more judicious terms will end up in prison. The consequence of the anomaly is pain and suffering for the people and revenge for him.

Equality under the law does not admit of a double standard. Free speech for me, but not for thee. The European institutions view Erdoğan's rampant suppression of speech as a violation of universal free speech norms and of the right of citizens to criticize the government.

Perhaps a fitting coda to this chapter is to draw attention to the fact that Erdoğan's bodyguard violently beat up peaceful Kurdish and Alevi protesters, who were demonstrating at the Turkish embassy in May 2017 when Erdoğan was visiting Washington. U.S. Secret Service agents who attempted to intervene also became victims of the bodyguards' violence. Erdoğan looked on and did nothing to stop the mêlée.[34]

Eleven individuals had to be hospitalized. The bodyguards fled the country immediately. A U.S. grand jury later indicted them. A diplomatic uproar ensued.[35] The incident magnifies Türkiye's brutal and oppressive history toward its minority populations and its callous disregard for fundamental human rights and civil liberties, which was again on show for the world.

Endnotes

1 Stephen Kinzer, "Fethullah Gulen: Turkish educator and Islamic scholar," *Time* (April 18, 2013), https://time100.time.com/2013/04/18/time-100/slide/fethullah-gulen/.

2 Muhammed Çetin, *The Gülen Movement: Civic Service Without Borders* (New York: Blue Dome Press, 2010), pp.166-167.

3 International Festival of Language and Culture (IFLC), https://intflc.org/.

4 Thomas Michel, "Eğitimci Olarak Fethullah Gülen," Fethullah Gülen Website (24 Feb. 2002), https://fgulen.com/tr/hayati-tr/hareketi-incelemeler/Dr-Thomas-Michel-Egitimci-Olarak-Fethullah-Gulen, ["Fethullah Gülen as an Educator"].

5 Gürkan Çelik, *The Gülen Movement: Building Social Cohesion through Dialogue and Education,* Eburon (Academic Publishers: Nieuwegein, 2011). *See also* Uğur Etga, "Religious Frames: The Gülen Movement," Oxford Research Encyclopedias (26 April 2019), https://oxfordre.com/politics/display/10.1093/acrefore/9780190228637.001.0001/acrefore-9780190228637-e-1345.

6 Caroline Tee, *The Gülen Movement in Turkey: The Politics of Islam and Modernity* (London: I.B. Tauris, 2016). *See also* Doğu Ergil, *Fethullah Gülen & The Gülen Movement In 100 Questions* (New York: Blue Dome Press, 2012). *See also* Bekim Agai, "Fethullah Gülen Hareketinin Eğitime İslamî Etik Kazandırma Projesi," Fethullah Gülen Sitesi (Fethullah Gülen Website) (2003), https://fgulen.com/tr/hayati-tr/hareketi-incelemeler/Bekim-Agai-Fethullah-Gulen-Hareketinin-Egitime-Islami-Etik-Kazandirma-Projesi ["The Fethullah Gülen Movement's Islamic Ethics to Education Project"]; *and see* Berna Turam, *Between Islam and the State: The Politics of Engagement* (Stanford: Stanford University Press, 2007); *and see* Elisabeth Özdalga, "Worldly Asceticism in Islamic Casting: Fethullah Gülen's Inspired Piety and Activism," *Critique: Critical Middle Eastern Studies*, Vol. 9, No. 17 (Fall 2000).

7 Charles H. Anderton, Jurgen Brauer, *Economic Aspects of Genocides, Other Mass Atrocities, and Their Prevention* (Oxford University Press: New York, 2016). *See also* Daniel C. Esty, et al., "State Failure Task Force Report: Phase II Findings," Wilson Center (1999), https://www.wilsoncenter.org/sites/default/files/media/documents/event/Phase2.pdf.

8 *See, e.g.*, "Erdoğan's Vile Campaign of Hate Speech Case Study: Targeting of the Gulen Movement," Stockholm Center for Freedom (May 2017), Erdoğans-Vile-Campaign-Of-Hate-Speech-Case-Study-Targeting-Of-The-Gulen-Movement_2017.pdf, Annex I, pp.26-33, Annex II, pp.34-50.

9 Barbara Perry, Davut Akca, Fatih Karakus. and Mehmet Fatih Bastug. "Planting Hate Speech to Harvest Hatred: How Does Political Hate Speech Fuel Hate Crimes in Turkey?," *International Journal for Crime, Justice and Social Democracy*, Vol. 9, No. 4 (2020), https://www.crimejusticejournal.com/article/view/1514.

10 Ruth Ben-Ghiat, *Strongmen: How They Rise, Why They Succeed, How They Fall* (London: Profile Books, 2021).

11 "Mahkeme, 'Hakan Şükür'e hakaret' davasında kararını Verdi," BirGün (26.02.2018), https://www.birgun.net/haber/mahkeme-hakan-sukur-e-hakaret-davasinda-kararini-verdi-205952 ["The court gave its decision in the 'Hakan Şükür insult' case"].

12 *See* Human Rights Violations Monitoring Project, https://turkeyrightsmonitor.com/en; "Resources," Solidarity with OTHERS, https://www.solidaritywithothers.com/resources; https://x.com/OthersInfo/status/1881669217797480875.

13 "Fuat Oktay'dan FETÖ ile mücadele açıklaması," Haber7 (14.07.2021), https://

www.haber7.com/guncel/haber/3120366-fuat-oktaydan-feto-ile-mucadele-aciklamasi ["Statement on the Fight Against FETÖ by Fuat Oktay"].

14 "Adalet Bakanı Bekir Bozdağ, gündemdeki merak edilen sorulara yanıt Verdi," CNN Türk (11.01.2023), https://www.cnnturk.com/turkiye/adalet-bakani-bekir-bozdag-gundemdeki-merak-edilen-sorulara-yanit-verdi-1879048 ["Minister of Justice Bekir Bozdağ answered questions on the agenda"].

15 "İşte kamudan atılanların isim isim listesi" ("Here is the list of names of those who were dismissed from the public sector"), Hürriyet (Sept. 02, 2016), https://www.hurriyet.com.tr/galeri-iste-kamudan-atilanlarin-isim-isim-listesi-40214111/1. *See also* "Report on the impact of the state of emergency on human rights in Turkey, including an update on the South-East, January–December 2017," Office of the United Nations High Commissioner for Human Rights (March 2018), https://www.ohchr.org/sites/default/files/Documents/Countries/TR/2018-03-19_Second_OHCHR_Turkey_Report.pdf. *See also* "2020 Country Reports on Human Rights Practices: Turkey," U.S. Department of State, https://www.state.gov/reports/2020-country-reports-on-human-rights-practices/turkey/.

16 "Dismissal of Public Servants by Emergency Decree Laws & HSYK/HSK Decisions," Solidarity with Others, https://www.solidaritywithothers.com/dismissal-by-decree-laws-and-hsk.

17 "Turkey Opinion on Emergency Decree Laws Nos. 667-676 Adopted Following the Failed Coup of July 15, 2016," European Commission for Democracy through Law (Venice Commission) (12 Dec. 2016), https://www.venice.coe.int/webforms/documents/default.aspx?pdffile=CDL-AD(2016)037-e.

18 "Closed and Confiscated Institutions by Emergency Decree Laws," Solidarity with Others, https://www.solidaritywithothers.com/closed-institutions.

19 "Turkey's Massive Crackdown on Healthcare Professionals," Advocates of Silenced Turkey (March 2019), https://silencedturkey.org/wp-content/uploads/2019/03/TURKEY%E2%80%99S-MASSIVE-CRACK-DOWN-ON-HEALTH-CARE-PROFESSIONALS.pdf.

20 Mustafa Yeneroğlu, "Hukuksuzluğun Sıradanlaşması: Silahlı Terör Örgütü Üyeliği Yargılamaları," Demokrasi ve Atılım Partisi Resmi Web Sitesi (Democracy and Atilim Party Official Website) (September 2021), https://cdn.devapartisi.org/422/Hukuksuzlugun-Siradanlasmasi.pdf ["Lawlessness Becoming Ordinary: Armed Terrorist Organization Membership Trials"].

21 "Hate Speech of the Erdoğan Regime: 'Fetö(!),'" Solidarity With Others (2023), https://www.solidaritywithothers.com/_files/ugd/b886b2_8da528792f2a47a89d-4e262659821d34.pdf. *See also* "Erdoğan's Vile Campaign of Hate Speech Case Study: Targeting of the Gülen Movement," **Stockholm Center for Freedom (May 2017),** https://stockholmcf.org/wp-content/uploads/2017/06/Erdoğans-Vile-Campaign-Of-Hate-Speech-Case-Study-Targeting-Of-The-Gulen-Movement_2017.pdf.

22 2021 Country Reports on Human Rights Practices: Türkiye, Bureau of Democracy, Human Rights, and Labor, U.S. Department of State, https://www.state.gov/reports/2021-country-reports-on-human-rights-practices/Türkiye/, https://www.state.gov/reports/2021-country-reports-on-human-rights-practices/turkey/.

23 *Id.*

24 2023 Country Reports on Human Rights Practices: Türkiye, Bureau of Democracy, Human Rights, and Labor, U.S. Department of State, https://www.state.gov/reports/2023-country-reports-on-human-rights-practices/Türkiye/. *See also* U.S. State Department's 2022 country report on Türkiye, https://www.state.gov/reports/2022-country-reports-on-human-rights-practices/Türkiye/.

25 "Human Rights in Türkiye," Amnesty International UK (18 May 2020), https://www.amnesty.org.uk/human-rights-turkey.

26 "Human Rights in Turkey: 2023 in Review," Stockholm Center for Freedom (March 4, 2024), https://stockholmcf.org/wp-content/uploads/2024/03/Human-Rights-in-Turkey-2023-in-Review.pdf. *See also* "Human Rights in Turkey: 2022 in Review," Stockholm Center for Freedom (Feb. 20, 2023), https://stockholmcf.org/wp-content/uploads/2023/02/Human-Rights-in-Turkey-Year-in-Review-2022.pdf. *See also* "Human Rights in Turkey: 2021 in Review," Stockholm Center for Freedom (Feb. 11, 2022), https://stockholmcf.org/wp-content/uploads/2022/02/Human-Rights-in-Turkey-2021-.pdf.

27 *See, e.g.*, "Reports," Advocates of Silenced Turkey, https://silencedturkey.org/reports-2.

28 "Turkey, Individuals associated with the Gülen Movement, The Finnish Immigration Service's Fact-finding Mission to Ankara and Istanbul 2–6 October 2023," Maahanmuuttovirasto Migrationsverket, Finish Immigration Service (June 2024), https://acrobat.adobe.com/id/urn:aaid:sc:EU:cdc8387c-0eef-4496-a333-d7d5fe396b02.

29 Mustafa Özmen, "Immigratie-en Naturalisatiedienst: The recent wave of mass arrests that have taken place in Turkey between 6 and 30 May 2024 (including minors and students - for providing support to families of detainees)," Justice Square (June 05, 2024), https://justicesquare.org/wp-content/uploads/2024/06/IND-MAY-NOTIFICATION_2.pdf.

30 Halit Turan, and İlker Turak, "FETÖ'ye 'Gazi Turgut Aslan' operasyonu: 59 ilde 543 gözaltı," Sabah (18.10.2022), https://www.sabah.com.tr/gundem/2022/10/18/fetoye-gazi-turgut-aslan-operasyonu-59-ilde-704-gozalti ["Operation 'Gazi Turgut Aslan' to FETÖ: 543 detentions in 59 provinces"].

31 "Turkey's Massive Crackdown on Healthcare Professionals Deepened the Country's Already Alarming Records of Human Rights Violations," Advocates of Silenced Turkey (Feb. 23, 2019), https://silencedturkey.org/turkeys-massive-crackdown-on-health-care-professionals-deepened-the-countrys-already-alarming-records-of-human-rights-violations.

32 *Id.*

33 Elmas Topcu, "Insulting Erdoğan is no laughing matter," DW Global Media Forum (02/12/2022), https://www.dw.com/en/turkey-marshals-law-to-defend-recep-tayyip-Erdoğans-honor/a-60733191; "Türkiye: End Prosecutions for 'Insulting President,'" Human Rights Watch (Oct. 17, 2018), https://www.hrw.org/news/2018/10/17/Türkiye-end-prosecutions-insulting-president.

34 Philip Bump, "Was Erdoğan personally involved in his bodyguards' attacks on protesters in D.C.?" Washington Post (May 19, 2017, https://www.washingtonpost.com/news/politics/wp/2017/05/19/was-Erdoğan-personally-involved-in-his-bodyguards-attacks-on-protesters-in-d-c/.

35 "Erdoğan guards attacked US Secret Service after protesters in 2017, new documents show," The Hill (11/9/19), https://thehill.com/policy/international/469705-Erdoğan-visit-stirs-memories-of-violent-protests/.

Chapter 2

The Quest for Hizmet's Eradication

Chronological Prelude

One important note to remember at the offset is that Fethullah Gülen, teacher and informal leader of the Hizmet movement, who had lived in self-imposed exile in Pennsylvania since 1999 until his death in October 2024, was indicted by the secularist government in 2000 under the Antiterror Law and criminal code of conspiring to change Türkiye from a secular state to a religious one. The 11th High Criminal Court acquitted him in 2006, finding in a detailed 50-page opinion that he had not formed or managed a terrorist organization bent on seizing power.[1]

Gülen won two appeals brought by the government, the last being before a plenary tribunal for criminal appeals in June 2008 on a 17-6 vote. The legal proceedings lasted eight years. He had gone into exile as the prosecution against him was beginning to ramp up and could never return home because of Erdoğan's eventual pursuit of him, even though the courts had exonerated him three times. Thirty-one judges had participated in the trial and appeals. Twenty-five ruled for Gülen.

This fact is important because the non-terrorist ruling was never overturned or reversed. Yet, the regime would ignore it and go on to label Hizmet as terrorist without proof, despite the standing high court ruling.

Another important prelude reminder, with more than a touch of irony. During the 2000-2010 era, under AKP leadership, Türkiye made enormous strides in implementing democratic reforms, augmenting human rights and civil liberties, and strengthening its judicial system with the European Union's help, as it contemplated joining the European

Union. The Gülen Movement, Hizmet, was a partner in this energetic endeavor.

Türkiye was chosen for President Barack Obama's first official foreign visit because of its prospect of becoming a secular democracy in a Muslim country. He addressed the parliament and praised the country's direction. Erdoğan turned the tables, though; and Obama eventually ended up years later denying his attempt to extradite Gülen for organizing the foiled coup because Türkiye could provide no evidence to support its assertion.

Transition of the Turkish Republic into the Erdoğan Regime

A brief review of the rise of the Erdoğan regime and the evolution of the state under his rule helps explain the origins of the hate policies and politicide directed toward Hizmet. Erdoğan and his collaborators initially identified with the innovative wing within the Virtue Party (Fazilet Partisi), an Islamist political party.

After the country's Constitutional Court banned the Virtue Party in June 2001 for violating the secularist articles of Türkiye's Constitution, he went on with others to establish the Justice and Development Party (AKP) two months later. Looking back a quarter century later, one can see more clearly now that Erdoğan's closely guarded, personal agenda was one-man rule by him, not one of philosophical or democratic principles.

The new AKP promised to pursue an innovative and liberal path, implement socio-economic reforms, protect human rights, advance relations and integration with the European Union, open the path to a democratic, conciliatory society, and oppose religious fundamentalism. These progressive goals garnered significant support for AKP from Turkish society, including from the Gülen Movement.

AKP came to power in 2002, following a tumultuous era in the country, which had involved counterterrorism measures and suspension of democratization. AKP was perceived as a welcome reform agent for society. Its initial years in power, buoyed by societal support, saw substantial democratization efforts and significant steps toward European Union accession. Reports prepared about Türkiye during that time reflected progress and offered hope.[2]

After eight years in power, however, AKP leaders gradually began transitioning to a different, more clandestine agenda. Once its cadre was in firm control, it implemented what may have been its covert agenda all along. It resurrected a hitherto dormant political Islamist ideology, more for electoral reasons than anything else, and began to show authoritarian signs.

Erdoğan, who had once advocated top-to-bottom democracy and used it to achieve his goals, slowly revealed himself in quite a different light. He expressed a view of democracy in the early years of his political career, which should have been a warning of things to come: "Democracy is a means to an end, not an end. We are committed to democracy until we achieve our goal.... Democracy is a tram for us. When we get to the stop we want, we get off."

Erdoğan repeated his belief that "democracy is not the goal, but the means"[3] to the Aegean Industrialists' and Businessmen's Association (ESİAD) in 2011. A wolf in sheep's clothing, he betrayed democracy's values and systems once he had the power to do so, and the nation's young democratic timbers were not strong enough to resist him.

As the regime began to re-gear itself, it pressed for allegiance from the strongly conservative religious communities it had supported. Even though having a relatively conservative religious foundation, Hizmet found itself at a crossroads with Erdoğan's political Islamist ideology, which clashed with Hizmet's contemporary and moderate Islamic discourse, emphasizing education, Westernization, dialogue, and tolerance.

After 2010, AKP leaders began to assiduously redesign the state apparatus and commandeer state resources to serve the party or, as they termed it, their causes and their allies' personal interests. Corruption and bribery networks targeting public assets became more overt.

Erdoğan abandoned the democratic and societal discourse that AKP had adopted during its rise and embraced aggressive political rhetoric aimed at consolidating groups identified as "his base." However, his policies disregarding democracy and the values of the Turkish Republic began to face backlash from society.

Hate speech became the medium to cover over the government's missteps and shore up Erdoğan's support structures. Hizmet took a clear stance against this lawlessness and hate speech, and the separation process accelerated in the fall of 2013 when Erdoğan began shuttering Hizmet-aligned college prep schools.

Initially, actions against Hizmet failed to gain widespread traction, especially among moderately conservative segments of society. The government, tarnished by rising corruption allegations and anti-democratic behavior, had lower public support than Hizmet, whose support came from various sectors, including social democrats, that also resisted the regime's illegal actions. Erdoğan desperately needed a strategy to discredit Hizmet and reverse its support.

28 May 2013: The Gezi Park Protest and National Uproar at Erdoğan's Violent Response

The first glimpse of Erdoğan's iron fist showed itself in his response to the Gezi Park protests that ran from May 28 to August 20, 2013. They began as a benign environmental pushback against plans to build a shopping center on top of the city's natural park next to Istanbul's iconic Taksim Square. The protests turned into country-wide resistance to Erdoğan, who was Prime Minister and out of the country at the time.

President Abdullah Gül tried for a peaceful solution; but, when Erdoğan returned to Türkiye, he moved swiftly to brutally put down the unrest. He branded the Gezi Park protesters as "looters," one of his first hate speech slogans to denigrate protestors or dissenters, however legitimate their cause. The unrest escalated into mass anti-government rallies across the country, which Erdoğan fiercely suppressed, leaving eleven people dead and more than 8,000 persons injured. The police arrest tally exceeded 3,000 individuals.

A premonition of things to come occurred during the Gezi Park uprising. A few days after the protests had begun, according to Erdoğan, a woman wearing a headscarf, 25-year-old Zehra Develioğlu, appeared in the pro-government press and made the fantastic and false claim that she and her baby had been attacked by dozens of protesters (mostly half-naked men with leather pants and gloves), who insulted her Islamic attire, kicked her baby, and urinated on her by the docks in Istanbul's middle-class Kabataş district and in broad daylight. She was the daughter-in-law of a mayor from the ruling AKP, whom Erdoğan called a "very close and important friend."[4]

Erdoğan often repeated Develioğlu's lie in his rallies to demonize the Gezi Park protesters, always playing the headscarf card for his conservative religious followers and repeating the same untruth: "They dragged my 'hijabi' sister on the streets near my office and attacked her and her child."

The assault was totally and utterly fabricated, and the government knew it—something that independent reporting thoroughly proved from security camera footage at the scene, police evidence (including videos), and testimony from a source close to the woman who conjured it up.

> "The people voiced democratic demands [during the Gezi Park protests] and, initially, there were innocent protests. These protests could have been tolerated. Officials could have visited the protesters and learned about their demands. Instead, the protests were violently suppressed. Is the shopping center that was to be built there worth a single drop of blood?"
>
> Fethullah Gülen

Skepticism was rampant from the beginning, given the unbelievable midday fact scenario, unwitnessed by anyone. However, the government claimed it had a video that supported her claim but would not release it because it was too horrific. Not many people believed that and faulted the regime's lack of transparency. In the end, there was no such video, and Erdoğan knew it; but he shoved ahead full speed with the false narrative, crassly playing the nationalist, xenophobic, and Islamist cards.

Even after it became public knowledge that the story was conjured up, Erdoğan repeated the same hate-baiting lie in early March 2015 at the Turkish Metal Workers' Union's 20th Grand Convention of Women Laborers.[5] Erdoğan's political use of hate language dressed in lies was beginning to ramp up and come into its own.

The pro-government media finally admitted in early March 2021 to the grotesque lie they had foisted on the nation for eight years. They could not accept responsibility for their own complicity but blamed the deception on the journalist who drafted the story and, of course, not on the government or Erdoğan. No *mea culpa* from the regime that foisted a gigantic falsity on the nation to denigrate a group of well-meaning young citizens. Even after that revelation, Erdoğan repeated the false story for his political use.

Underlining the regime's hegemony over the media by then, fifteen columns in five different pro-government newspapers bore the same headline: "Your language is rude; your conscience is as hard as a stone," a cute wordplay in Turkish.[6] The government spoon-fed the words to the press, and the media lapped it up without its own *mea culpa* for having reported and perpetuated the lie.

Türkiye's largest protest in modern history unnerved Erdoğan. Hizmet, which once had generally supported him in the initial phase of his leadership ten years earlier, was critical, which must also have alarmed him. The animosity between them began to percolate after the vicious crackdown on the Gezi Park protesters.

Equally disconcerting for Erdoğan was that the courts acquitted the Gezi Park protest leaders in 2015. This legal slap in the face validated his search, already in progress, for ways to manipulate the judges and sharply bend the judiciary to his will.

People only learned much later how deeply he loathed the courts that freed the Gezi protesters and how he would take reprisals even after years had passed. Erdoğan never forgot something for which he wanted to exact vengeance, as he often reminded his audiences.

Even twelve years later, his government is still seeking revenge by continuing to prosecute people seen as Gezi supporters or organizers, not that they perpetrated any kind of violence but for "intensive communication" with the acquitted Gezi Park protestors during their trial, according to an arrest made on January 28, 2025.[7]

December 17-25, 2013: Caught in Brazen Corruption, the Government Sends Out a Smoke Screen

The question of the great wealth that Erdoğan, family, and friends ("cronies," might fit better) were accumulating began to come into sharp focus, a question that became heavier as time went on. As head of state, his annual salary is equal to $65,000. He was financially broke and had no wealth when entering politics decades earlier.

Yet somehow, Erdoğan and his family acquired incredibly valuable assets, allegedly hidden in overseas trusts. He is one of the world's richest heads of government. The American Enterprise Institute has designated him as a "billionaire many times over" and published several exposé articles about his mysterious and sudden extreme personal and familial wealth.[8] Given the general truth of the adage "where there's smoke, there's fire," it was not surprising that questions of possible corruption would bubble to the surface.

In the ego department, speculation, not credibly denied by Erdoğan, has it that he aspires to occupy a 21st Century position comparable to the Ottoman Caliph. That desire seems to be operative in his foreign policy decisions and displays of wealth and power. He built an outsized presidential palace in 2014, for which he received sharp criticism for heavily spending public funds and in an environmentally sensitive area and a legally protected site near Ankara, where the law permitted no construction. The government put the price for the 920,000-square-foot palace at $615 million, but the cost was significantly more, $1.2 billion according to reliable sources.

Erdoğan also reportedly spent upwards of $70 million to construct a lavish 27.600-square-foot vacation property in Marmaris, Türkiye, complete with an artificial beach. The elite presidential pomposity and vacation property money could have been better invested in Türkiye's insufficient healthcare and education systems, which have greater need and less negative impact on the country's economy and welfare.

The widening cleavage between Hizmet and Erdoğan yawned further with the immense corruption scandal in December 2013, a few months after Gezi Park, which suddenly enveloped Erdoğan's family, friends, and government officials. The Hizmet Movement and Fethullah Gülen were critical of the moral failure presented by the corruption, no doubt further alarming Erdoğan, who had already begun his anti-Hizmet trajectory to cut back its influence in Turkish civil society.

The more Hizmet called him to task, the more Erdoğan loathed Hizmet and sought to suppress it. The fact that Hizmet held him and the regime accountable for the scandal set off flares across the darkening sky. They were now solid enemies, not just antagonists. His path to power was getting shaky; and he acted in the only way he knew, with a hammer. What was best for Türkiye was not part of the calculus.

Following the judiciary's investigations into government bribery and corruption December 17-25, 2013, the Erdoğan regime dramatically demonized Hizmet as a group to be ostracized and eliminated. This process involved a meticulously crafted hate policy aimed at erasing, devaluing, and alienating Hizmet from society at large. Politicide, in other words.

Under the cover of a hate campaign, the government levied laws, regulations, administrative procedures, and judicial actions against Hizmet. These included extraordinarily oppressive government inspections and closure of Hizmet-affiliated educational institutions, sanctions on Bank Asya (founded and operated by Hizmet-sympathizing businesspeople), seizure of assets of Hizmet-associated businesspeople, and the appointment of state trustees over Hizmet schools and businesses.

After Gezi Park, the government's favorite pejorative nouns for Hizmet evolved with increasing venom from "Parallel Organization" in 2012, to "Parallel State Organization" (PSO), then later "FETÖ/PSO," and finally settling on "FETÖ" ("Fethullahist Terrorist Organization") in 2016. The term is broad and sweeps within it any people who might have favorably spoken about the Gülen Movement or its organizations (such as the schools). "FETÖ" became a noun to which defamatory adjectives were frequently appended.

The December 17-25 corruption and bribery scandal propelled Erdoğan's full-throttle assault on Türkiye's democracy and judiciary and his war on Hizmet.[9] The scandal began unfolding as a criminal investigation, involving key government officials. All fifty-two people, whom the prosecutors detained on December 17 for investigation, were related to AKP.

Prosecutors formally accused fourteen people, including Süleyman Aslan, CEO of state-owned Halkbank, Iranian businessman Reza Zarrab, and several family members of cabinet ministers of bribery, corruption, fraud, money laundering, and gold smuggling with Iran in violation of an international embargo.

On December 21, a court ordered their arrest. At the heart of the scandal was an alleged "gas for gold" scheme with Iran, involving Aslan, who had $4.5 million in cash stored in shoeboxes in his home when arrested. Zarrab eventually was arrested in the United States and pleaded guilty to the scheme in 2017 as part of the prosecution and conviction of Mehmet Hakan Atilla, deputy head of Halkbank regarding the same scandal.[10]

In 2016, Erdoğan unsuccessfully asked then-Vice-President Joe Biden to remove Preet Bharara, the U.S. attorney in New York who would go on to indict Zarrab. Following continued lobbying by Erdoğan, President Donald Trump later fired Bharara in 2017. In late 2018, Erdoğan personally lobbied Trump twice to drop further investigations into Halkbank. Trump agreed. Erdoğan's actions speak for themselves as to his own guilt or innocence vis-à-vis the scandal.

In total, ninety-one people were detained in the investigation, twenty-six of them arrested by court order. Erdoğan, then Prime Minister, and the government moved quickly to purge the police force, sacking dozens of police chiefs, including the Istanbul Chief of Police, and thus de-fang the criminal proceedings.

Then, on December 25, several newspapers reported a further investigation was about to commence, involving Erdoğan's son Bilal and others. However, police, newly appointed by the government just a few days previously, refused to carry out their orders; and the prosecutor behind the second investigation was summarily dismissed on the same day. A heated controversy erupted after the YouTube release of audio recordings in which Erdoğan allegedly was heard telling Bilal to urgently get rid of tens of millions of dollars from his home.

Four ministers implicated in the scandal resigned. One of those ministers called on Erdoğan to also step down, accusing him of having approved everything. At midnight on January 7, 2014, the government published a decree, removing 350 police officers from their positions, including the chiefs of units dealing with financial crimes, smuggling, and organized crime, and reassigning them across the country in inconvenient locations far from home, which caused officers to resign rather than uproot their families.

Not only did the officers who conducted the corruption investigations lose their jobs, but, after Erdoğan cemented control of the judiciary, the courts convicted them of a judicial coup aimed at bringing down the elected government regardless of whether the facts were established beyond doubt that the defendants in the corruption cases committed the alleged acts (as noted, one the main actors was arrested in the United States and pleaded guilty). The courts gave these officers aggravated life prison sentences.

An aggravated life sentence entails thirty years' imprisonment, after which prisoners are eligible for parole on condition of good behavior. People with aggravated life sentences face harsher conditions than other prisoners: solitary confinement for twenty-three hours/day, one phone call every fifteen days to immediate family members, visitation by immediate family for one hour every fifteen days, and no permission to leave under any circumstances.

According to the United Nations Standard Minimum Rules for the Treatment of Prisoners ("The Nelson Mandela Rules"), prolonged solitary confinement amounts to torture or other cruel, inhuman, or degrading treatment or punishment and must not be imposed under any circumstances. The rules also prohibit discriminatory sentencing on the grounds of political or other opinion, among other grounds.[11]

Gülen, whose relationship with Erdoğan had become so frayed as to be beyond repair, strongly criticized the unwarranted purge of civil servants, while Erdoğan continued to describe the corruption investigation as a "judicial coup" by those jealous of his success, backed by an international conspiracy (United States and Israel), and a "dirty plot" of Hizmet. Erdoğan threatened to expel U.S. ambassador Francis Ricciardone from Türkiye. Erdoğan and his government accused Gülen and Hizmet followers of treason and started referring to them as "terrorists."[12]

Eventually, AKP saw to it that parliament swept the scandal under the rug and returned the bribery money to the culprits—with interest. Another event that says much about the regime's integrity.

Erdoğan could have accepted responsibility for the scandal and tried to repair the damage, but he and his cohorts were too deep into the mud. He went on a ferocious offensive, marshaling as much government power as he could to turn the tables on those who sought to clean up the mess. This was to be a series of pitched battles, the first of which was creating the official regime narrative, no matter how false it might be. He would do everything possible to keep—and expand—power and protect the corruption.

Interpreting Hizmet's principled reaction against the corruption scandal as a personal undertaking against himself, Erdoğan and his government let loose vicious sentiments of hatred, vengeance, and animosity toward the Movement, not only to alter the national narrative but to forever ostracize and vilify Hizmet members, politicide.

This included manipulating the judiciary and other organs of government to obliterate their rights. Hizmet's brand of clean government and civil society were incompatible with Erdoğan's agenda. He needed them out of the way. Hizmet was too much of a threat to him and his group who were scamming Türkiye.

Erdoğan's own words to Parliament on February 25, 2014, laid out the new narrative that he wanted the country to embrace and for which he would be the avenging angel:

> ...This is an independence struggle. We will not hesitate for a moment to put our lives on the line for our independence. On December 17, a clear attack was made on our national will, our institutions, and our values. On December 17, followed by the December 25 attack, they were going to sideline the government and once again seize control. This coup attempt will not go unanswered. First, the people, then the judiciary, will hold them accountable for this coup attempt. We will unveil all the disgraces of this parallel organization, making those associated with them so condemned that they won't be able to step foot outside. We will make them condemned to the point they cannot walk the streets....[13]

His use of coup language at the time was curious, particularly in retrospect.

Two months later, after AKP did well in municipal elections, Erdoğan had even more vituperative comments to the AKP annual general assembly in November:

> .... On 30 March, our nation gave us the mandate to combat the "parallel structure." Before March 30, we labeled it as a new struggle for our future. Our country faced a treacherous, despicable, and

> unforgivable attack on our unity and independence. Rest assured, the survival of this structure, inflicting more harm on Türkiye, is no longer possible. The main resources of this structure have been dulled. Our citizens, thinking there was a Gülen organization in Anatolia and Thrace, started to distance themselves from this organization. They started to withdraw their children from schools and educational institutions. The schools haven't been closed yet, not everyone has made a definite decision. Courageous prosecutors and judges in Adana, Istanbul, Ankara have patriotically taken steps to fulfil their professional and conscientious duties. They often talk about the fight against the parallel structure turning into a witch hunt. If changing the duties of those who betrayed this country is called a witch hunt, then know that we will conduct this witch hunt. This fight is not an ordinary one. Anyone who knows where and what is being done in this regard should inform us. We will sterilize this filthy water, whether by boiling it or breaking it down to molecules. I say to all my citizens, you will inform us, and we will act accordingly. History won't forgive those who remain silent. So long as I breathe, I won't forget or forgive….[14]

His language embraced a witch hunt and said nothing about due process.

Then, to journalists six weeks later, on a return flight from France, he began to telegraph his agenda more explicitly:

> .... The steps of the executive are being hindered by the "parallel judiciary." Some legal arrangements we've made are in front of the President. Once approved by him, swift steps will be taken...[15]

> …. There are those inside and outside. There are those who have fled. Everything from issuing red bulletins [Interpol] to opening cases will happen. Just like they filed hundreds of lawsuits against us, we will file hundreds, thousands of lawsuits against them. Then the situation will develop differently.... We are developing a project; the process will accelerate....[16]

The 2015 Election

A year later General elections were held in June 2015 to elect 550 members to parliament. This was the 24th general election in the history of the Turkish Republic, electing the country's 25th Parliament. The result was the first hung parliament since 1999. AKP's unsuccessful attempts to form a coalition government resulted in a snap general election for November 2015. AKP plunged into the snap election and won it, but the demonstrated tenuousness of his power could have only unsettled Erdoğan.

We now turn to how he "accelerated his project" against Hizmet.

The Attempted Coup: a "Blessing from God" or Curse for Türkiye?

On July 15, 2016, a faction within the Turkish Armed Forces, allegedly organized as the Peace at Home Council, attempted a coup d'état against the government. They tried to seize control of places in Ankara, Istanbul, Marmaris, and elsewhere, such as the Asian-side entrance of the Bosphorus Bridge but failed after forces and civilians loyal to the state defeated them.

During the slipshod coup attempt, as many as 251 people were killed and more than 2,100 were injured. Government buildings, including the parliament and the presidential palace, were bombed from the air. The main opposition parties in Türkiye condemned the attempt, as did Gülen and Hizmet.

The alleged rebellious council cited an erosion of secularism, elimination of democratic rule, disregard for human rights, and Türkiye's loss of international credibility as reasons for the coup. Erdoğan, within hours, blamed Gülen and began purging civil servants.

The government said it had evidence linking the coup leaders to the Gülen Movement, but it never produced any proof at the time and never has since. The government, playing to its nationalist base, alleged also that the United States, not an infrequent whipping boy, had a role in the attempted coup. Smoke and mirrors.

The New York Times and some other Western media such as *The Economist*,[17] described the purges as a "counter-coup," with the *Times* presciently expecting Erdoğan to "become more vengeful and obsessed with control than ever, exploiting the crisis not just to punish mutinous soldiers but to further quash whatever dissent is left in Türkiye."[18]

No one knows what to make of the coup attempt because it was so incompetently executed and had so few participants. There were peculiar pre-coup meetings within the government and associates, as well as seemingly coordinated responses post-attempt that appeared planned.

It was also odd that the coup began at 10:00 pm on a hot Friday evening while the country was still awake. Most coups occur in the early morning hours when people are asleep at home and immediately sequester the political leaders, which did not happen in this event. This was nothing like the 1960 and 1980 military coups that assumed power in Türkiye.

The "coup plotters" trials afterward demonstrated no real leaders or any post-coup plan. Parliament established an inquiry commission but did not invite key figures, such as the chief of the intelligence service and the army chief of staff to testify despite the insistence of commission members from the opposition parties. Parliament never published the final report, and it has since mysteriously disappeared.

Superiors mobilized military school students to take part in the coup event. Those who gave the orders were later promoted while the students were sentenced to aggravated life in prison. No post-mortem examinations were performed on those killed on the bridge; and no forensic ballistics were conducted on the guns to determine who was responsible for the killings. Video footage that emerged later appears to show snipers on the bridge, who killed both protesting civilians and soldiers. Some alleged that the snipers were members of paramilitary SADAT teams, a secretive private military enterprise.

The government immediately arrested those journalists who began investigating what happened and seized their computers, papers, and other items.

Because no independent and impartial court or forum has investigated the incident, no one will know until Erdoğan leaves power, if then.[19] Former AKP parliament member and pro-government journalist Şamil Tayyar stated in a TV interview: "If the July 15 coup attempt is thoroughly unraveled one day, you will see that those you view as traitors today were indeed the true patriots, and those whom you view today as patriots were indeed the real traitors."[20]

Even as the coup attempt was thwarted, Erdoğan appeared in public with his son-in-law Berat Albayrak, and unabashedly called the attempt "a divine gift, a blessing from God,"[21] which cynically played into the hands of hardcore Islamists. Derailing of a growing democracy and causing untold suffering to believers are not generally considered attributes of the Deity, but rather of a man, who, as Voltaire once cryptically remarked, tried to create God in his own image and likeness instead of the other way around.

This event marked the ballooning of Erdoğan's well-honed hate speech into sudden, actionable consequences. His hatred propelled hate crimes. The regime filled prisons, detention centers, police stations, and sports halls overnight with members and supporters of Hizmet, whom the government suddenly accused as terrorists and coup plotters.

A key figure during the state of emergency, declared six days after the coup attempt, was Prime Minister Binali Yıldırım. As he was leaving office after the country's transition to the presidential system, he made a farewell visit to the state news Anadolu Agency. During an interview with the Editor's Desk, when asked if there was a project of the government that had been particularly challenging for him, he responded, "The project I did not like was July 15th. I wish it had not happened.... And those who made this [coup] attempt were faced with a problem that they could not have calculated. Otherwise, the projects we do outside of that, they are all nice things."

The interviewer did not follow up on his enigmatic comment, which perhaps suggested that Hizmet's eradication was a government project.[22]

"FETÖ" Hate Speech Turned into State Politicide Policy

Before the December 2013 corruption and bribery scandal, the government commonly referred to Hizmet derogatorily as the "community" or "congregation" ("cemaat," in Turkish), Gülen Movement, or simply Hizmet. Following publication of news about the December scandal in Hizmet-associated media outlets, the regime, ever more at odds with Hizmet, ramped up its state-sponsored hate speech campaign with disparaging terms like "parallel state structure," "assassins," "seemingly legal but illegal structures," and, ultimately, the "Fethullahist Terror Organization (FETÖ)."

Driven by the delusional or paranoid idea that Hizmet possessed the power to overthrow his government through elections or parliamentary means, Erdoğan quickly and aggressively set his target sights on the movement. The courts were also creating pressure on him, something that rankled and concerned him enough that he publicly complained about it.

> "As someone who suffered under multiple military coups during the past five decades, it is especially insulting to be accused of having any link to such an attempt. I categorically deny such accusations."
>
> Fethullah Gülen
> July 16, 2016

The regime portrayed the July 15 coup attempt as Hizmet-orchestrated. Erdoğan did not believe that (nor did anyone else), but it was the ideal chance to step up his war on Hizmet and get it out of his way. It was the perfect opportunity to consolidate even more power and further gut Türkiye's democratic institutions.

The acronym "FETÖ" was a quintessential destructive expression of hate speech, and the Erdoğan regime imposed it on society without any supporting court decision. The term eventually passed unchallenged into rulings by judges, who had become government "lapdogs," as Erdoğan supporter Doğu Perinçek candidly admitted.[23] Perinçek leads the small minority left-wing nationalist Patriotic Party. He has been an influential informal foreign policy adviser to the Turkish government with a largely anti-West and pro-China bent.

"FETÖ" was used widely to target Hizmet-associated individuals and demean them, presenting them as guilty enemies of the nation and secret terrorists without any evidence or any due process, and promoting discrimination and violence against them and their families. Calling Hizmet an "armed terrorist organization" and "treasonous" without a single supporting fact were frequent recitals in the regime's litany of hatred.

Unfortunately, tying the "terrorist" label to a particular person, Gülen in this case, was a savvy move. It is always easier to generate public hostility toward a "malevolent" individual who is leading others down the primrose path to perdition than to attack one's individual friends, neighbors, and acquaintances who belong to a particular civil society association. However, that could be (and was) the eventual outcome. Once enmity toward the group has taken hold, individual dissociation from the villainous organization becomes problematic in the eyes of others who were once friends, neighbors, and acquaintances.

Added to this, Erdoğan stirred up xenophobia by playing off the fact that Gülen resided in the United States at the time, rather than in Türkiye, which fit into his nationalist rhetoric and is sometimes part of his "blame the United States" game, as during the December 2013 corruption scandal.

Gülen was in self-exile for a reason. He would certainly have been in prison had he gone back to Türkiye, even if his ill health could have borne a return to his homeland. Nor would he have been able to exercise his spiritual leadership for the movement. Given what the regime has shown in how it treats Hizmet folks and the hate language it spun against Gülen personally, the outcome would not have been in doubt.

Even when Fethullah Gülen died in late October 2024, Erdoğan could not pause the hate speech but railed forth, saying Gülen had suffered a "dishonorable death" and labeling him a "demon in human form." He reiterated his agenda to eradicate and "completely" eliminate Hizmet.[24]

Türkiye's state broadcasting regulator warned the media against praising Gülen, when he died, saying no broadcaster can honor a "terrorist." Foreign Minister Hakan Fidan said Gülen's death "will not make us complacent or relaxed. This organization has been a threat rarely seen in the history of our nation." He called on Gülen's followers to turn away from "this treasonous wrong path."[25]

Journalist Kazım Güleçyüz, the editor-in-chief of the *Yeni Asya* newspaper and no supporter of Hizmet, was arrested and spent 57 days incarcerated on charges of disseminating terrorist propaganda for conveying condolences on social media when Gülen passed away. Jail time for a customary act of basic humanity and civil society.[26]

Transforming Hate Speech into State Policy

Hizmet as a "terrorist organization" became the official political discourse of the Erdoğan regime and the core material for his "witch hunts." An apparatchik media, government bureaucracy, judiciary, and religious leaders rapidly disseminated this hate speech to society. It was a roadmap for civil death, politicide."[27]

The extent to which a country has become democratized speaks to its ability to resist autocrats and demagogues bent on obtaining and consolidating power. Türkiye's democracy was nascent when Erdoğan began clawing up the political ladder. He followed the authoritarian playbook adeptly, paying lip service to democracy while stabbing it in the back. Act One of the playbook was adopting hate speech.

Political authorities, even when they do not personally believe in the rhetoric they utter publicly, often employ hate speech to reign in democratic tendencies. They discredit and marginalize dissenters and use hate speech to vilify them. Hate speech legitimizes autocratic interventions, witch hunts, and social persecution. For anti-democratic authorities, hate speech masks their failures, validates illegal actions and corruption, and paves the way to neutralize opposing factions through government oppression.[28] Erdoğan and AKP followed the script.

The next phase, sometimes in tandem with the first, is utilizing hate-filled propaganda to generate negative societal reactions and biases against the target group. If the propaganda is strong enough, it can create sinister narratives devoid of factual bases. It legitimizes and incites hatred toward the targeted individuals.

Executors of hate policies deliberately spread provocative, discriminatory, and violence-framed rhetoric, intending harm, whether a criminal act or discriminatory action. Hate speech constructs the foundation for hate crimes that society or the state could commit, motivating and justifying these actions.[29] Hate speech can become an explicit precursor to violence. A systemic hate strategy inevitably leads to crimes, often crimes against humanity, which is the final stage of the hate-propelled policy,[30] or politicide.

This slogan-like hate speech against Hizmet spread widely in Türkiye through written, visual, and social media. As politicians and others reiterate this hate speech, the media become purveyors of hate policies, demonization, and marginalization. They are co-actors in politicide.

Once society acquiesces in hate policies, the state proceeds to build its politicide structure through a discriminatory legal framework. That, in turn, overrides fundamental universal rights and protections. Judicial institutions come to operate within this framework and protect it.

Wrap-Up: The Strategy for Implementing FETÖ Hate Speech

This hate speech, systematically constructed by the government and adopted by opposition and society at large, operates on four core policies targeting Hizmet:

1. Eradicating societal tolerance by exaggerating negative notions and distorting perceptions

2. Attacking the community's rights and dignity by using derogatory terms like "coup plotter," "traitor," "terrorist," "unpatriotic," "agent," and the like

3. Instigating hostility and discrimination and inciting violence by using inflammatory rhetoric

4. Escalating hostility to the extent of endorsing violence, even potential crimes against humanity or genocide, by using phrases like "uprooting," "cleansing," and "denying the right to live"[31]

Despite all the years passing since the coup attempt, this narrative continues in full force, spewing hatred and encouraging violence. The quest for politicide carried on to this day in undiminished vigor, in violation of both international law and Turkish law.

The following two chapters describe how Erdoğan stepped up his power grab through the massive purge of public employees, prosecutors, and judges simultaneously with his invoking a state of emergency and then ruling by decree for two years. All steps in his compulsive desire to annihilate Hizmet.

Endnotes

1 *See* James C. Harrington, *Wrestling with Free Speech, Religious Freedom, and Democracy in Turkey: The Political Trials and Times of Fethullah Gulen* (Lanham, MD, USA: University Press of America, 2011).

2 *See, e.g.*, "Commission Staff Working Document, Turkey 2010 Progress Report, accompanying the Communication from the Commission to the European Parliament and the Council" European Commission, Brussels (9.11.2010), https://eur-lex.europa.eu/LexUriServ/LexUriServ.do?uri=SEC:2010:1327:FIN:EN:PDF, İET: 23/06/2023.

3 "Demokrasi Amaç Değil Araçtır," *Hürriyet* (March 06, 2011), https://www.hurriyet.com.tr/gundem/Erdoğan-demokrasi-amac-degil-aractir-17197745 ["Democracy is not the goal, but the means"]. *See also* "Recep Tayyip Erdoğan: 'Demokrasi bizim için amaç değil araçtır,'" Posted Jan 22, 2013, TarihUnutmaz, YouTube, 1 min., 6 sec., https://www.youtube.com/watch?v=qY52kEMQyBA ["Democracy is like a train; you get off once you reach your destination"].

4 "Pro-gov't daily admits 'fake' reports of attack on headscarved woman by Gezi protestors," Stockholm Center for Freedom (July 30, 2021), https://stockholmcf.org/pro-govt-daily-admits-fake-reports-of-attack-on-headscarved-woman-by-gezi-protestors/. *See* also Berivan Orucoglu, "Turks, Lies, and Videotape: Today's Turkey is a place where fictitious news reports live on long after they've been debunked," Foreign Policy (FP) (March 13, 2015), https://foreignpolicy.com/2015/03/13/turks-lies-and-videotape-turkey-Erdoğan/.

5 "Turkish President Erdoğan reawakens Kabataş attack claims," *Hürriyet Daily News* (March 7, 2015), https://www.hurriyetdailynews.com/turkish-president-Erdoğan-reawakens-kabatas-attack-claims-79280.

6 The words "shameless" (kaba) and "stone" (taş) make up the word "Kabataş," referring to the scene of the fabricated attack.

7 "Turkey arrests talent manager over trying to overthrow the government," Reuters (Jan. 28, 2025), https://www.reuters.com/world/middle-east/turkey-arrests-talent-manager-over-trying-overthrow-government-2025-01-28/.

8 *See* Abdullah Bozkurt, "Insider: Erdoğan Has Made Billions from Bribes and Kickbacks, Middle East Forum (June 1, 2023), https://www.meforum.org/insider-erdogan-has-made-billions-from-bribes.

9 Mahmut Cengiz, "How the Corruption Investigations of 2013 Still Shape Turkey's Bleak Future," Vocal Europe (22/12/2017), https://www.vocaleurope.eu/how-the-corruption-investigations-of-2013-still-shape-turkeys-bleak-future/; *and see* Berivan Orucoglu, "Why Turkey's Mother of All Corruption Scandals Refuses to Go Away," Foreign Policy Magazine (6 Jan. 2015, https://foreignpolicy.com/2015/01/06/why-turkeys-mother-of-all-corruption-scandals-refuses-to-go-away/.

10 "Turkish Opposition Launches Inquiry into Government Bribery," Organized Crime and Corruption Reporting Project (OCCRP) (24 Sept. 2020), https://www.occrp.org/en/daily/13168-turkish-opposition-launches-inquiry-into-government-bribery.

11 "The Nelson Mandela Rules," United Nations Standard Minimum Rules for the Treatment of Prisoners, https://www.un.org/en/events/mandeladay/mandela_rules.shtml.

12 "2013 corruption scandal in Turkey," Wikipedia, https://en.wikipedia.org/wiki/2013_corruption_scandal_in_Turkey.

13 "Başbakan: Robot lobisi tweetlerle vuracaktı," *Hürriyet* (Feb. 25, 2014), https://www.hurriyet.com.tr/gundem/basbakan-robot-lobisi-tweetlerle-vuracak-

ti-25887710 ["Prime Minister: The robot lobby would hit with Tweets"].

14 "Erdoğan'dan önemli açıklamalar," *Hürriyet* (May 11, 2014), https://www.hurriyet.com.tr/gundem/Erdoğandan-onemli-aciklamalar-26397831 ["Important statements from Erdoğan"].

15 "Erdoğan: Köşk adaylığı konusunda ters köşe yapabiliriz," T24 (23 June 2014), https://t24.com.tr/haber/Erdoğan-kosk-adayligi-konusunda-ters-kose-yapabiliriz,262043.

16 ¨Erdoğan: 'Bu iş burada bitmez,'" Star (24 June 2014), https://www.star.com.tr/politika/Erdoğan-bu-is-burada-bitmez-haber-900227/.

17 "After the coup, the counter-coup," *The Economist* (July 23, 2016), https://www.economist.com/briefing/2016/07/23/after-the-coup-the-counter-coup.

18 "The Counter-Coup in Turkey," New York Times (July 16, 2016), Opinion | The Counter-Coup in Turkey - The New York Times (nytimes.com).

19 Michael Rubin, "Did Erdoğan Stage the Coup?" AEIdeas (14 April 2017), https://www.aei.org/foreign-and-defense-policy/middle-east/did-Erdoğan-stage-the-coup/.

20 Necip F. Bahadir, "Unveiling the Truth of July 15: A Critical Examination," Politurco (July 15, 2024), https://politurco.com/unveiling-the-truth-of-july-15-a-critical-examination.html.

21 Marc Champion, "Coup was 'Gift from God' for Erdoğan Planning a New Turkey," Bloomberg (July 17, 2016), https://www.bloomberg.com/news/articles/2016-07-17/coup-was-a-gift-from-god-says-Erdoğan-who-plans-a-new-turkey.

22 ¨Binali Yıldırım: Hoşuma gitmeyen proje 15 Temmuz¨ (05.07.2018), https://www.cumhuriyet.com.tr/haber/binali-yildirim-hosuma-gitmeyen-proje-15-temmuz-1017813 ("Was there a project that challenged you a lot? So, the project I don't like is July 15th. I wish it had not happened, thank God, the determination of our president, our nation's protection of the flag... Patriotic policemen, soldiers to carry out orders, and above all, you media. He did a great job that night. And those who made this attempt were faced with a problem that they could not have calculated for. Otherwise, the projects we do outside of that, they are all nice things.").

23 "Perinçek: Hukuk siyasetin köpeğidir," posted June 8, 2021, by Kaç Saat Oldu?, YouTube (2 min., 14 sec), https://www.youtube.com/watch?v=8apwDkbWPcA ["Perinçek: Law is the dog of politics"]. (Perincek, on Habeturk TV discussion panel, "Enine Boyuna" by Ece Guner in October 2017, that the judicial system [judges and their verdicts] are the dog of politics [the government]). *See also* "D.Perinçek E.Şen 'Hukuk siyasetin köpeğidir' Tartışması...," posted Oct. 27, 2017, by Adalet Ve Özgürlük Hareketi, YouTube (2 min, 14 sec), https://www.youtube.com/watch?v=RTSUoPSEACM ["D.Perinçek - E.Şen 'Law is the dog of politics' Debate..."] ("Justice and Freedom Movement").

24 Michael Rubinkam, "Thousands mourn Fethullah Gülen, a Turkish spiritual leader who died in the US," Associated Press (Oct. 24, 2024), https://apnews.com/article/fethullah-gulen-turkey-dead-funeral-burial-69336b5a23988b0c-2c350a4799ff6c51.

25 *Id.*

26 "Turkish court releases editor arrested for conveying condolences for Erdoğan foe," Stockholm Center for Freedom (Dec. 19, 2024), https://stockholmcf.org/turkish-court-releases-editor-arrested-for-conveying-condolences-for-Erdoğan-foe/.

27 "Erdoğan Rejiminin Nefret Söylemi: 'FETÖ,'" Solidarity with Others (2023),

https://tr.solidaritywithothers.com/_files/ugd/b886b2_a19495c590774e08a3bec-5433be47b02.pdf (pp.6-7).

28 *Id.* p.6.

29 Karaduman, Murat/Akbulutgiller, Betül: Yeni Medyada Nefret Ve Ayrımcı Söylem: Gazetelerin Twıtter Hesapları Üzerine Bir Analiz, Yeni Medya Çalışmaları II. Ulusal Kongre Yeni Medya Yayıncılığı, 26-27 Şubat 2015, İstanbul Kongre Kitabı, s.374 vd., https://ekitap.alternatifbilisim.org/pdf/ymk-2.pdf, İET:16/08/2023 (Karaduman, Murat/Akbulutgiller, Betül. “Hate Speech and Discriminatory Discourse in New Media: An Analysis of Newspapers' Twitter Accounts.” In Proceedings of the II. National Congress on New Media Broadcasting, February 26-27, 2015, Istanbul Congress Book, pp. 374 *et seq.*

30 *Id.*

31 “Hate Crimes,” Hate Crime Monitoring Project Against Gulen Movement Members, https://en.nefretsucu.com/.

Chapter 3

The Purge

Erdoğan seized on the botched coup as a pretext to proceed full speed against Hizmet associates, sympathizers, and other adversaries (secular dissidents and Kurdish leaders) whose names were on extensive "enemy" lists already prepared long before the coup attempt. This raises significant questions about why the lists even existed and how the government had gone about compiling them.

The regime, capitalizing on the coup chaos, instantly activated "watch" lists, previously assembled by officials from public institutions and intelligence agencies, beginning in February 2016 during Prime Minister Ahmet Davutoğlu's tenure. They targeted public servants associated with organizations and structures posing "a threat to national security." There was never an operative precise definition of "a threat to national security," although it encompassed legitimate liberties and activities, dissenting however mildly from the regime, with which the government took political umbrage.

The government had prepared lists of thousands of people whom it suddenly identified as "coup plotters" without an ounce of evidence. The initial list was 669 pages long and inadvertently released at 1:00 am as an attachment of a prosecutor's warrant for the arrest of 2,745 judges and prosecutors, three hours after the coup attempt began.

The list had obviously been in existence for quite some time. That the names of deceased, retired, and resigned judges and prosecutors were on the list underscores its prior preparation.[1] The obvious intent was to use it in some fashion at a propitious time, which turned out to be a post-coup "witch hunt," in Erdoğan's words.

The input into the list must have come from government surveillance and informants. Informants can be quite unreliable by providing names of people against whom they have a grudge, with whom they disagree, or for a host of other purposes, whether innocent mistake or not. The regime intended to cut a wide swath.

Expelling Judges from Office

Early on July 16, 2016, just three hours after the coup attempt had begun, Serdar Coşkun, a Turkish prosecutor in Ankara, who gained notoriety for going after Hizmet and critics of Erdoğan, emailed a letter to the chief public prosecutors' offices of all eighty-one provinces and the General Directorate of Security, giving "instructions" for the arrest of thousands of judges and prosecutors: "All provinces should be contacted and the judges and prosecutors on the list should be taken into custody immediately" and "the detained judges and prosecutors should be arrested."[2]

That Coşkun could somehow have immediately identified all the perpetrators while the attempt was still in progress is quite suspicious. Another dubious feature of this letter, which found its way into the files of all judge-prosecutor cases, is that it lacked a document with an official authenticating fiche. Worse, though, he was establishing regime tutelage over the courts by declaring the judges and prosecutors on the list guilty in advance and ordering their arrest.

When the Ankara Chief Public Prosecutor's Office for the Investigation of Offences Committed Against the Constitutional Order failed to explain how it so swiftly obtained the list from which to arrest so many judiciary members, the Supreme Board of Judges and Prosecutors (HSYK), which oversees the judiciary, assembled on July 16 with Ministry of Justice Undersecretary Kenan İpek presiding as chair. Chapter 5 describes how Erdogan attained control over HSYK.

Rather than safeguarding judicial independence and asserting itself as an autonomous branch of government, HSYK's 3rd Chamber decided to suspend and initiate investigations of the judges and prosecutors on the list. HSYK's 2nd Chamber then issued a removal order for them.

Some members of the 2nd and 3rd Chambers, detained because of the overnight order, were absent during these decision-making sessions, rendering the meeting procedurally irregular. They were unable to defend themselves and had no semblance of due process accorded to them.

Altogether, detention orders were issued for two Constitutional Court judges (out of seven judges), 48 Council of State members (Türkiye's highest administrative court) (out of 156 members), 140 Court of Cassation members (out of 250 appellant judges and 144 prosecutors), and 2,745 administrative and judicial judges and prosecutors and support staff). This was the largest expulsion of judiciary members in Turkish history, about one-third of the roster.[3] This opened the door for the government-friendly HSYK to appoint replacements amicable to the regime, the agenda all along.

The data in the 2016 Türkiye Report of the Council of Europe are different, but no less egregious. In the days after the bungled coup, according to CoE information, HSYK suspended 3,508 judicial officials, constituting one-fifth of the total number of judges and prosecutors, of whom 3,390 were subsequently dismissed.

The Council of Europe (CoE) is an international organization with the goal of promoting human rights, democracy, and the rule of law in Europe and beyond. Türkiye is one of the forty-six member states, which altogether encompass seven hundred million people.[4]

According to CoE data, the regime detained 2,386 judges and prosecutors, including 2,229 from the first-level courts, 109 from the Court of Cassation, forty-one from the Council of State, two members of the Constitutional Court, and five members of HSYK (the judiciary's governing agency). The dimensions, pace, and criteria of these measures, which included a brazen attack on the highest courts of the land, raised doubts for the CoE about the legitimacy of their application.

The mass dismissals and rapid recruitment of new judges and prosecutors as replacements was designed to, and did, undermine the judiciary's performance and independence.[5] The summary expulsions included stripping the judges and prosecutors of their licenses, impeding their future ability to earn a living as attorneys and mediators in private practice.

The regime unconscionably disseminated decisions concerning the judges and prosecutors on government-friendly written, visual, and social media platforms, along with personal information about their families, all without advance notice to the individuals. This was invasive of their personal and family privacy and slurred their reputations. That was the Erdoğan's intent.

Erdal Demir, the pro-Erdoğan former HSYK General Secretary Deputy at the time of the massive judicial purge, posted on his Twitter account:

> We will gather all the lowlifes who attempted the coup and were members of the "parallel organization," no matter what position they hold.... We will punish these parallel lowlifes with a severity they cannot imagine, with no mercy.... Today is the day we stood by the state. It is the day we cut off their heads and hands and make the FETÖ bastards vomit blood.[6]

An astonishing ferocity of hate language, invoking hate crimes, all in the service of politicide, by a principal administrator of an organization charged with selecting and overseeing an impartial, unbiased judiciary.

For Erdoğan, the judiciary was the focal point of his drive to implement systematic practices aimed at Hizmet's politicide. He had to neutralize the courts or, even better, turn them into faithful servants. He could not risk them becoming an institutional obstacle to him as they had at times in the past. The judiciary was his first target. He had already begun his project, as described in Chapter 5, but it was moving slowly. The coup event let him rev up the motor.

A month before the suspicious July 15 coup attempt, on June 14, Turgay Ateş, another HSYK member and Erdoğan ally, said in a speech, "The judiciary will not be able to get up from where it has fallen until the structure in question within the judiciary is cleansed. To realize this goal, HSYK has a variety of procedures at its disposal, but it can only find a solution within the framework of legislation, and that process takes too long."[7]

Perhaps Ateş was tipping his hand or setting the stage for what was to come in terms of "cleansing" the judiciary, since HSYK could not accomplish the task. The rapid purges sought by Ateş and the extraordinary methods for quickly reshaping the judiciary had devastating personal effects on those suddenly without employment and on their families.

One should note the 2024 European Court of Human Rights decision *Affaire Sözen c. Türkiye*,[8] eight years later, holding that HSYK violated the rights of Bekir Sözen, a member of the powerful Council of State, by abolishing his term of office and removing him without due process following adoption of a court restructuring law in 2016. Sözen was put in pretrial detention for alleged Hizmet links following the coup fiasco and one of the 4,000 judiciary members removed summarily from their positions for alleged relationship with Hizmet. The Constitutional Court denied his appeal, but the ECtHR ruled in his favor in strong language.

The European Court of Human Rights (ECtHR) enforces the European Convention on Human Rights (ECHR), which is a supranational convention to protect human rights and political freedoms in Europe. Drafted in 1950 by the newly formed Council of Europe, the convention entered into force in 1953. Türkiye is one of the forty-six countries that has obligated itself to abide by the convention and voluntarily honor and enforce judgments of the court. Aggrieved residents of a country can appeal to the court if their country has violated their rights under the convention.[9] The Council of Europe's Parliamentary Assembly elects the ECtHR judges. The formal title for the ECHR is the Convention for the Protection of Human Rights and Fundamental Freedoms

The *Sözen* case is emblematic of the attack on the independence of the courts. There are many other ECtHR cases on this issue. As *Sözen* demonstrates, however, there is no immediate relief from the ECtHR for transgressions of the human rights convention. It takes years to litigate to conclusion at the ECtHR, long after the harm has occurred, and even then, Türkiye typically ignores the court's judgments and refuses to implement them. A classic situation of having a right without a remedy.

Mass Terminations of Public Servants

Besides the myriad judges and prosecutors, tens of thousands of public servants found themselves on lists added to state of emergency decrees and summarily dismissed from employment without any chance to defend themselves. The palace regime, as part of its hate policy and politicide, utilized these lists to expel them from their jobs solely because of alleged Hizmet affiliation. The purges were based on pre-prepared, but legally groundless, profiling lists.

Thousands of individuals, uninvolved in any coup activity and employed within state-regulated institutions, private enterprises, or just engaged in private commerce, sought justice in vain upon learning of their impending arrests. Rather, in the days following, the regime subjected them to severe and inhumane treatment instead of swift exoneration upon proof of innocence.

High-ranking officials and the media unfairly joined the frenzy and unjustly branded them as "coup plotters" and "terrorists," among other pejorative epithets, with the malicious intent of denying them due process and a fair trial. Amnesty International labeled this as "professional annihilation."[10]

Numerous individuals critical of the Erdoğan regime, who had no connection to Hizmet, were also classified as "FETÖ supporters" solely because it was the easiest way to remove them from their positions. Thousands were dismissed from public service due to illegitimate justifications, for such innocuous reasons as depositing money in Bank Asya, sending their children to Hizmet-associated schools, or attending Hizmet preparatory schools, even though these actions do not imply Hizmet membership. Young adults just wanted a good education to get ahead, and the Hizmet gave them that opportunity.

One list annexed to a decree comprised more than 50,000 thousand public servants from various institutions. The government permanently sacked more than 150,000 public servants in this way, many of the victims being in academia.

There were other devastating consequences for expelled public servants. Termination from public service meant that the person could not only not work in government but also could not do any kind of public service. For example, a law professor and lawyer could not practice as a private lawyer or teach at a private university because those were public-nature jobs.

The dismissal decrees also revoked people's passports so they could not leave the country to pursue professional employment as they had before being stripped of their jobs.

The government changed the Military Service Law so that police officers dismissed due to affiliation with Hizmet could be called for military service. The regulations retrospectively annulled the right of police officers to be exempt from national mandatory military duty by virtue of their police service.

Likewise, the Notary Law, the Law on Mediation in Legal Disputes, and the Law on Expert Witnesses were altered to ban anyone from these professions connected with or in contact with a terrorist organization (i.e., Hizmet).

The emergency decrees aimed to expel everyone associated with the Gülen Movement or supportive of its principles from public service, even though they had not engaged in any unlawful activities, leading to their economic and social exclusion, civil death, and politicide.

Given the absence of any objective indication of disloyalty to the democratic legal order in performing their public duties, these individuals suffered unlawful expulsion from their employment. The reasons proffered did not prove illegal activity or affiliation with a violent terrorist organization. No specific reasons were given for the dismissal of any individual, simply that the discharges were taking place according to lists attached to the emergency decrees.

In a November 2019 interview on Hadi Özışık's program on Internet News' YouTube channel, AKP Deputy Chairperson Numan Kurtulmuş, a prominent regime figure, defended the unlawfulness of dismissing hundreds of thousands of people without any evidence after July 15.[11] He called it a "state reflex" and acknowledged the emergency decrees as a tool for eradication:

> .... If we had attempted to dismiss them through normal processes, from July 15 until 2020, until 2030, we would not have been able to remove them from public service. The state took such an urgent extraordinary measure to protect itself....

Had the government not acted, he said, "...a large portion of those dismissed by decrees today would have been given duties at the highest levels of the state."

Asked about decree victims who were eventually acquitted, albeit few, Kurtulmuş continued showing little regard for the rule of law, "The person who was subjected to a Statutory Decree may be acquitted, but this does not mean that the person is free from the charge of membership in an organization. There is other evidence for membership in an organization." These comments carry weight since Kurtulmuş was Deputy Prime Minister from 2014-2017 (and Spokesman for the Government, 2015-2017). He then served as cultural minister for a year and became the parliament Speaker in 2023.

Only a few spoke out against the summary dismissals. Nor was there any effort to form a coalition opposing the government's actions. The few who raised questions or lifted a contrary voice suffered the consequence of doing so and ended up behind the same prison walls of those whom they defended.

Objections of the Venice Commission

The Venice Commission (officially, European Commission for Democracy through Law), an advisory body of the Council of Europe, comprised of independent experts in constitutional law from sixty-one countries, expressed concern regarding the dismissal process in the context of emergency decrees and the insufficiency of abstract terms such as "relationship, connection, or affiliation" as reasons to terminate a person's employment.

The commission underscored the necessity for concrete evidence for objectively questioning a public servant's loyalty.[12] The commission emphasized Türkiye's need to change these regulations, allowing only judgments based on concrete actions indicating a public official's clear departure from allegiance to the democratic legal order.

The Commission further faulted the flawed decision-making process, leading to the dismissal of the public officials, noting the absence of specific justifications for their dismissal, rendering meaningful judicial review impossible. Likewise, individuals identified and convicted of illegally-obtained profiling used against them in court were not allowed to suppress the evidence. Had the courts allowed the challenge to illegal evidence, most, if not all, discharged workers would have had their employment restored.

The Inquiry Commission: Smoke and Mirrors

Under international pressure, state of emergency Decree 685 established the Inquiry Commission on State of Emergency Measures in January 2017 with the expressed intent of correcting any errors that had occurred through implementing state of emergency decrees. It had a semi-adjudicatory appellate function.

However, the commission, instead of judging cases consistent with international due process principles or those in Turkish law, acted in sync with the regime's expectations and decisions. The process and results were a far cry from due course of law and equity. That was not surprising, given the makeup of the seven-member commission: three members appointed by the prime minister, one by the Justice Ministry, one by the Interior Ministry, and two by the Supreme Board of Judges and Prosecutors (HYSK). Nary an independent person or non-political member. Moreover, the commissioners had immunity for their decisions and actions, assuring they would freely do the regime's bidding, no matter what kind of injustice they wreaked.

The Inquiry Commission began its decision-making in May 2017 and concluded in January 2023. The commission rendered 127,292 decisions, including 17,960 approvals of appeals and 109,332 appeals rejections. Out of the approved appeals, only seventy-two concerned reopening closed institutions (associations, foundations, schools, TV channels, newspapers).[13]

The commission only granted the appeals of 14% of dismissed individuals and returned them to their employment,[14] though typically to a different job than the one in which they were working when discharged. The commission averaged seventy-one decisions per workday (or one decision every six minutes, at best), hardly enough time to consider each case on its merits.

The Inquiry Commission rejected appeals related to dismissals based on untenable legal reasons (such as subscribing to *Zaman* newspaper), being a member of a state-controlled union or association, sending children to Hizmet-associated schools later closed by decrees, making donations to the previously legally-authorized, Hizmet-associated charitable organization "Kimse Yok Mu?" or depositing money in the Hizmet-associated Bank Asya. The commission cemented the Erdoğan regime's hate policies and politicide practices against the Gülen Movement rather than engaging in sound legal reasoning or administering justice.[15]

Rejecting the reinstatement of thousands of acquitted individuals, those against whom no investigation was initiated and those against whom no prosecution was undertaken, underscored the commission's real agenda, to ratify and paint over what the government had done, not to rectify it. It was hardly a fair adjudicatory process. "Kangaroo court" might be a good fit.

Amnesty International's report "Türkiye: Purged beyond return? No remedy for Türkiye's dismissed public sector workers" nailed the Catch-22 syndrome at play. It underscored the systematic denial of effective remedial processes for almost 130,000 public sector workers whom the Erdoğan regime arbitrarily dismissed and permanently banned from working in the public sector or even in working in their profession altogether.

Beyond losing their jobs, many faced insurmountable obstacles to housing and healthcare and providing their families with an adequate livelihood. The report faulted the Inquiry Commission as a cosmetic "rubber stamp" measure designed to deceive international opinion and was not remedial or intended to be remedial.[16]

The purge was going at the same time as the state of emergency was active. They interacted with each other, as laid out in the following chapter, always to the detriment of the people.

Endnotes

1 *See* Robert Bartunek, “Turkey Government Seemed to Have List of Arrests Prepared: EU’s Hahn,” *Reuters* (July 18, 2016), https://www.reuters.com/article/us-turkey-security-eu-hahn-idUSKCN0ZY0EA.

2 “15 Temmuz’un skandal belgesi: Binlerce hakim, savcıyı fişleme yazısıyla tutuklatmış,” TR724 (20 Feb. 2019), https://www.tr724.com/15-temmuzun-skandal-belgesi-binlerce-hakim-savciyi-fisleme-yazisiyla-tutuklatmis/ [“July 15th scandal document. Prosecutor has thousands of Judges arrested through a ‘labeling’ letter.”].

3 Hâkimler Ve Savcılar Yüksek Kurulu, Genel Kurul Kararı, Karar No : 2016/426, Tutanak No : 17, Karar Tarihi: 24/08/2016, https://www.resmigazete.gov.tr/eskiler/2016/08/20160825-5.pdf [“Judges and Prosecutors High Council, Plenary Decision No: 2016/426, 24/08/2016.”].

4 *See* Council of Europe, https://www.coe.int/en/web/portal/home.

5 “Commission Staff Working Document, Turkey 2016 Report, Accompanying the document Communication from the Commission to the European Parliament, the Council, the European Economic and Social Committee and the Committee of the Regions” (p.17), European Commission, Brussels (9.11.2016), https://neighbourhood-enlargement.ec.europa.eu/document/download/e703a769-bf7f-46d1-8a13-6a836683e838_en?filename=20161109_report_turkey.pdf.

6 “Adalet Bakanlığı Daire Başkanı, 15 Temmuz gecesi nefret saçmış: Başlarını ve ellerini kesip, kan kusturacağız!,” TR724 (22 Nov.r 2021), https://www.tr724.com/adalet-bakanligi-daire-baskani-15-temmuz-gecesi-nefret-sacmis-baslarini-ve-ellerini-kesip-kan-kusturacagiz/ [“The Head of Department of the Ministry of Justice spread hatred on the night of July 15: We will cut off their heads and hands and make them vomit blood!”].

7 “Hakim ve savcılar iftarda buluştu: ‘Devletin yanındayız,’” CNNTurk (14.06.2016), https://www.cnnturk.com/turkiye/hakim-ve-savcilar-iftarda-bulustu-devletin-yanindayiz-548037 [“Judges and prosecutors met at the Iftar: ‘We are with the state’”].

8 *Sözen c. Türkiye* (No. 73532/16), European Court of Human Rights (9 April 2024), https://hudoc.echr.coe.int/eng#{%22itemid%22:[%22001-231998%22]}.

9 *See* European Court of Human Rights (homepage), https://www.echr.coe.int/.

10 “Türkiye: Professional annihilation of 100,000 public sector workers in post-coup attempt purge,” Amnesty International (May 22, 2017), https://www.amnesty.org/en/latest/news/2017/05/turkey-professional-annihilation-of-100000-public-sector-workers-in-post-coup-attempt-purge/#:~:text=May%2022%2C%202017-.

11 “Numan Kurtulmuş’un KHK itirafı: ‘Hukuk uygulansaydı 2030’a kadar bu insanları atamazdık!,’” TR724 (Nov. 18, 2019), https://www.tr724.com/numan-kurtulmusun-khk-itirafi-hukuk-uygulansaydi-2030a-kadar-bu-insanlari-atamazdik/ [“Numan Kurtulmuş’s confession regarding the Statutory Decree: ‘If the law was implemented, we would not be able to dismiss these people until 2030!’”].

12 “Turkey: Opinion on Emergency Decree Laws Nos. 667-676 Adopted Following the Failed Coup of July 15 2016,” European Commission for Democracy Through Law (Venice Commission) (9-10 December 2016), https://www.venice.coe.int/webforms/documents/default.aspx?pdffile=CDL-AD(2016)037, (paras.119-131).

13 “OHAL İnceleme Komisyonu tüm başvuruları karara bağladı: İstatistiklerle kabul ve ret oranı,” Euronews (20/01/2023), https://tr.euronews.com/2023/01/20/ohal-inceleme-komisyonu-tum-basvurulari-karara-bagladi-istatistiklerle-kabul-ve-ret-orani [“State of Emergency Review Commission has decided on all applications:

acceptance and rejection rate with statistics"].

14 *Id.*

15 "Avrupa Hukuk Yoluyla Demokrasi Komisyonu (Venedik Komisyonu), 15 Temmuz 2016 Başarısız Darbe Girişimi Sonrasında Çıkarılan 667 ilâ 676 Sayılı Olağanüstü Hal Kanun Hükmünde Kararnameleri Hakkında Görüş," European Commission for Democracy through Law (Venice Commission) (12 Dec. 2016), https://www.venice.coe.int/webforms/documents/default.aspx?pdffile=CDL-AD(2016)037-tur, pp.130-131 ["Turkey Opinion On Emergency Decree Laws Nos. 667-676"].

16 "Türkiye: Purged beyond return? No remedy for Türkiye's dismissed public sector workers," Amnesty International (Oct. 24, 2018), https://www.amnesty.org/en/documents/eur44/9210/2018/en/.

Chapter 4

Manipulating the State of Emergency

The failed July 15 putsch was a U-turn for Türkiye's struggling democracy. Erdoğan capitalized on the crisis to consolidate power and eviscerate political opponents through a two-year state of emergency that quickly morphed into authoritarian control. Erdoğan exploited the coup attempt to quash dissent through mass detentions and arrests and bending the organs of state to his will.

Erdoğan's self-proclaimed fizzled coup as "a grace from God" swiftly turned into a capricious opportunity, a pre-planned one. By declaring a state emergency, Erdoğan, already having a docile parliamentary majority and in the process of fashioning a compliant judiciary, adeptly crafted a mechanism to dominate his opposition and rid himself of the Hizmet thorn in his side. He opened the door to unabated politicide.

The nation's constitutional order was a casualty of the coup that never was.[1] Erdoğan engineered its degradation, seeking a pickaxe to dig Hizmet's grave. Even before the attempted coup, the regime had engaged in unlawful practices targeting the movement. The major crackdown occurred in the botched coup's aftermath.

Unlawful Derogation

On July 20, 2016, Türkiye formally declared a three-month state of emergency, which laid the foundation for systematic human rights violations, negating constitutional and international legal protections. As part of the declaration, the government formally advised the Council of Europe, to which Türkiye belonged, as required, that it was suspending basic rights under the European Convention on Human Rights (ECHR).

This derogation, as it is formally called, allows a state to temporarily obviate certain international rights and guarantees as necessary for its survival. Besides only being as temporary as necessary, the suspension is to be as narrow and limited as possible. By the government's admission, it quickly brought everything under control after the coup fiasco. Thus, the need for derogation under the ECHR should have been short-term and limited. Erdoğan turned it into a long-term, draconian measure, a political ploy to accomplish illegally what he could not achieve legally.

While states are permitted to derogate from certain obligations under the ECHR and the International Covenant on Civil and Political Rights (ICCPR), to each of which Türkiye is a signatory, where strictly required to address an officially proclaimed state of emergency that threatens the life of the nation, the authorities are still under an obligation to respect and protect fundamental rights.

They must ensure that restrictions imposed under the state of emergency are only those strictly required by the emergency, proportionate to the legitimate aim pursued, and are exceptional and temporary in nature. Türkiye followed none of these proscriptions and severely abused derogation to implement the state of emergency it never needed in the first place. Erdoğan stage-managed the derogation pretext to violate the fundamental rights of Hizmet people and consolidate their annihilation.

Neither the ECHR nor the ICCPR, to both of which Türkiye is a signatory, allow the wholesale suspension of fundamental rights. The International Covenant on Economic, Social and Cultural Rights (ICESCR), to which Türkiye is also a party, admits no suspension of rights at all.[2]

The UN Human Rights Committee, composed of independent experts who monitor states' ICCPR compliance, has elaborated on these points in General Comment 29 regarding ICCPR Article 4 on Derogations during a State of Emergency.[3]

State of Emergency Without Justification

Declaring a state of emergency let the government go after the previously identified people, thousands upon thousands of individuals and terminate their employment or subject them to other penalties. That also raised questions about surreptitious government surveillance and cultivation of informants over a lengthy stretch of time to identify whom they wanted to remove from its rolls, for which the regime put forward no response.

This dubiousness belies the regime's contention. Indeed, if so many tens of thousands of people were engaged in a coup plot, it is unfathomable that not a single person took any action supporting a coup or that one did not see any pockets of activity before, during, or afterward.

Nor were any caches of arms found or anything of suspect nature that would indicate potential participation in a coup. As the Venice Commission eventually noted with a degree of sharpness, no specific factual allegations linked any terminated public servants to activities that would destabilize the state. Just blanket employment dismissals; and, of course, the only ones named were potential opponents of a corrupt regime, mostly Hizmet-associated people and sympathizers and dissenters.

The cache of creative ideas and moral uprightness were the arms the government feared. The Venice Commission (officially, the European Commission for Democracy through Law) is an advisory body of the Council of Europe, comprised of independent experts in constitutional law. It has closely followed events in Türkiye.

Three-Month State of Emergency Turns into Two Years

The Turkish Constitution limits a state of emergency to four months, subject to renewal. Erdoğan invoked the proviso for eight three-month periods, which parliament had to, and did dutifully, ratify. The Constitution's drafters obviously contemplated that four months would be sufficient to deal with an emergency and had not anticipated the need of having to prevent someone like Erdoğan from so starkly debasing the emergency proviso repeatedly.

The ill-fated coup attempt ended quickly, within hours. By July 17, 2016, two days later, the government was issuing public statements, bragging that it had suppressed the coup attempt and had completely restored security in the country. Part of the bragging might have been a tactical warning to any other presumptive usurpers, but no facts indicate any on-going challenge to government authority.

With peace and domestic tranquility reestablished, none of the requisite constitutional conditions for invoking a state of emergency were present but Erdoğan nonetheless did so three days later, on July 20, assuming authority to issue decrees with the force of law.

There certainly was no constitutional justification for extending the state of emergency every three months for two years other than to thoroughly bat down Hizmet and create the levers of a totalitarian state. Nor was abrogation of the protection of rights rescinded or lessened during the two years; it continued in full force. Erdoğan conjured up the state of emergency and its aftermath to conduct a *de facto* coup d'état against the democratic order of the Turkish state.

Erdoğan would have continued to extend the state of emergency had not the European countries and organizations to which Türkiye belonged begun to rigorously question whether it was becoming a subterfuge to eliminate political opposition and install an ever more authoritarian regime. Of course, that was exactly how Erdoğan used the state of emergency, to suppress people's rights in general and annihilate the Hizmet Movement in particular, which was his most potent potential opposition at the time.

Legal Parameters of a State of Emergency

The Turkish Constitution's state of emergency provisions gave Erdoğan the legal-appearing artifice he needed: the advice of the National Security Council (MGK) and the vote of the Council of Ministers, his cabinet, which have ten and eighteen members respectively, five of whose positions overlap.[4] A handful of people, ideologically in sync and under Erdoğan's tutelage, assumed rule over the country to achieve what they could not otherwise legally accomplish under the nation's normal democratic processes.

Parliament transformed a number of the emergency decrees into law, such as the revamped criminal procedure laws. The parliamentary majority since 2002 consisted of Erdoğan's AKP ruling party in coalition with the ultra-nationalist MHP (Nationalist Movement Party) (the Cumhur Alliance) long before the coup attempt. MHP has provided unconditional support for Erdoğan's policies.

Erdoğan has absolute control over his party. Given his despotic tendencies, no one in his cabinet or AKP parliament members would dare act against his will. Cabinet ministers have responsibility and liability for their decisions but apparently did not know (or risk asking) what the state of emergency decrees or orders that they were signing entailed.

Ali Babacan, then economy minister, after leaving office made that startling admission in May 2024 to the BirGün press network: "At the time I left the government, the Council of Ministers was signing blank papers, and the content was filled in later. They were published in the Official Gazette with Mr. Erdoğan's signature. In reality, these decisions were made with just one signature.... All these decree laws were like that. You should inquire about these matters in private conversations with the ministers at that time. Otherwise, no one will come out and confess to this...."[5] It was a classic palace regime operation.

Babacan left AKP in 2020 to found the Democracy and Progress Party (DEVA), which advocates a return to the country's previous parliamentary system and abandoning the newer strong presidential system.

Ruling by Decree for Two Years

State of emergency decrees, also known as decrees having the force of law, are issued by the Council of Ministers, chaired by the President, and are not subject to review by the Constitutional Court.

During the two-year state of emergency, the government emitted thirty-two emergency decrees, seventeen of which targeted certain people and legal entities (organizations, companies, associations, schools, and the like), and enacted a total of 131,922 measures. More precisely, 125,678 individuals were summarily dismissed from public service without due process; and 2,761 legal entitites were closed and their assets confiscated without compensation and due process.[6]

The emergency decrees obliterated basic human rights protections with abandon, violating the right to life, the prohibition of torture, the right to a fair trial, the rights to freedom of movement, free speech, and association, and the right to property—all guarantees protected by the Turkish Constitution and international accords to which Türkiye is signatory.[7]

People were tortured in prison, and some died because of deficient medical attention in prison. More than one hundred individuals were abducted and disappeared. Government decrees discharged 133,792 people from public and private sector employment and seized thousands of companies and non-governmental organizations, leaving tens of thousands of individuals in those organizations unemployed.

Through state of emergency decrees, the regime accused more than one million individuals of crimes that it created to operate retroactively, subjecting them to trials and imprisonment for crimes that had never hitherto existed. The government, through decrees, detained more than two hundred thousand people and arrested more than a hundred thousand people. Nothing of this scale had ever happened before in Turkish history.

The retroactively applied, vague, and overly broad criminal criteria to persecute Hizmet-associated individuals fell into these categories:

- Being employed in a workplace closed by decree
- Holding an account at Hizmet-related Bank Asya
- Sending children to Hizmet-related schools
- Having received education in Hizmet-related university preparation courses, schools, and universities, or having resided in Hizmet educational-related dormitories
- Using the ByLock smartphone application
- Reading books by publishers shut down by decree or having the books at home
- Reading and subscribing to newspapers and magazines banned by decree
- Having membership in Hizmet-related associations, participating in the activities of these associations, and having provided past financial aid; and,
- Being the spouse, child, or parent of someone dismissed from their job by decree.

These criteria starkly illustrate the government's punitive measures against constitutionally protected activities, directed against Hizmet and anyone else in opposition to the government. Criteria designed for politicide.

Ministers implemented decrees through circulars, which are regulations directing how public servants and officers in their ministries should act in a particular situation. Normally, circulars may not regulate any area of the public sphere that conflicts with other regulations or laws. For example, the government may not regulate, in the absence of a statute enacted by the parliament, whether detainees can hold private meetings with their lawyers because such regulations relate to a person's fundamental rights and freedoms. This became an issue. Only parliament may enact such laws, provided they meet legal muster.

Under Turkish law, courts are supposed to repeal such regulations/circulars upon application or objection by an affected individual. However, as the courts have become the government's pliant servants, individual rights now exist only in the law books and have become illusory in reality. Courts upheld the circulars.

Changing Criteria for Defining a Terrorist Organization

In action directed toward Hizmet, the Erdoğan regime, before the coup events, began consistently referring to Hizmet as an illegal structure, as a "parallel state structure." State institutions adhered to this narrative through laws, regulations, and administrative measures.

An October 30, 2014, declaration by the Turkish National Security Council (MGK) listed Hizmet as a "legal-appearing illegal structure," a strange twist of phrasing. Fourteen months later, on January 8, 2016, MGK included Hizmet under the name "FETÖ on its list of existing terrorist organizations," a decision approved by the General Command of the Gendarmerie. Another MGK declaration five months later reaffirmed that it took measures against Hizmet as a parallel state structure, which it considered to be a terrorist organization posing a national security threat.

Unlawfully, without a court decision and in terms contrary to international law definitions, MGK unilaterally proclaimed Hizmet to be an armed terrorist organization, sanctioning a process intended to annihilate the group through an illegal witch hunt. Hundreds of thousands of individuals were terrorized, detained, arrested, and subjected to torture, inhumane treatment, and human rights violations.

No one even knew exactly where the line of criminality was drawn in the sand. The definitional ambiguity extended greater flexibility to the regime, which the courts approved and allowed.

The emergency decrees sanctioned real and legal persons for having "membership, affiliation, relation, or connection (cohesion) to "the

Gülen movement/structure, which was outlawed by the government. The decrees also criminalized having "membership in, or affiliation, link or connection with terrorist organizations or structures, formations, or groups that MGK determine engaged activities against national security of the State."

The Turkish word "*iltisak*,"' which can be translated into English as "cohesion" or "connection" was undefined in the emergency decrees although it was the essential reason for the employment terminations and property seizures. The term is vague, and its vagueness encompasses the lawful exercise of a host of legitimate, protected fundamental rights. The government did not preoccupy itself with narrowly applying the definition so as to not trample on people's rights. It did just the opposite. That was its goal.

Not until April 2019 was there a court definition. The Ankara Regional Administrative Court defined the *iltisak* (connection or cohesion") as:

> ...moving as conjoined to one another, voluntarily submitting, facing the same direction, interpreting circumstances from the same viewpoint, conducting oneself with suggestions, instructions and directions of an organization or structure, and in doing so anticipating worldly or unworldly gains; as well as communication i.e. establishing voluntarily or involuntarily and for personal gains, one's own course of action by taking into account messages one receives either through personal contact or through the press, mass media or social media.[8]

The court definitions were no better. They, too, were overly broad, exceedingly vague, and penalized legitimate exercise of fundamental rights. They criminalized whatever the regime wanted to criminalize to oppress the Gülen Movement.

The rule in Turkish law had been that, when a court tries an alleged perpetrator in the context of the existence of an armed terrorist organization, the court issues a decision delineating the elements of the offense. The government ignored these requirements when it came to cases against Hizmet. Instead, an MGK administrative decision simply declared Hizmet to be *ipso facto* a terrorist organization. There was not even a façade of due process.

To keep this in focus, the 11th High Criminal Court acquitted Fethullah Gülen in 2006, finding that he had not formed or managed a terrorist organization bent on seizing power. The government had indicted him in 2000 under the Anti-Terror Law and criminal code of conspiring to overthrow the secular state and establish a religion-based government.

Gülen won two appeals brought by the prosecutor, the last before a plenary tribunal for criminal appeals in June 2008 on a 17-6 vote.[9] The courts all wrote detailed opinions and findings of fact (68 pages in total) that vindicated Gülen, a telling commentary on how MGK decided the opposite. Thirty-one judges had participated in the trial and appeals. Twenty-five ruled for Gülen.

That court verdict has not been rescinded or overturned. It is still good law, that Gülen was neither a terrorist nor attempting to overthrow the state, although neither the courts nor the government pay it heed.

Somehow, however, the regime would have the public believe that, within but a few years of acquittal, the Hizmet Movement suddenly transitioned into an enormous, dangerous terrorist organization. Virtually overnight, hundreds of thousands of individuals, who were unarmed, unaware of any coup attempt, and who in some point in time had gathered for social, religious, and other legitimate reasons abruptly became classified as members of a terrorist organization.

Legitimate social and economic activities included subscribing to *Zaman* newspaper, depositing money into Bank Asya, sending SMS donations to Kimse Yok Mu, attending religious conversations, sending children to Hizmet-affiliated private schools, possessing Hizmet literature or books, joining associations and unions or working in institutions related to Hizmet—in reality, anything associated somehow with Hizmet, no matter how innocent or tenuous—came to be construed as organizational terrorism. People were cast as "terrorists" not because of their actions to overthrow the state but by virtue of an MGK administrative edict.

Similarly, using ByLock, a communication application publicly available to download on any smartphone, or even downloading the program or just calling or receiving a call from someone who used ByLock was sufficient evidence of belonging to a terrorist organization and led to arrests and convictions accordingly. (Given that the government unlawfully obtained ByLock records, they should never have been admissible evidence in any regard).

The principles of "legality" and "no punishment without law" aim at clearly describing conduct that constitutes a crime before its commission so that people know which acts and omissions will carry criminal liability. Yet, Turkish judicial authorities have accepted innocent non-criminal daily activities that entail the exercise and enjoyment of fundamental rights as evidence of being a terrorist. Nor could laws be retroactive. An action done when it was not a criminal act cannot retroactively become a crime. Nor can a higher punishment for a crime be imposed *post-factum*. Türkiye started doing both.

A 2022 report by the Stockholm Center for Freedom discusses the elements that comprise an illegal "armed terrorist organization" under Turkish law and how an individual's relationship to an armed terrorist organization (Hizmet, in this case) is implicated and imputed through innocent non-criminal daily activities.[10] Essentially, the government infers criminal intent from innocuous conduct and penalizes it. It is *de facto* criminalizing activity *ad hoc* without formally *de jure* criminalizing conduct that it could not otherwise legitimately criminalize.

Although the European Court of Human Rights has made it clear that the rule of law may not be derogated even in times of emergency under Article 15 of the European Convention on Human Rights, criminal prosecutions and trials in Türkiye have been carried out *en masse* in violation of this principle since 2016.

According to Turkish Ministry of Justice statistics, a sharp increase in "terrorism" charges under Article 314 of the Turkish Criminal Code occurred in the aftermath of the coup attempt. While 8,416 charges were filed under Article 314 in 2013, the number soared to 146,731 in 2017, 115,753 in 2018, 54,464 in 2019, and 33,885 in 2020. More than 265,000 individuals were sentenced under Article 314 between 2016 and 2020. With this number of people charged with terrorism, one would think that the government would have found a shred of evidence somewhere, but it has not.

Türkiye has the largest population of inmates convicted of terrorism-related offenses, according to a Council of Europe (CoE) report showing that, in 2020, of 30,524 inmates in CoE member states sentenced for terrorism, 29,827 of them were in Turkish prisons (97.7%).[11] It is important to recall that, when the government began its post-coup mass incarceration of "terrorists," essentially prisoners of conscience, it had to free 38,000 inmates convicted of actual crimes from prison to make room.[12]

The government released criminals convicted of nonviolent offenses, such as thieves and drug smugglers, and put them back on the street so that 40,000 journalists, teachers, attorneys, judges, police officers, state bureaucrats, and even airline employees could take their places. They were not dangerous or merit jailing, but at political odds with Erdoğan and his regime and this deserved incarceration and gross maltreatment.

On the international level, Türkiye's decision to convict a United Nations judge from that country was a breach of diplomatic immunity and caused internation consternation.[13] Judge Aydın Sefa Akay of the UN's Mechanism for International Criminal Tribunals was arrested and convicted of being a member of a designated terrorist group, Hizmet. He had used ByLock and had two Hizmet-related books in his extensive personal library, neither of which indicated terrorist ties.

The ECtHR ruled in Akay's favor and awarded him €28,000 ($31,080), which was not much, given his loss of employment. Nor did the UN reappoint Akay, to considerable internal and external criticism.[14]

The Inquiry Commission: Smoke and Mirrors

Under international pressure, Türkiye established the Inquiry Commission on State of Emergency Measures in January 2017 with the articulated intent of rectifying any errors that had occurred through implementing state of emergency decrees. It had a semi-adjudicatory appellate function. A Mexican proverb fits well here: "Between what is said and what is done lies a deep chasm."

The previous chapter provides a detailed discussion of the commission and how it did not function other than to give scattered relief to some non-Hizmet claimants. Overall, the commission was a rubber stamp, providing a veneer of justice while summarily ratifying the regime's actions. Hizmet-associated individuals and entities found no relief. The previous chapter described the commission as a "kangaroo court," which it was.

Summary

State of emergency decrees were the vehicle to immediately discharge more than two hundred thousand dedicated public servants, including judges, police, military personnel, academics, and lawyers, from their employment because of their alleged association with Hizmet and likely lack of support for Erdoğan. Prepared secretly and signed by uninformed ministers, the emergency decrees sidestepped legal procedures for dismissing public employees, offering no protections or recourse.

The decrees were used to shut down unfriendly press outlets, non-supportive NGOs, private schools, and companies with Hizmet connections, and then confiscate their assets, and transfer them to the state. Manipulating the decrees to disregard constitutional rights and legal frameworks, Erdoğan staged his own coup, demolishing constitutional checks and balances under the thin guise of saving the nation. His efforts at creating an aura of legitimacy, however, failed the transparency test, at home and abroad. Various comprehensive overviews are harshly critical of the state of emergency structure and decrees.[15]

The regime issued thirty-two decrees to purge alleged Hizmet members from public and private sectors, seize their assets, and enable their arrests. And, while the state of emergency officially ended on July 17, 2018, after prolonged public and European pressure,[16] its legal impact endured, crippling the judiciary and undermining constitutional order through permanent legislation codifying decrees that should never have existed and, in any respect, should have expired in due course.

The measures of oppression continue to this day, relentlessly.

Endnotes

1 "Turkey: State of Emergency Ends, but Not Repression," Human Rights Watch (Jan. 17, 2019), https://www.hrw.org/news/2019/01/17/turkey-state-emergency-ends-not-repression. *See also* Peter Kenyon, "Turkey's State of Emergency Ends, While Erdoğan's Power Grows and 'Purge' Continues," NPR (July 26, 2018), https://www.npr.org/2018/07/26/632307755/turkeys-state-of-emergency-ends-while-Erdoğans-power-grows-and-purge-continues; "The State of Emergency has ended but urgent measures are now needed to reverse the roll back of human rights," Amnesty International (18 July 2018), https://www.amnesty.org/en/latest/campaigns/2018/07/turkey-state-of-emergency-lifted/.

2 ECHR Article 15, ICCPR Article 4, and ICESCR Article 5.2 (*see* Appendix A for texts).

3 "CCPR General Comment No. 29: Article 4: Derogations during a State of Emergency," UN Human Rights Committee (31 Aug. 2001), https://www.refworld.org/legal/general/hrc/2001/en/30676.

4 The National Security Council of Turkey (MGK) includes the President (as the chair), Vice-President, Ministers of Justice, National Defence, Interior, and Foreign Affairs, Chief of General Staff of the Armed Forces, and commanders of the Turkish Land, Naval, and Air Forces.

5 "Babacan'dan itiraf: Bakanlar Kurulu'nda boş kağıtlar imzalanıyordu, üstü dolduruluyordu; KHK'lar da öyle," BİRGün (10.10.2021), https://www.birgun.net/haber/babacan-dan-itiraf-bakanlar-kurulu-nda-bos-kagitlar-imzalaniyordu-ustu-dolduruluyordu-khk-lar-da-oyle-361625 ["Confession from Babacan: Blank Papers Were Being Signed at the Council of Ministers, and Then Filled In; Decree Laws Were Also Like That"].

6 "Factsheet on Turkey's Emergency Measures Inquiry Commission," Arrested Lawyers Initiative, https://arrestedlawyers.org/wp-content/uploads/2020/07/soe-inquiry-com_47656916.pdf.

7 *See* Ufuk Yesil, "The Cases of Dismissal Under State of Emergency (OHAL): The Right to a Fair Trial as a Human Right," in Hasan Aydin and Winston Langley (eds), *Human Rights in Turkey: Assaults on Human Dignity* (New York: Springer, 2021), pp. 227-260, https://doi.org/10.1007/978-3-030-57476-5_11.

8 "Factsheet on Turkey's Emergency Measures Inquiry Commission," Arrested Lawyers Initiative, https://arrestedlawyers.org/wp-content/uploads/2020/07/soe-inquiry-com_47656916.pdf [Decision No: 2019/246, April 24, 2019].

9 James C. Harrington, *Wrestling with Free Speech, Religious Freedom, and Democracy in Turkey: The Political Trials and Times of Fethullah Gulen* (Lanham, MD, USA: University Press of America, 2011).

10 "Rule of Law(lessness) in Erdoğan's Turkey: Violation of the principle of legality and no punishment without law in post-coup trials," Stockholm Center for Freedom (March 22, 2022), Rule of Law(lessness) in Erdoğan's Turkey - Stockholm Center for Freedom (stockholmcf.org) (p.5).

11 *Id.*

12 Tim Arango and Ceylan Yeginsu, "Turkey to Release Tens of Thousands of Prisoners to Make Room for Coup Suspects," *New York Times* (Aug. 17, 2016), https://www.nytimes.com/2016/08/18/world/europe/turkey-prisoners-Erdoğan.html?smid=nytcore-ios-share&referringSource=articleShare.

13 "Turkey jails UN judge in 'breach of diplomatic immunity,'" BBC (15 June 2017), https://www.bbc.com/news/world-europe-40285658.

14 Levent Kenez, "European court rules Turkey violated immunity of UN judge,"

Nordic Monitor (April 24, 2024), https://nordicmonitor.com/2024/04/european-court-rules-turkey-violated-immunity-of-un-judge/.

15 "Emergency Decree Laws and Their Impact on Human Rights in Turkey," Human Rights Association (December 2021), https://ihd.org.tr/en/wp-content/uploads/2022/05/EmergencyDecreeLawsReport.pdf. *See also* "Constitutional and Legal Provisions Governing Curfew in Turkey," European Commission for Democracy Through Law (Venice Commission) (19 April 2016), https://www.venice.coe.int/webforms/documents/default.aspx?pdffile=CDL-REF(2016)028-e.

16 "Turkey ends state of emergency after two years," BBC (18 July 2018), https://www.bbc.com/news/world-europe-44881328.amp.

Chapter 5

Bending the Judiciary

The next three chapters focus on how Erdoğan turned three major state and societal organs into auxiliaries of his manipulation: the judiciary, the religious establishment, and the media. They became instruments for undermining whatever democratic rule Türkiye had managed to build up between 2000 and 2010. They became a patina of legitimacy for illegitimate actions. In retrospect, one can see how Erdoğan was at this effort for years but played his hand close to his vest.

Erdoğan turned other aspects of government into engines of his capriciousness, of course. But these three warrant special attention for being key players in Erdoğan's brutish campaign to perpetrate and perpetuate hatred, oppression, and politicide toward a group, Hizmet, which was dedicated to improving civil society and democracy and at odds with the regime for trying to do so.

Overview

Erdoğan's capture of the country's judiciary was one of his most critical moves against Hizmet. Not only did he make the nation's legal machinery subservient to his will; and, by doing so, he used judges and prosecutors to cow all other state institutions to stay in step.

The Turkish judiciary does not have a solid history of having an independent and impartial legal structure that can fully protect human rights. Only during the first decade of this century did the country take major steps to create a court system that is both fair and appears to be fair and protects people's rights. The quest for European Union accession provided the needed impetus, and the EU helped with training judges and prosecutors. Erdoğan has erased and reversed that progress.

Erdoğan had long had antipathy toward the judiciary. He does not philosophically believe in the democratic separation of powers, and he had seen the courts in action enough to know they were not always his friend, as in the Gezi Park protests, and would not likely hold open the door to his ambition.

The December 2013 scandal was an even ruder awakening for him when his family, friends, and inner-circle ministers suddenly came under judicial scrutiny for corruption. He ramped up his assault on the judiciary. December 2013 is the milestone transition for the abject about-face of the Turkish judiciary.[1]

Capturing the judiciary entailed restructuring Türkiye's court system and punishing non-compliant judicial officials. Revamping the judicial system had three distinctive steps: creating Criminal Judgeships of Peace with its new procedure of collateral appeals from regular judges; taking institutional control of the Supreme Board of Judges and Prosecutors (HSYK); and amending the Constitution. Erdoğan also later orchestrated changes to the country's criminal justice system, to the detriment of people's rights.

After the abortive July 2016 coup, the collapse became complete with the sudden massive purge of one-third of the nation's judges and prosecutors. Within days, the judicial system lost its independence and became the regime's "sword of politics," "suspending justice" more than any time in the past, in the words of Ertuğrul Günay, former AKP Minister of Culture and Tourism.[2]

Retaliation and Retribution

The mass summary employment purge was but one way of assuring a compliant and loyal judiciary. A second, more brutal way was jailing and torturing "errant" judges and prosecutors. The chapter on detention centers and prisons provides accounts of this.

It is unfathomable that the state could terminate, punish, jail, and torture judges for making a wrong decision, that is, a decision not to the regime's liking. But so it happened. Such retaliation is antithetical to democracy. The message is clear: you are our pawns; you and your family will pay a heavy price if you forget it.[3] This was the death knell of whatever judicial independence had existed, and it cemented Erdoğan's tutelage over the legal system.

A total of 4,296 judges and prosecutors (3,392 men and 904 women) were dismissed based on State of Emergency Decree 667 as implemented by ten different HSYK decisions. The number exceeds 5,000 when one includes military judges, rapporteurs of the Constitutional Court, and auditors of the Court of Accounts.[4] These purges suddenly crippled the country's legal system and left it "reeling."[5]

Most of the judges and prosecutors abruptly removed from the judiciary were not necessarily associated with Hizmet. The coup attempt provided the cover to get rid of them for not supporting the Judiciary Unity Platform, engineered by the Erdoğan regime, during the 2014 HSYK membership elections. They branded all non-supportive judges and prosecutors as "FETÖ" and unjustly discharged them for their political views and not for any lack of integrity or competence. To the contrary, the government feared their integrity and competence.

Restructuring the Judiciary: Earlier Steps Before the Purge

The massive judicial purge was the culmination of Erdoğan's efforts. He had initiated the judicial takeover process earlier on, years before; but it was more gradual than the sudden colossal post-coup purge. Inasmuch as his earlier changes were also directed against Hizmet, they are informative steps in finally taking the judiciary hostage. He had little resistance as he unfolded his plot. The political establishment was fully behind him, solid team members. They were all feeding at the trough. One cannot fault Erdoğan for not being a masterful tactician.

Taking Control of the Council of Judges and Prosecutors

To get where he wanted to get, Erdoğan had to overhaul the Supreme Board of Judges and Prosecutors (HSYK), which later in this narrative becomes the Council of Judges and Prosecutors (HSK). It is an elected governmental body that selects, regulates, and disciplines judges, prosecutors, and other legal functionaries for the entire country (referred to as the judiciary). HYSK was created by the 1982 Constitution and significantly amended by a constitutional referendum in 2010 (including an expansion from seven members to twenty-two to create a more diverse group). A 2017 constitutional referendum engineered by Erdoğan reconfigured HYSK into HSK and reduced its members to thirteen.

Of HSK's thirteen members, parliament appoints seven, the president appoints four, and the Minister of Justice and the Ministry Undersecretary serve *ex officio*, giving the president virtual control if the same political party controls parliament.

The 2017 constitutional amendment abolished all non-political, professional input and made the Council purely an agency of the president and parliament. It reversed the 2010 constitutional amendment, widely seen as a progressive step in professionalizing the judiciary and making it more independent; only six of its twenty-two members were political appointees until the 2017 amendment, and the remaining members were elected by the judiciary at large.

After the 2010 constitutional referendum, international organizations, particularly those in Europe, acknowledged HSYK's new, reformed structure as a crucial step toward ensuring the judiciary's independence and impartiality. The last thing, though, that Erdoğan and the power structure wanted was judicial oversight. It interfered with their long-term plans. They had to change the system that was beginning to flex muscle and jeopardized the corruption into which a number of them had already dipped their hands wrist deep.

They began their plan with some initial steps through parliament which passed a law in 2014 that initiated changes in HSYK and empowered the Minister of Justice with broad authority in appointing judges, prosecutors, and inspectors, as well as in disciplinary investigations.[6] The law restructured HSYK's internal departments and discharged all staff, effectively purging HSYK.

To rid themselves of "problematic" judicial officials. Erdoğan's regime initiated a process similar to that used by the country's top generals in their February 28, 1997 "post-modern" coup ("we need you to resign for the 'good of the country'"—without, of course, any other option), this time, however, targeting those with perceived Hizmet sympathies and other nonconformists.[7]

Despite strong reaction to these unconstitutional legal actions and President Abdullah Gül's statement—"I observed fifteen contradictions in twelve articles of the proposal with the Constitution and warned the Minister of Justice.... Besides rectifying these overt contradictions, I found it appropriate for the other debated provisions of the law, both in favor and against, to be assessed by the Constitutional Court"[8]—expressing potential violations of the Constitution, this law, designed to interfere with the judiciary, was put into effect.

Given the popularity and respect he enjoyed, Gül could have vetoed or quashed the legislation, but he did not; and the rest is history. He and Erdoğan were cofounders of AKP. A wrong decision that threw democracy in Türkiye off track and into the ditch.

Although the Constitutional Court nullified non-substantial aspects of these changes in October 2014, it allowed the legislative and executive branches to successfully intervene in re-organizing the judiciary, thus terminating the employment of HSYK employees associated with Hizmet to reset the personnel structure administratively.

The Erdoğan government knew how to play the Constitutional Court. Under the national constitution, court annulments do not have retroactive effect. So, the AKP parliament could (and did) pass sketchy laws that would not pass constitutional muster. However, they would be in effect until nullified; no retroactive correction. It was quite a charade, a legislative operation to undermine judicial authority.

This gamesmanship drew severe criticism for not complying with the principles of the "rule of law" and "separation of powers," which the European Commission, the primary executive arm of the European Union, highlighted in a major 2014 critique. Other authorities and domestic public opinion articulated concern about handling corruption allegations and the courts' impartiality, transparency, and non-discrimination.[9]

The European Commission Report also contained other substantial critiques of Türkiye's human rights record. Türkiye at the time was still a candidate for admission to the European Union, and the report was measuring its progress toward EU accession. Türkiye has since effectively jettisoned its candidacy. Hizmet had promoted EU accession.

The gamesmanship continued. The Erdoğan regime intervened in the HSYK election process, for which provincial judges and prosecutors had an electoral majority, to assure HSYK's restructuring. The Justice Ministry interposed itself and helped organize the Judiciary Unity Platform to orchestrate a plan for the government to win the HSYK election, which succeeded.

The newly elected HSYK, in cooperation with the regime, then made hundreds of judicial appointments, issued dozens of decrees, effective immediately, and reassigned judges and prosecutors who had been involved in significant investigations and trials with which the government took issue, such as the December 2013 bribery and corruption files, investigation of the Iran-backed Selam Tevhid group, the questioning of then MİT Undersecretary Hakan Fidan, and the Ergenekon and Balyoz trials.[10] It appointed judges and prosecutors affiliated with the Judiciary Unity Platform, who explicitly supported the Erdoğan regime in written, visual, and social media, contradicting the ethical neutrality of judges and prosecutors.

Besides its extraordinary decrees, HSYK, with its new structure and goals aligned with the Erdoğan regime, created lists of questionable origin, profiling judges and prosecutors who did not vote for them and were alleged to be Hizmet members or too independent to trust, as reported by inspectors and individuals within the judiciary. These lists became a means of evaluating appointments, promotions, and disciplinary investigations before the 2016 coup attempt.

Considering the constitutional guarantees that remained in place, however, HSYK leadership believed that only extraordinary methods would "cleanse" the judiciary. Turgay Ateş, a leading HSK member, already discussed in this book, was alarmingly candid about this at an Iftar dinner event organized by the Judiciary Unity Association in June 2016.[11] The Judiciary Unity Association dates to the Judiciary Unity Platform of 2014. Even before the July 15 coup purge, various Ateş administrative measures unjustly and detrimentally affected judges and prosecutors.[12]

Creating Criminal Judgeships of Peace

Taking control of HYSK, which appointed new judges and prosecutors who were government-friendly was not a big enough prize for Erdoğan. Another step was hand-crafting a new component of the judiciary, the Criminal Judgeships of Peace. Erdoğan, while Prime Minister, was clear about his agenda:

> ...We are developing a project. We are building the infrastructure for this. Once that' done, the process will speed up. Just as they filed hundreds of lawsuits against us, we will file hundreds, thousands of lawsuits against them. Then the situation will develop differently.[13]

Erdoğan created a parallel judiciary that would give him the result he wanted and when he wanted. They had extraordinary power to pursue "terrorists," that is, the Gülen Movement. They had collateral appellate power, allowing them to overrule decisions by regular judges on the same level. The government could immediately appeal unfavorable rulings to this cadre of special judges. This process minimized the chance of initial decisions adverse to the regime. No judge would want to risk a ruling that would be overturned immediately, leaving the judge to face retaliation for the government-adverse ruling.

These courts were single-judge courts, which made them more susceptible to political strings. The new judges were young and inexperienced, as much as thirty-forty years younger than the more seasoned regular judges and were appointed by HYSK.

Erdoğan's remarks when the new Criminal Judgeships of Peace infrastructure went into operation in July 2014 were quite telling: "The judicial process begins now. Criminal Judgeships of Peace will manage this process."[14]

The Criminal Judgeships of Peace, from their inception, functioned in line with the expectations of the political establishment, leaving an array of human rights violations in the dust. These judgeships are a solid touchstone of discriminatory regime practices, serving as a hub for illegal activity under the guise of a court. These courts were designed, and politically guided, to legitimize the suppression of Hizmet—politicide, civil death.

Rather than prosecuting government officials for the politicide prohibited by the Turkish Penal Code (Article 77), the judges have become criminal misfeasors, exercising judicial authority in an illegal and improper manner and not abiding by the law. The courts are protecting the lawbreakers and helping them punish their victims.

Article 77 of the Turkish Penal Code defines crimes against humanity. It specifies that the systematic perpetration of certain acts against a part of society, driven by political, philosophical, racial, or religious motives, according to a plan, constitutes this crime. Among others, the acts include intentional injury, torture or inhuman treatment, and deprivation of liberty.

A state prosecutor must bring criminal charges of Article 77 violations, but the chances of that ever happening with the current state-captured judiciary are so close to zero as to be imperceptible. Even more remote, if that is possible in this context, is bringing charges against Erdoğan, which, under Turkish law, would be tried in the Constitutional Court since he is president. To paraphrase Macbeth's famous words, the words of Article 77 and the Turkish Constitution may be "full of sound and fury, signifying nothing."

That parallel judiciary sprang into action when Erdoğan wanted "legal" cover for his full-scale hate war on Hizmet and its allies and sympathizers after the coup attempt. These newly minted and politically chosen judges and prosecutors were short on legal experience and had no qualms about arresting their colleague judges and prosecutors whom they linked to "Hizmet." Nor did these judges hesitate a moment from jumping onto the politicide bandwagon. They became an arm of the executive branch, pursuing dissenters and the Gülen Movement, rather than serving as unbiased and neutral jurists.

The Venice Commission highlighted criticisms about the functions, powers, and operations of Criminal Judgeships of Peace, noting that those judges issued tens of thousands of arrest warrants following the coup attempt, operated on a closed-loop appeal system, made decisions on objections to arrest and requests for release during the state of emergency based only on file review and not live testimony, failed to adequately convey the reasons for detention decisions to the concerned parties, and did not adequately justify decisions that significantly impacted individuals' fundamental rights and freedoms.[15]

The commission likewise expressed deep skepticism about the subsequent detention and arrest of judges and prosecutors after their summary employment termination because of Criminal Judgeships of Peace decisions, which the commission did not view as competent courts.

The new judgeships also drew scathing attention from other respected organizations, such as the International Commission of Jurists, composed of sixty eminent judges and lawyers from all regions of the world, which minced no words and refused to recognize them as authentic courts capable of administering justice.[16]

None of the criticism caused Erdoğan to blink. He had what he had long wanted and was not going to backtrack a bit. Rather, full speed ahead to obliterate his foes.

Amending the Constitution

As noted earlier, one of the 2017 constitutional amendments engineered by Erdoğan restructured HYSK as the Council of Judges and Prosecutors (HSK), which abolished all non-political, professional input in the selection and governance of judiciary members and made the council purely an agency of the president and parliament. It reversed the 2010 amendment, widely seen as a progressive step in professionalizing the judiciary and making it independent. The amendment constitutionalized the regime's earlier capture of HYSK.

Suppressing Lawyers: Arrest, Restrictions

When William Shakespeare wrote his famous and oft-quoted line in Henry VI (Part 2), "The first thing we do, let's kill all the lawyers," he did not write it to foster dislike for attorneys but because the legal system is the only backstop to autocracy and despotism.

Erdoğan has proven that point once again in history. Attorneys and human rights organizations have faced all sorts of harassment, obstacles, and, quite often, incarceration.[17] The regime even shut down the well-respected Union of Judges and Prosecutors (YARSAV) and imprisoned its chair Murat Arslan.[18]

Tahir Elçi, a prominent human rights lawyer and Diyarbakır Bar Association president, was assassinated after a press conference, shot in the head, in late November 2015. Three police were acquitted nine years later for murdering him, despite video and forensic evidence that emerged. Elçi was an outspoken voice against the government. He assisted victims of human rights violations and campaigned vigorously for the rights of the Kurdish people.[19]

Dinushika Dissanayake, Amnesty International's Deputy Regional Director for Europe, summarized it well, "It is a bitter irony that Tahir Elçi's life was cut short by the very violence he was campaigning to end, and justice has been sidestepped because of the endemic impunity that he had dedicated his life to eradicate.[20]

In November 2023, a British lawyers group conducted an international fact-finding mission to Türkiye to monitor the treatment of lawyers detained, arrested, and imprisoned by the Turkish government for terrorism. They published their blistering report in February 2024.[21] Former President of the Texas State Bar association Richard Pena had published an earlier similarly unfavorable, if not scathing, report after a 2013 visit by a delegation he led of eleven U.S. lawyers to Turkish attorneys and bar associations.[22] Little had changed in ten years.

Both groups found a worrying pattern of violations of international human rights law and standards, and a blatant disregard for the protection of lawyers. Lawyers in Türkiye have been arbitrarily arrested, detained, and imprisoned following unfair trials, simply due to their legal work, including clients they represent and professional bodies to which they belong.

The British mission also found that criminal law and human rights lawyers have been charged with national security offences and face long sentences with very restrictive measures in prison. Lawyers are held in conditions that violate internationally accepted standards for prisons, including the U.N. Standard Minimum Rules for the Treatment of Prisoners.

Detentions were arbitrary and prolonged with little justification or explanation. Imprisoned attorneys have restricted access to family members and are held in isolation conditions, often able to interact with only two or three other detainees. Disciplinary measures are also being applied to undermine and deny the lawyers' early release.

Legitimizing Discriminatory Prosecutions and Civil Death

The consequence of the state's legal apparatus coming under regime control led all social and governmental elements to embrace the government's policies, including expressed hatred. Judges reiterated, word for word, the regime's hateful propaganda statements in their decisions.[23]

Erdoğan used incendiary and vile words to declare that the judiciary would effectuate his campaign of hatred, animosity, and annihilation of Hizmet. He has succeeded. Judges and prosecutors, who should be independent, impartial, and duty-bound to protect people's fundamental rights and freedoms and the rule of law, have not refrained from articulating the regime's severe expressions of hate speech in written, visual, and social media, as they dance to the government's rhythm.

Yunus Süer, for example, the former Ankara 5th Criminal Peace Judge, who oversaw anti-Hizmet criminal cases and appointed trustees over media outlets critical of the government and sympathetic to Hizmet, ordered the arrest of hundreds, if not thousands, of people associated with Hizmet. He posted on his Twitter account (@yunussuer) that, "Traitors to the state will not cease their betrayal until their heads are cut and the soil is watered with their blood."[24]

Süer's language is utterly reprehensible for a judge whose obligation is to be fair and impartial and abide by legal principles, but it underscores the complicity of Erdoğan's special judges with the regime. Süer was not unique. He represented the norm, as it was.

Starting with the December 2013 scandal and extending past the ill-fated coup attempt into the present day, the judiciary issued thousands of indictments and decisions, which mirrored the government's political rhetoric. Their decisions violated their constitutional duties no matter how prettily wrapped in legal rhetoric. Individuals seeking relief had no recourse. Judicial rulings sanctioned constitutional violations, including torture and discriminatory actions against Hizmet prisoners. The judiciary legalized politicide.

The decrees during the state of emergency altered Türkiye's legal system to the detriment of all citizens and diminished the protection of everyone's rights across all facets of life. The Constitutional Court, Court of Cassation (appeals court), and Council of State (the country's highest administrative court), theoretically entrusted with upholding justice against an unlawful system, failed in their duties, and instead issued rulings legitimizing the regime's illegal actions.

The high courts, designed to guide the legislative and executive branches and local courts with their precedents and serve as a check on the other two government branches, buckled under intense pressure and acted according to Erdoğan's desires. Their rulings deviated from a century's worth of established practice and precedent, traveling on the roadmap sketched out for them by the regime. The courts abandoned their role in the checks and balances of democratic governance.

This process, orchestrated through the nation's highest courts, covered over the regime's unlawful conduct with a patina of legitimacy. The most striking examples are decisions by the Court of Cassation and the Constitutional Court, departing from previous precedents to radically redefine the legal definition of an armed terrorist organization and membership therein.

The Constitutional Court, with obviously strained reasoning, summarily dismissed requests for annulment (injunction) based on international legal principles and denied individual appeals alleging infringement on constitutional rights. Although occasionally issuing judgments of rights violations because of public pressure from domestic and international communities, the Constitutional Court overall set itself up as a shield for the palace regime.

That the high court did not crater completely offers a bit of hope, if any, that, step-by-step, it may slowly reclaim its stature in the future as a co-equal branch of government for the good of Türkiye. That said, the court unabashedly abandoned its role during this epoch, sanctioning great misery on its watch.

Even worse for the country's legal structure, the Constitutional Court reversed its ruling of a quarter-century earlier that state of emergency decrees were subject to judicial review.[25] In October 2016, three months after the bumbling coup attempt, the court ruled that it lacked the authority to review state of emergency decrees,[26] essentially handing over free and unchecked reign to Erdoğan.

During this dark period of Turkish justice, the Court of Cassation and Council of State similarly mirrored the Constitutional Court's role. Instead of safeguarding individuals' constitutional guarantees, both high courts overlooked the irregularities, relinquishing their power and ignoring their hitherto consistent precedent. Rather than rejecting legal irregularities in criminal and disciplinary processes, the courts bowed to the government's arbitrary behavior.

The Council of State, the country's highest administrative court, reversed its precedent during the state of emergency. Despite previously prohibiting the dismissal of employees in professional occupations without allowing them a proper defense and giving them appropriate procedural safeguards in disciplinary investigations, the council decided that state of emergency measures overrode these procedural safeguards and made them inapplicable. This jeopardized the well-being of purged employees and their families.

Instead of scrutinizing practices that undermine international legal principles in Türkiye, the Court of Cassation legitimized emergency decrees that nullified Code of Criminal Procedure protections and approved new criminal law definitions regarding terrorist organizations, such that they undermined people's freedoms of speech, association, and assembly and swept innocent conduct within a broad terrorist organization definition.

These decisions, parroting the government's position in these cases, were not rooted in legality but instead utilized the law as a guise to validate their illegal practices. HSK and the high courts paved the way for lower courts to act arbitrarily, transforming them into instruments of pressure and intimidation, not of justice, and wounding many individuals in the process.

The country's top courts discarded and disregarded the jurisprudence that the European Union had helped them fashion and instead tailored their revised rulings to the regime's will. Türkiye's courts refused to apply ECtHR decisions that invalidated the detentions and arrests of judges, including two Constitutional Court judges, and faulted Türkiye for other human rights violations.[27]

Two other prominent ECtHR rulings that Türkiye courts and Erdoğan disregarded involved human rights activist Osman Kavala[28] and Kurdish leader and former parliament member Selahattin Demirtaş.[29] discussed in other sections of this book. Kavala's case is described in a few pages going forward.

It came to be that no legal outcome was possible that did not legitimize the framework of the government's systemic anti-Hizmet discrimination.

The entire country, directly and indirectly, suffered damage in myriad ways from Erdoğan's singular war on Hizmet, not the least of which was the wrecked legal system.

Major Ruling by the European Court of Human Rights

It took several years, but the ECtHR issued a milestone ruling in September 2023 on behalf of Yüksel Yalçınkaya, a public-school teacher. Türkiye's Constitutional Court had reviewed the case and found no ECHR violations.

This powerful decision by the Grand Chamber, the highest level of the ECtHR, lays out a comprehensive analysis and strong denunciation of what is transpiring in Türkiye's court system. It is well-reasoned with a thorough grasp of the facts. It is a solid rebuke of the systemic unlawfulness of Turkish judicial proceedings. The seventeen judges of ECtHR's Grand Chamber faulted court proceedings in Türkiye, particularly those after the coup attempt that alleged Hizmet affiliation, as arbitrary and lacking in fundamental fairness.

The sweeping 183-page decision, *Yüksel Yalçınkaya v. Türkiye,*[30] concluded that the Turkish court proceedings violated Article 6 of the European Convention on Human Rights (guaranteeing the right to a fair trial), Article 7 (prohibiting punishment without due process), and Article 11 (freedom of assembly and association and the right to join a trade union).

Yalçınkaya was convicted solely for using the ByLock application. The ECtHR ruled that such a reason, standing by itself, could not sustain a conviction and was protected free speech activity. The investigation against him began as an anonymous report to authorities lodged against him by phone, making it all the more suspicious.

The court also decided that Yalçınkaya did not have a fair trial, procedurally or substantively, in that MİT (National Intelligence Organization) surreptitiously obtained evidence of his use of ByLock and did not disclose having done so until the prosecutor used it in court against him.

This denied him the ability to prepare a proper defense and raised legal questions about MİT violating Yalçınkaya's privacy rights.

Further damning in ECtHR's eyes, the Türkiye courts likewise ruled that Yalçınkaya's membership in a trade union and his association with Bank Asya, both considered as Hizmet-affiliated, impermissibly corroborated his conviction. The court censured the Turkish courts for their unprecedented narrowing of protected free association rights.

The ECtHR took pains to emphasize the necessity of scrutinizing the mental element of "knowledge and intent" in Türkiye's terrorism cases, especially given that Fethullah Gülen, Hizmet's spiritual guide, had previously been acquitted in 2008 of the charge of forming a terrorist organization and there was no final court decision before Yalçınkaya's indictment in 2017 changing that holding. That begged the question of how he could be convicted of belonging to a terrorist organization that the courts had ruled was not one.

The court found that, under ECHR Article 7, the first-level Turkish judge and the appellate Court of Cassation had engaged in impermissible assumptions rather than identifying any actual material or mental elements of being a terrorist organization member or security threat to the country. Nor may someone be punished for criminal activity that was not a crime at the time of the person's actions. A law may not retroactively create a crime and punish someone for violating it.

The monumental ruling also strongly delimited the state-of-emergency derogation argument that Türkiye had put forward as a defense. The court narrowed the reach of derogation to what is essential in the security situation at the time and made it quite clear that the invocation of derogation is not a complete derogation of the rule of law or fundamental rights. This decision reined in derogation and brought its use within the scope of court review, a significant ruling of first impression since it asserted judicial oversight over the possible abuse of derogation, as indeed was the case with Türkiye and its lengthy two-year state of emergency.

The court had already pointed in the direction of narrowing derogation in the case of *Şahin Alpay v. Turkey,*[31] six years earlier. *Alpay* is instructive in that he was not a Hizmet member but a columnist for *Zaman.* He was a respected and prominent journalist and critic of the government. His sympathies were with what Hizmet stood for in terms of civil society. He published a critical column on the December 2013 corruption scandal on the day before the coup disaster.

The ECtHR was clear that the bare invocation of a public emergency threatening the life of the nation could not be used as a pretext to constrain political debate and criticism against state authorities. Journalistic activities in that context *per se* could not be subject to criminal charges for terrorist-related activities.

In a similar case, *Mehmet Hasan Altan v. Turkey*, decided in parallel with *Alpay* on the same day, the ECtHR ruled in favor of a journalist critical of the government. The court emphasized that a "public emergency threatening the life of the nation must not serve as a pretext for limiting freedom of political debate, which is at the very core of the concept of a democratic society."[32]

In both the *Alpay* and *Altan* cases, the ECtHR focused on the fact that trial courts refused to implement the ruling of the Constitutional Court that the two journalists' free speech rights had been violated and that they should be freed. This set the country further on the path of the regime's and lower courts' non-implementation of Constitutional Court rulings.

Non-implementation was a message to the Constitutional Court that deciding adversely to the government is risky because other courts and the government will ignore its authority, undercutting the rule of law. It also puts the judges in an awkward, perhaps precarious, position, given the earlier summary dismissals of their two court colleagues during the purge. Maybe those fears and realities played a part in their *Yalçınkaya* decision that ECtHR reversed.

Yalçınkaya's situation was not unique but representative of how tens of thousands of Hizmet people and those with alleged Hizmet association were prosecuted and jailed with the Turkish courts' jaundiced blessing for actions that are not prohibited by law but were nevertheless used to justify incarceration in violation of ECHR Article 7 ("no crime and punishment without law" and no retroactive laws or punishment). There were forty-seven other previous decisions in which the ECtHR found Article 7 violations against Türkiye.

The *Yalçınkaya* decision applied to more than 100,000 jailed people at the time. As the court pointed out, thousands of cases are pending in

Türkiye based on ECHR Article 7 violations. More than 8,000 cases were pending before the Constitutional Court, and the court had already forwarded 3,000 similar case files to the government in December 2023 and April and July 2024 for response.

The *Yalçınkaya* case is one of the most substantial human rights judgments against Türkiye. Erdoğan strongly attacked the landmark ruling as "the final straw" that broke the camel's back,[33] although he did not elucidate what he meant, other than again showing disdain for the court. There was no promise of reform or correction with respect to the ruling, just full-throated rejection.

Yalçınkaya is not only a landmark decision and an indictment of what Türkiye's judiciary had become but also the plaintive voice of a society in search of justice and freedom.[34]

Other ECtHR Decisions Reversing Turkish Courts

One of the most important ECtHR cases (and by its Grand Chamber, the plenary court assembly), that goes to the heart of Türkiye's democratic structures is *Selahattin Demirtaş v. Turkey* in late 2020.[35] Demirtaş was an outspoken Kurdish leader and a parliament member from the opposition Peoples' Democratic Party (HDP). Erdoğan brooks no opposition, not even from parliament members elected by the people.

The AKP-dominated parliament stripped Demirtaş of parliamentary immunity and that of other opposition members of parliament so that the government could prosecute them under Türkiye's catch-all terrorism law scheme. Demirtaş was also charged with insulting the president. The Constitutional Court, with bowing and genuflecting, acquiesced in the scheme.

This action by parliament and the court undermined, if not gutted, the country's constitutional separation of powers. The ECtHR's 156-page opinion ruled against Turkey. Erdoğan's reaction was to disdainfully call the grand chamber's ruling "non-binding," despite ECHR Article 46, Section 1, requiring otherwise ("The High Contracting Parties [of which Türkiye is one] undertake to abide by the final judgment of the Court in any case to which they are parties.").

The European Court of Human Rights has also taken unfavorable note of the decisional shifts in both the Constitutional Court and the

Court of Cassation. In two cases especially, those concerning two former respected judges Alpaslan Altan and Hakan Baş, the ECtHR rejected rulings by the Constitutional Court and the Court of Cassation as contravening international principles, the judges' only "crime" being an accusation of association with Hizmet.

The *Alparslan Altan vs. Türkiye* decision in 2019 highlighted violations of the well-established principle of legal certainty, that courts do not suddenly create a new and different application of a law divergent from its established interpretation and precedent. Otherwise, court decisions become arbitrary; and people have no idea of what conduct is legal and what is prohibited.[36]

Judge Altan, formerly of the Constitutional Court, complained that his unjustified arrest resulted from an investigation that violated international human rights guarantees under ECHR Article 5.1 (right to liberty and security). He argued that the regime prosecuted and penalized him for alleged peaceful association with Hizmet, a protected right, and not for actual terrorist conduct.

To uphold the state's position against the former judge, the Court of Cassation did a disingenuous legal acrobatic and re-interpreted the principle of *in flagrante delicto* (being caught in the actual act of committing a crime). The ECtHR faulted the Court of Cassation for expanding the concept's scope beyond its traditional legal definition and, going even further to the core of the case, ruled that mere membership in, or association with, an alleged terrorist organization could not itself be considered *in flagrante delicto*. There had to be a concrete act against state security. Thus, the government had no basis for the arrest and detention of the judge.[37]

In another case, Judge Baş, while serving in Kocaeli, was arrested and held in detention for fourteen months without trial. When the trial finally arrived, he was convicted and sentenced to seven and a half years in prison for alleged Hizmet association. The European Court of Human Rights ruled that the Turkish government violated Baş' right to liberty and security and lacked reasonable suspicion to detain him in the first place and had no incriminating evidence to justify its action.[38]

This case in 2020, coming seventeen months after *Alparslan Altan*, was more attentive to the Erdoğan regime's attack on the judiciary. The

82-page opinion expressed concern about the number of judges terminated by the government and the impact that such expulsions had, and would have, on the judiciary's independence.

A third case, brought by one of the country's former highest-ranking judges, is instructive. In March 2024, the European Court of Human Rights (ECtHR) ruled that Türkiye violated the rights of Judge Adem Kartal, the former vice president of the HSYK inspection board.

Kartal was appointed in late 2011 as the inspection board vice-president and dismissed after the parliament adopted Law No. 6524 in February 2014 to restructure HSYK according to Erdoğan's predilections. HSYK appointed his replacement within days, all a well-planned maneuver.

HSYK then appointed him as a public prosecutor at the Court of Cassation in March. Although the Constitutional Court (the nation's highest court) annulled the applicable section of Law No. 6524 in April 2014, Kartal was not reappointed to his position as he should have been. On July 16, 2016, the day after the abortive coup, HSYK suspended Kartal from the Court of Cassation. In August, HSYK fired him and rejected his administrative appeal in November.

A year later, in October 2017, an Erzurum court convicted Kartal of membership in Hizmet and sentenced him to more than seven years in prison. The Court of Cassation upheld his conviction three years later on appeal. The Constitutional Court refused to hear his case.

Kartal had already applied to the ECtHR for relief in July 2014, arguing that he had not been afforded any effective remedy regarding his HSYK termination and that, although the Constitutional Court had annulled the provision under which he was discharged, the fact that HYSK did not follow the court's judgment meant that he had no effective right of access to court, thus violating Article 6.1 of the European Convention on Human Rights. The ECtHR agreed and ordered Türkiye to pay the former judge €9,567 ($10,619).[39] but it was ten years after the fact and much less than he would have otherwise earned. A moral victory, at least, but not much more.

As noted earlier, applying to the ECtHR, even when successful, brought no immediate relief. Procedurally, the case has to wind its way through the Turkish courts, which can go on for years, before the ECtHR has jurisdiction to hear it, which can often take years. The slowness of the judicial process worked to the government's advantage.

Non-Implementation of Judicial Decisions

During the state of emergency, the relatively few individuals dismissed by emergency decrees and later reinstated to their positions through the Inquiry Commission or court rulings were not allowed to resume their duties by the relevant authorities, an obvious abuse of power and a snub at judicial process.

During this period, individuals whose dismissal decisions were reversed or revoked due to lack of evidence by the Inquiry Commission or a court were either kept waiting without their reinstatement orders being processed or were assigned different employment positions. This effectively continues to treat individuals as guilty and is part of the Erdoğan regime's effort to keep animosity churned up against them.

The following are examples of many, keeping in mind that Türkiye's Constitution (Article 138) mandates implementing court rulings without delay.

A Chief Police Officer removed from duty in 2016 while serving in the General Directorate of Security won his case, and the administrative court ordered him reinstated. Despite a prolonged waiting period, the directorate did not reinstate the officer. He then lodged a complaint with the Office of the Ombudsman, which, in accord with the court ruling, sent a recommendation to the ministry for the officer's reinstatement. Regardless of these efforts, the directorate did not allow the officer to resume duty.[40]

Other individuals reinstated at the interior ministry were not re-employed in their original positions at the General Directorate of Security. Instead, after a long delay following their reinstatement order by the Inquiry Commission or a court, they were employed within the ministry's research center, a different kind of employment. A substantial number of grievances regarding this issue surfaced in the media.[41]

The Ministry of Interior's defense in a court case illustrates the practices of public institutions to disregard court decisions, in line with the official posture of the Erdoğan regime:

> Although the State of Emergency [Inquiry] Commission has decided to reinstate the plaintiff to public service, part of the process involves consideration and investigation as to whether the person is suitable for the position to which they will be appointed, with the Minister retaining the discretion to make the appointment accordingly. This discretion is specifically and consciously applied, particularly for appointments to armed institutions because of the importance of ensuring state and public security.

Yet another instance involved police officer H.Ö., suspended in April 2017, during the state of emergency and dismissed in February 2021, almost four years later. An appellate court granted a stay of the dismissal and eventually rejected the Ministry of Interior's objection to the court decision.[42] According to Article 28 of the Administrative Procedure Law, H.Ö. should have been reinstated within 30 days. However, nearly ten months after the court decision, H.Ö. still was not reinstated. Consummate recalcitrance.

Educators were also adversely affected, 5,000 of whom were snared by profiling immediately after the fraught coup attempt and dismissed from their positions through emergency decrees.

Following their dismissals, the regulations establishing the Inquiry Commission were amended, allowing the commission to reinstate dismissed public employees, but stipulating that restored educators could not return to their former workplaces.[43] The Constitutional Court ruled, though, that there was no lawful or factual obligation barring these individuals categorically from returning to their previous positions before their dismissal.

Despite the high court's decision, the Higher Education Council (YÖK) refused to reinstate some educators, stating flatly that the "Constitutional Court decision would not be implemented." The refusal to immediately reinstate Hizmet-associated individuals, who were few in number, despite the court ruling is another example of the government's politicide policies. Complaints in this regard have not yielded results, highlighting the extent of discriminatory administrative practices in Türkiye and the Constitutional Court's inability to rein them in, even if it wanted.

Gezi Park Revenge Redux

Six years later, in February 2019, still smarting from the 2013 Gezi protests, after reshaping the judiciary, Erdoğan went after sixteen people, including a prominent philanthropist, long-time civil society activist, and businessman Osman Kavala for allegedly financing the Gezi protests and "attempting to overthrow the government," even though the courts had acquitted the actual protesters of those charges.[44] Erdoğan was determined to get even with the judges, protestors, and those who supported the protests and had embarrassed him.

Kavala received aggravated life imprisonment, the most severe sentence under Turkish law. He is still imprisoned despite two judgments of the European Court of Human Rights (including one by the seventeen judges of the Grand Chamber), ordering his release. He is one of thousands of political prisoners, but high profile enough to show Erdoğan's lack of respect for the court and that his ego, when offended, will bow to none.

When the ECtHR first ruled in Kavala's favor in late 2019, it acquitted him of the charges and ordered his release,[45] Türkiye dismissed the charges but immediately filed added charges, kept him in prison, and convicted him of the new charges. The ECtHR's Grand Chamber then ruled in July 2022 that Türkiye, even with the new charges and conviction, was still in violation of the original court order.[46] Türkiye took no action thereafter. Kavala remains in prison.

Erdoğan never forgot or forgave anyone of something for which he wanted to exact retribution, as he often reminded people. As noted earlier, even twelve years later in 2025, his government is still seeking retaliation by prosecuting people seen as Gezi supporters or organizers, not for any violence but to get even for challenging him.[47] This speaks much of the psychology and personality at play in the persecution of Hizmet.

Summary

The process of stigmatizing, eradicating, and criminalizing Hizmet, fast-tracked following the suspicious coup attempt, engulfed the judiciary and made it a primary actor. With the establishment of Peace Criminal Judgeships, control of the Council of Judges and Prosecutors (HSK), and the declaration of a state of emergency, Erdoğan accelerated and consolidated his persecution of Hizmet and bankrupted the integrity of the courts.

A 2016 report on Türkiye by the European Commission, the primary executive arm of the European Union, raised concerns about the ongoing institutional and structural changes in the composition and formation of the Court of Cassation and the Council of State and their effect on the independence of the judiciary.[48] The report highlighted alterations frequently made within the judicial system, particularly in the criminal court system, causing legal uncertainties. Legal certainty is an anchor of democratic governance.

In June 2024, the Special Rapporteur on the independence of judges and lawyers, appointed by the United Nations Human Rights Council, released a comprehensive twelve-page inquiry to Erdoğan about the situation in Türkiye, detailing many of the issues discussed in this chapter and adding others, clearly concerned about the direction of the country's judiciary and legal system.[49] No response thus far from the regime.

Erdoğan changed the country's legal landscape and concentrated more unchecked power into his position, undercutting democracy and civil society to the country's detriment. The most significant setback overall was the judiciary's erosion and reversal of progress it had made in the 2000-2010 period in alignment with the European Union accession process. Lawlessness and arbitrariness became ascendant in Turkish courts, and independence bowed out.

Endnotes

1 "Turkey: the Judicial System in Peril: A briefing paper" International Commission of Jurists, Turkey-Judiciary-in-Peril-Publications-Reports-Fact-Findings-Mission-Reports-2016-ENG.pdf (icj.org).

2 "Günay: Yargı hiçbir dönemde bu kadar siyasetin kılıcı olmadı," Kronos37 (9 August 2021), https://kronos37.news/ertugrul-gunay-yargi-hicbir-donemde-bu-kadar-siyasetin-kilici-olmadi/ [Günay: Jurisdiction has never been such a sword of politics"].

3 Mustafa Doğan, "Torture Report on Judges and Prosecutors in Turkey," Cross-border Jurists' Association (March 2022), https://justicesquare.org/wp-content/uploads/2023/09/TORTURE-REPORT-ON-JUDGES-AND-PROSECUTORS-IN-TURKEY-.pdf. *See also* "How Turkey's courts turned on Erdoğan's foes," Reuters (May 4, 2020), https://www.reuters.com/investigates/special-report/turkey-judges/.

4 "Dismissal of Public Servants by Emergency Decree Laws & HSYK/HSK Decisions," Solidarity with Others, https://www.solidaritywithothers.com/dismissal-by-decree-laws-and-hsk.

5 Carlotta Gall, "*Erdoğan's Purges Leave Turkey's Justice System Reeling,*" New York Times (June 21, 2019), https://www.nytimes.com/2019/06/21/world/asia/Erdoğan-turkey-courts-judiciary-justice.html.

6 Law No. 6524 (enacted 15 Feb. 2014). *See also* "Turkey: New Amendments to Laws on Judiciary," Library of Congress (Mar. 10, 2014), https://www.loc.gov/item/global-legal-monitor/2014-03-10/turkey-new-amendments-to-laws-on-judiciary/.

7 *See* Sevgi Akarcesme, "Hizmet unmasks 'undemocratic' Erdoğan," Al Jazeera (2 March 2014), Hizmet unmasks 'undemocratic' Erdoğan | Opinions | Al Jazeera.

8 "Turkey's Gul signs divisive bill," Deutsche Wells (02/26/2014), https://www.dw.com/en/turkish-president-gul-signs-controversial-judiciary-bill/a-17457590.

9 "Commission Staff Working Document, Turkey 2014 Progress Report, Accompanying the Document Communication from the Commission to The European Parliament, The Council, The European Economic And Social Committee and The Committee of the Regions," European Commission, Brussels (8.10.2014), https://neighbourhood-enlargement.ec.europa.eu/document/download/351f7f4d-8530-43c5-840f-147cfc0a5a8e_en?filename=20141008-turkey-progress-report_en.pdf (p.13).

10 "Former prosecutors, judge overseeing Iran-backed Tevhid-Selam network detained in Istanbul," Turkish Minute (February 18, 2017), https://www.turkishminute.com/2017/02/18/former-prosecutors-judge-overseeing-iran-backed-tevhid-selam-network-detained-istanbul/; and see "Turkish court sentences 10 to life in prison over 2012 summoning of intel chief Hakan Fidan," duvaR.english (March 03, 2021), https://www.duvarenglish.com/turkish-court-sentences-10-to-life-in-prison-over-2012-summoning-of-intel-chief-hakan-fidan-news-56492.

11 "Hakim ve savcılar iftarda buluştu: "Devletin yanındayız,"" CNNTurk (14.06.2016), https://www.cnnturk.com/turkiye/hakim-ve-savcilar-iftarda-bulustu-devletin-yanindayiz-548037 ["Judges and prosecutors met at the Iftar: 'We are with the state'"].

12 "Turkish Judiciary in the International Arena Reports after 17/25 December Investigations Report Published," Crossborder Jurists' Association (Jan. 28, 2024), https://www.crossborderjurists.org/turkish-judiciary-in-the-international-are-

na-reports-after-17-25-december-investigations-report-published/.

13 "Erdoğan operasyonu yönettiğini ağzından kaçırdı" Siyaset Cafe (22 July 2014), https://www.siyasetcafe.com/Erdoğan-operasyonu-yonettigini-agzindan-kacirdi-6005h.htm, İET: 30/07/2023 ["Erdoğan let out of his mouth that he was running the operation"].

14 Leighann Spencer, "Should the ECtHR Consider Turkey's Criminal Peace Judgeships a Viable Domestic Avenue?," Verfassungsblog on Matters Constitutional (10 Oct. 2018), https://verfassungsblog.de/should-the-ecthr-consider-turkeys-criminal-peace-judgeships-a-viable-domestic-avenue/.

15 "Turkey: Opinion on the Duties, Competences and Functioning of the Criminal Peace Judgeships," European Commission for Democracy through Law (Venice Commission) (13 March 2017), https://www.venice.coe.int/webforms/documents/default.aspx?pdffile=CDL-AD(2017)004.

16 "The Turkish Criminal Peace Judgeships and International Law," International Commission of Jurists (2018), https://www.icj.org/wp-content/uploads/2019/02/Turkey-Judgeship-Advocacy-Analysis-brief-2018-ENG.pdf. *See also* "Factsheet on Turkey's Criminal Peace Judgeships," Arrested Lawyers Initiative (25 July 2019), https://arrestedlawyers.org/wp-content/uploads/2019/08/factsheet-criminal-peace-judgeships.pdf.

17 "Report of an Independent International Fact-finding Mission to Turkey: Examining the Treatment of Lawyers Deprived of their Liberty and Observing Trial Proceedings 6-10 November 2023," The Law Society (23 Feb 2024), https://www.lawsociety.org.uk/campaigns/international-rule-of-law/news/results-of-our-recent-fact-finding-mission-in-turkey. *See also* "Briefing: Prosecution of 11 Human Rights Defenders," Amnesty International (Oct. 19, 2017), https://www.amnesty.org/en/wp-content/uploads/2021/05/EUR4473292017ENGLISH.pdf.

18 "MEDEL at the side event Revisiting the functioning of democratic institutions and rule of law in Turkey – Role of judiciary in current situation of Turkey in honouring the obligations deriving from CoE membership," MEDEL (June 23, 2023), https://medelnet.eu/medel-at-the-side-event-revisiting-the-functioning-of-democratic-institutions-and-rule-of-law-in-turkey-role-of-judiciary-in-current-situation-of-turkey-in-honouring-the-obligations-deriving/.

19 Liemertje Sieders, "Turkey: Tahir Elci death must be investigated amid questions over rule of law," International Bar Association (2016), https://www.ibanet.org/article/fb931eb4-28bb-42b3-8fc1-4e74cbd52359.

20 "Türkiye: Acquittal of three police officers for involvement in killing of human rights lawyer a huge blow to justice," Amnesty International (June 12, 2024), https://www.amnesty.org/en/latest/news/2024/06/turkiye-acquittal-of-three-police-officers-for-involvement-in-killing-of-human-rights-lawyer-a-huge-blow-to-justice/.

21 "Report of an Independent International Fact-finding Mission to Turkey Examining the Treatment of Lawyers Deprived of their Liberty and Observing Trial Proceedings 6-10 November 2023," The Law Society (23 Feb. 2024), New report details results of our recent fact-finding mission in Turkey | The Law Society.

22 Richard Pena, "Lawyers Under Attack in Turkey: A commentary by Richard Pena," State Bar of Texas (2013), https://www.texasbar.com/Content/NavigationMenu/NewsandPublications/TexasBarJournal1/OnlineMaterial/Pena.pdf.

23 Hasan Dursun, Mustafa Dogan, *Bir Soykırım Silahı Olarak Türk Yargısı* (Nordic Publishing House, 2021), s.140 (available as an eBook at Barnes & Noble Digital Books, https://www.barnesandnoble.com/w/bir-soykirim-silahi-olarak-turk-yargisi-hasan-dursun/1140950169) ["Turkish Judiciary as a Genocide Weapon."].

24 "Turkey Seizes Media Outlets Critical of Government," Freedom House (Oct. 26, 2015), https://freedomhouse.org/article/turkey-seizes-media-outlets-critical-government. *See also* "UK court rejects Turkish extradition request for media boss," Guardian (28 Nov. 2018), https://www.theguardian.com/law/2018/nov/28/uk-court-rejects-turkish-extradition-request-for-media-boss.

25 Turkish Constitutional Court, K.1991/1 (10 Jan. 1991).

26 *Id.* E.2016/166, K.2016/159 (12 Oct. 2016).

27 *Alparslan Altan* v. Turkey (No. 12778/17), European Court of Human Rights (16 April 2019), https://hudoc.echr.coe.int/eng#{%22itemid%22:[%22001-192804%22]}. *See also Baş v. Turkey* (No. 66448/17), European Court of Human Rights (3 March 2020*)*, https://hudoc.echr.coe.int/eng#{%22itemid%22:[%22001-201761%22]}. *See also* "Türkiye: Constitutional Court should uphold decisions by the European Court of Human Rights," Norwegian Helsinki Committee (12.10.2023), https://www.nhc.no/en/turkiye-constitutional-court-should-uphold-decisions-by-the-european-court-of-human-rights/. *See also* "The European Court of Human Rights condemns Turkey for the detention of 427 judges and prosecutors," CrossBorderJurists (December 1, 2021), https://www.crossborderjurists.org/the-european-court-of-human-rights-condemns-turkey-for-the-detention-of-427-judges-and-prosecutors/.

28 *Kavala v. Türkiye [GC]* (No. 28749/18), European Court of Human Rights (11.7.2022), https://hudoc.echr.coe.int/eng?i=002-13743. *See also Kavala v. Türkiye* (No. 28749/18), European Court of Human Rights (10 Dec. 2019), https://hudoc.echr.coe.int/eng#{%22itemid%22:[%22001-199515%22]}.

29 *Selahattin Demirtaş v. Turkey* (No. 14305/17) (No. 2), European Court of Human Rights (22 Dec. 2020), https://hudoc.echr.coe.int/fre?i=001-207173.

30 *Yüksel Yalçinkaya v. Türkiye* (No. 15669/20), European Court of Human Rights (26 Sept. 2023), https://www.courthousenews.com/wp-content/uploads/2023/09/Yuksel-Yalcinkaya-v.-Turkiye.pdf. For an overview of the court's operation, *see* "European Court of Human Rights," International Justice Resource Center, https://ijrcenter.org/european-court-of-human-rights/#:~:text=Grand%20Chamber%3A%20composed%20of%2017,directly%20to%20the%20Grand%20Chamber.

31 *Şahin Alpay v. Turkey* (No. 16538/17), European Court of Human Rights (20 March 2018), https://hudoc.echr.coe.int/eng?i=001-181866.

32 *Mehmet Hasan Altan v. Turkey* (No. 13237/17), European Court of Human Rights (20 March 2018), https://hudoc.echr.coe.int/eng?i=001-181862.

33 Emre Turkut, "'Article 7' Shockwaves, ByLock and Beyond: Unpacking the Grand Chamber's Yalçinkaya Judgment," Strasbourg Observers (Oct. 13, 2013), https://strasbourgobservers.com/2023/10/13/article-7-shockwaves-bylock-and-beyond-unpacking-the-grand-chambers-yalcinkaya-judgment/. *See also* Coşkun Yorulmaz, "Beyond the Verdict: Yalçınkaya v Türkiye and the Quest for Justice in the Shadow of Terrorism Charge," Human Rights in Context (Dec. 26, 2023), https://www.humanrightsincontext.be/post/beyond-the-verdict-yal%C3%A7%C4%B1nkaya-v-t%C3%BCrkiye-and-the-quest-for-justice-in-the-shadow-of-terrorism-charge.

34 *Id. See* Coşkun Yorulmaz, "Beyond the Verdict."

35 *Selahattin Demirtaş v. Turkey* (No. 14305/17) (No. 2), European Court of Human Rights (22 Dec. 2020), https://hudoc.echr.coe.int/fre?i=001-207173.

36 *Alparslan Altan v. Turkey* (No.12778/17*)*, European Court of Human Rights (16 April 2019), *https://hudoc.echr.coe.int/eng#{%22itemid%22:[%22001-192804%22]}*.

37 Emre Turkut, "The Discovery in Flagrante Delicto, The Kafkaesque Fate of a

Supreme Judge and the Turkish Constitutional Court: The Alparslan Altan Case In Strasbourg," Strasbourg Observers (May 6, 2019), https://strasbourgobservers.com/2019/05/06/the-discovery-in-flagrante-delicto-the-kafkaesque-fate-of-a-supreme-judge-and-the-turkish-constitutional-court-the-alparslan-altan-case-in-strasbourg/.

38 *Baş v. Turkey* (No. 66448/17), European Court of Human Rights (7 Sept. 2020), https://hudoc.echr.coe.int/fre#{%22itemid%22:[%22001-201761%22]}.

39 *Kartal v. Türkiye* (No. 54699/14) European Court of Human Rights (26 March 2024), https://hudoc.echr.coe.int/eng?i=001-231738.

40 "İçişleri Bakanlığı hukuk tanımıyor," Gerçek Gündem (13 May 2023), https://www.gercekgundem.com/siyaset/icisleri-bakanligi-hukuk-tanimiyor-goreve-iade-kararlari-dikkate-alinmadi-422495 ["Ministry of Interior does not recognize law"].

41 E.g. Can Bursali, "Mahkeme göreve iade etti, İçişleri Bakanlığı 10 aydır kararı uygulamıyor... Ödenecek tazminat, idari amirlerden tahsil edilebilir mi?" Independent Turkçe (6 April 2022), https://www.indyturk.com/node/494371/haber/mahkeme-g%C3%B6reve-iade-etti-i%CC%87%C3%A7i%C5%9Fleri-bakanl%C4%B1%C4%9F%C4%B1-10-ayd%C4%B1r-karar%C4%B1-uygulam%C4%B1yor-%C3%B6denecek ("The court reinstated him, the Ministry of Internal Affairs has not implemented the decision for 10 months... Can the compensation to be paid be collected from the administrative supervisors?").

42 *Id.*

43 Law No. 7145 (25 July 2018), amending Law No. 7075,

44 "Türkiye: Convictions of Osman Kavala & four others needs urgent international response," Amnesty International (Oct. 11, 2023), https://www.amnesty.org/en/latest/news/2023/10/turkiye-convictions-of-osman-kavala-four-others-needs-urgent-international-response/.

45 *Kavala v. Türkiye* (No. 28749/18), European Court of Human Rights (10 Dec. 2019), https://hudoc.echr.coe.int/eng#{%22itemid%22:[%22001-199515%22]}.

46 *Kavala v. Türkiye [GC]* (No. 28749/18), European Court of Human Rights (11 July 2022), https://hudoc.echr.coe.int/eng?i=002-13743.

47 "Turkey arrests talent manager over trying to overthrow the government," Reuters (Jan. 28, 2025), https://www.reuters.com/world/middle-east/turkey-arrests-talent-manager-over-trying-overthrow-government-2025-01-28/.

48 "Commission Staff Working Document, Turkey 2016 Report, Accompanying the document Communication from the Commission to the European Parliament, the Council, the European Economic and Social Committee and the Committee of the Regions" (pp.17-10), European Commission, Brussels (9.11.2016), https://neighbourhood-enlargement.ec.europa.eu/document/download/e703a769-bf7f-46d1-8a13-6a836683e838_en?filename=20161109_report_turkey.pdf.

49 Margaret Satterthwaite, "Mandate of the Special Rapporteur on the independence of judges and lawyers," UN Human Rights Council (21 June 2024), AL TUR (3.2024).

Chapter 6

The Media

Journalism in Türkiye has had a long, painful history of struggle with the government and with itself. Objectivity and fairness are distant goals, if goals at all. That struggle has sharpened under Erdoğan. The country consistently finds itself on the list of the world's leading jailers of journalists, often in first place.

According to Reporters Without Borders (RSF), between 2014 and 2024, five Turkish journalists were killed, 131 imprisoned, 77 convicted of "insulting the president," and hundreds of others prosecuted in one fashion or another for their work.[1] In 2023, Türkiye ranked 165th out of 180 countries in the RSF World Press Freedom Index.

Erdoğan's war on the media began with his suppression of the Gezi Park protests as prime minister when police attacked 150 reporters in Izmir, Ankara, and Istanbul and walked away with immunity for their ruthless deeds. He was out of the country when the discord erupted; but, as soon as he returned, he reversed President Abdullah Gül's conciliatory overtures and went fiercely full steam ahead after the protestors. Eleven people died, and more than 8,000 people suffered injuries. The police arrested more than 3,000 protesters.

Tightening his grip on the press was essential to Erdoğan's rise to power, and he undertook a variety of tactics, as he moved upstream.[2] He learned well from the textbook for autocrats, the same edition they all seem to use. Moving through the December 2013 corruption scandal and into the coup debacle, his grip became tauter.

The regime, which pursued an agenda based on political Islam that it could control and manipulate, identified Hizmet, which it could not control, as the prime target of one of the most intense, extensive, and systematic hate speech campaigns in the country's history. It was a vital part of Erdoğan's politicide agenda.

The government-"guided" media took on the task of promoting and ingraining hate speech throughout the country. The social media apparatus, often referred to as the "AK troll army," did its part, too, unleashing waves of hatred against Hizmet across all media domains.

Seizing Media Outlets

For Erdoğan to take hold of the press and succeed in his systemic campaign to demonize and erase Hizmet, he needed badly to be rid of prominent and respected independent media outlets with Hizmet connections or sympathies like *Zaman*, *Today's Zaman*, *Meydan*, *Bugün*, and *Millet* newspapers, along with Kanal Türk, Bugün TV, Cihan News Agency, and *Aksiyon Magazine*. So, the government, without blinking, outright seized them early on and appointed trustees or receivers to manage their parent companies.

Government-chosen trustees also took over the Koza-Ipek Media Group, Feza Media Group, and suspended broadcasts of TV channels with Hizmet affiliation. Altogether, after the coup attempt, emergency decrees shut down thirty-three TV channels, seventy newspapers, twenty magazines, thirty-four radio stations, thirty publishing houses, and countless distribution companies.[3]

Decree 668 mandated the transfer of all movable and immovable assets, rights, documents, and real estate of the shuttered media outlets to the state treasury without any legal proceedings, court orders, or compensation. This was a brazen denial of due process and illegal seizure of private property.

The assets of other major companies—whose owners openly identified with Hizmet initiatives, projects, and institutions—such as Boydak, Dumankaya, Akfel, Kaynak, and Naksan, which held some of Türkiye's largest firms, were seized by the TMSF (Savings Deposit Insurance Fund) and later sold off far below their value, favoring regime supporters. Again, seizure without compensation. Instant wealth for the oppressors, and a smelly odor of corruption.

Altogether, following the December 2013 corruption events and post-coup measures, 179 media institutions, including TV channels, news agencies, printing houses, magazines, newspapers, and radio stations, associated with dissident circles, especially Hizmet, were summarily shuttered.[4]

The United Nations High Commissioner for Human Rights finally sounded the alarm in 2022 that seizing critical sources of independent journalism posed an extraordinary threat to press freedom and pluralism in Türkiye,[5] but by then it was too late. The die was cast.

Eventually Controlling 85% of the Country's Media

Even before his full-scale seizure of the media related to Hizmet, Erdoğan, since becoming prime minister in 2002, had been steadily reshaping media ownership. He created a financial system that appropriated media companies struggling to repay their debts to the state and ultimately allocated these outlets to private companies allied with the government. As a result of this careful strategy and later post-coup appropriations, companies that support the government or are bound to it by shared strategic interests control more than 85% of private sector national media.

TV channels like Star TV and ATV, and digital platforms, ended up in the portfolios of pro-Erdoğan businesspeople amid controversial tender processes. It was mutual backscratching, devoid of justice and equity. Going a step further, a network of TV channels and newspapers formed a partisan media army under Erdoğan's control, including *Sabah*, *Takvim*, *Habertürk*, *Yeni Şafak*, and more.

Erdoğan's grip on the public sector media includes tight control over the Turkish Radio and Television Corporation, the national public broadcaster (TRT), and the Radio and Television Supreme Council (RTÜK) regulatory agency, both of which, despite being charged with objective neutrality, assisted his third presidential election victory in May 2023 with biased media coverage.[6]

The regime now controls a very sizeable portion of Türkiye's written, visual, and social media. Whatever opposition media there are, and they almost non-existent, hold an ineffectual position in the country, which is why the government tolerates them.

Holding the Purse Strings

And, if the message was not clear enough, the Press Advertisement Agency (BIK), which manages state advertising in the media, modified its press ethics code provisos to penalize newspapers critical of the government.

RTÜK, the broadcast media regulator, likewise undermines TV channels that show government-critical or outspoken material by fining them colossal sums. Three-quarters of RTÜK's fines in 2022 were imposed on the seven leading critical TV channels (Halk TV, Fox TV, Tele1, KRT, Habertürk TV, Flash TV, and TGRT Haber).[7]

The government's machinations obliterated press freedom and jettisoned property rights by unlawfully confiscating assets worth billions of dollars, mostly targeting entities associated with Hizmet.[8] The non-impacted media shamelessly kept a silent voice against this wholesale attack on their industry.

Directorate of Communications: A Propaganda Hub

Through government operations like RTÜK and TMSF, the captured media began functioning like Erdoğan's propaganda ministry. In 2018, it became official. Erdoğan, by decree, formed the Directorate of Communications, directly under him, which became the center for developing and promoting hate speech policies against Hizmet through government-controlled media. The directorate took on the role of Erdoğan's *de facto* Ministry of Propaganda.

Crackdown on Media Reportage

Erdoğan's suppressive policies intimidated the media, muting them from critiquing Türkiye's hate-driven politics and discriminatory government practices. The pro-regime media, on the other hand, depicted all this as legitimate. After the constitutional amendments were adopted in 2017, fashioning a new presidency model of government, RTÜK obtained expanded powers, such as enabling temporary and permanent suspensions of broadcasts, further enhancing government hegemony over media outlets.

New regulations clamped down on describing terrorist attacks in the media under the pretext that such coverage served the interests of terrorism. The actual purpose was to prevent journalists and writers, who, under the guise of reporting counterterrorism efforts, might express opinions or offer comments (even criticism) about government operations targeting the Gülen Movement, differentiating it as a nonviolent organization from actual violent terrorists.

These interventions extended beyond the broadcast media and led to severe repercussions for all Turkish journalism. Columnists and journalists from newspapers like *Cumhuriyet* and *Sözcü*, despite lacking any affiliation with Hizmet, received hefty penalties for reporting on Hizmet's unjust treatment. This eradicated any possibility of informing the public about the role of hate speech, crimes against humanity, and discriminatory practices against Hizmet, transforming major media outlets into propaganda adjuncts for the palace regime. The drumbeat goes on and has its intended effect on the populace.

The centralization of media resulted in uniform headlines, almost verbatim, across the media and avoidance of specific topics banned by the government press center. A prime example of this was the fabricated Kabataş daytime violent assault on a woman during the Gezi Park protests, discussed earlier. When the pro-government media finally confessed eight years later to the damaging falsehood they had helped palm off on the country, they blamed the journalist who authored the story (and, of course, not Erdoğan, who perpetrated it).

In case of any doubt of the regime's dominance of the media, fifteen columns in five different pro-government newspapers bore the same headline for the retraction story: "Your language is rude; your conscience is as hard as a stone," a cute wordplay in Turkish.[9] Such was the government's clutch on the media that it parlayed the exact words to the press, and the press lapped it up.

The media helped poison the well about the Gezi Park protesters' legitimate democratic activity and helped generate a false narrative of violence that Erdoğan played off.

Restricting Reporting of Arrests and Trials: Beating Up Journalists

Judicial harassment is another of the government's favorite methods to intimidate journalists and prevent media coverage of the state's authoritarianism, corruption, political cronyism, and Kurdish issues and to prevent investigative reporters from uncovering stories embarrassing to the regime and its allies.

Mass arbitrary arrests were conducted across media outlets, including the daily newspapers *Cumhuriyet, Sözcü,* and *Özgür Gündem.* The most common criminal charges against media personnel were "spreading propaganda for a terrorist organization" and "exposing a counter-terrorist official to the threat of terrorist organizations" under the terrorism law and "insulting a public official," "insulting the president," and "denigrating state institutions." These ambiguous and vague laws are perfect for arbitrary enforcement.

According to the website of Bianet, an independent news agency in Istanbul, RSF's partner in Türkiye, the courts, beholden to Erdoğan, censored at least 550 pieces of online journalistic content in 2022 alone--articles, editorials, and investigative reports that in most cases dealt with corruption, political clientelism, or questionable practices within circles allied with the government.[10]

To make life even more problematic, the "Disinformation Combat Act," commonly known as the "Censorship Law," was to go into effect in October 2023.[11] Yet another law to keep journalists reined in was under consideration by the Turkish parliament. It would have added a new proviso to the "Crimes Against State Secrets and Espionage" section of the criminal code that "Those who commit crimes against state security or domestic and foreign political interests in line with the strategic interests or instructions of a foreign state or organization are sentenced to imprisonment from three to seven years."

The proposed law was like the one that Russian President Vladimir Putin passed in 2012, which Western analysts called an attempt to curb opposition and civil society. Fortunately, enough pressure compelled the parliament to withdraw the proposed legislation. The Turkish Journalists Association opposed the law since it established *de facto* government control over journalists' content and provided a stiff penalty if the regime decides a journalist broke the law.[12] The fact that Erdoğan wanted this law is significant, even if he did not get it. That he failed to get it offers some hope.

One noteworthy criminal case is that of Erol Önderoğlu, RSF's Türkiye representative. He is a co-defendant with fellow journalist Ahmet Nesin and human rights defender Şebnem Korur Fincancı. The case has dragged on for more than eight years. They are charged with propaganda in favor of the outlawed Kurdistan Workers' Party (PKK) by being part of a journalistic solidarity campaign in support of *Özgür Gündem*, a pro-Kurdish newspaper forcibly closed in 2016. They were acquitted at trial, but the court later overturned their acquittals after Erdoğan publicly chastised the acquittal.[13]

The regime's persecution of journalists recognizes no borders, even when they have fled abroad. For years, the government has subjected disfavored journalists to judicial proceedings *in absentia* or administrative reprisals for their journalism.

Can Dündar, former editor-in-chief of the daily newspaper *Cumhuriyet*, was personally threatened by Erdoğan and forced to flee into exile abroad. He was sentenced *in absentia* to twenty-seven and a half years in prison for an exclusive 2015 report headlined "Here are the weapons that Erdoğan says do not exist," alleging that Türkiye's intelligence service sought to send weapons to Syrian rebel groups.[14]

Purveyors of Hate Speech

Many in the media, hemmed in by Erdoğan, opted to jump in with him wholeheartedly and often with vigor. Expressions that endorse, support, or justify hate speech, of course, become complicit in the hate policies and the politicide. A journalist who justifies a politician's hate-filled speech against a group shares the blame for the hate policies and their result. One might argue that the media blame is quite broad since it provided the means that the regime did not possess to do its dirty work.

The regime spewed out hate speech to the public through its controlled central media bureaucracy. It was a sophisticated process that ensured the discourse's lasting impact and sustained its continuity. Every negative image aimed at erasing, excluding, and disregarding Hizmet was encoded as a message and projected to the public. The media jumped on board and gave this rhetoric significant negative resonance in society.

The transformation of hate speech into state policy and its preaching by the media remains consistent to this day.

Turkish society, under the sway of hate speech, if not at times bombarded with it, began to accede to the illegal state practices, measures, and decisions and internalize the government's agenda, accepting it as necessary if not correct. Unfortunately, government-driven and media-supported hate speech was not new. Certain individuals, groups, and entities in Türkiye historically have been targets of hate speech and vilified at various periods, often because of ethnic, cultural, and religious differences. That the ground was already soft made the government's work easier.

Hate speech in the media intensified. Sevda Noyan, for example, known for her allegiance to the Erdoğan regime, referring to the attempted coup, said on Ülke TV, "July 15 is still stuck in our throats. It left us wanting to do more. We could not do what we wanted. My family can take down fifty people. My list is ready."[15] Charges were filed against her for the threatening language, but the parties and the government "reconciled" with her and dismissed the case.

She was not the only media person to call for violence.[16] There were others. One was Fatih Tezcan, a writer for the online T24 newspaper, known for his closeness to the government. He was taken to court for a graphic online violent diatribe against the CHP, Hizmet, and anyone opposing Erdoğan. The court acquitted him on the charge of "threatening to cause fear and panic among the public" due to "lack of intent."

The courts infer intent to find people Hizmet guilty when they have nothing concrete on which to base their findings but can acquit for "no intent" when they have concrete words of violent threats.

Another example of how the courts stack up against Hizmet people when threats are levied against them involved reputed organized crime figure Sedat Peker, who, during a July 15, 2017, patriotic event, railed, "They think that, one day, prisons will also be raided. However, I swear it will not be as they imagine. After hanging all those we catch outside on trees and flagpoles, we will also enter the prisons. We will hang them in prisons too. We will hang them by their necks from flagpoles...."[17] Given Peker's criminal record and shady reputation, the threat may well be quite real.

Despite his explicit threats of violence, Peker was acquitted a year later in July 2018 of "openly inciting the commission of a crime." The court's rationale was that every Turkish citizen has the duty to stand alongside the nation against terrorist organizations and Peker's words did not threaten a crime because the addressees of his tirade were members or sympathizers of the so-called FETÖ/PDY terrorist organization and thus criminals. Twisted logic and twisted judicial integrity. Nor did the media raise any questions about the trial or its peculiar result.

Not only was there never a chance of Hizmet people having their voice heard, but the media was quick to sensationalize their arrests and trials, which was a way of smearing individuals and prejudicing judicial investigations and proceedings involving them. The media made no effort to be objective or present "all sides" of the story. As George Orwell framed it in *1984*, the media became Erdoğan's "Newspeak" in selecting and fashioning "news" for Türkiye.

Spreading Hate Speech: Social Media and Internet

Hate speech, by nature, eradicates societal tolerance and ultimately encourages violence, whether physical, psychological, or societal. Repetitive hate speech progressively transforms itself into a process of societal acceptance. Increased communication channels these days facilitate the rapid spread of hate expressions throughout society, accelerating their acceptance, even by those who might not themselves use or accept the language—a numbing effect, as it were, which still plays to the state's advantage.

The European Commission against Racism and Intolerance (ECRI) has zeroed in on the internet becoming an unwelcome, even precarious, booster of racism and intolerance. Hate speech relayed through social media has precipitously expanded and reaches a significantly broader audience than print media.

Theoretically, the media in a democratic society have the professional duty to inform, educate, and contribute to individual access to information. However, when the media lacks independence or functions in an anti-democratic context, such as operating like a government mouthpiece, it can turn into a weapon against society.

With today's widespread use of the internet, the media have become one of the primary channels for generating and circulating hate speech. Use of social media platforms has expanded globally and in Türkiye. Pro-government internet journalism has also rapidly expanded. Media outlets' social media postings often become more effective than traditional print and visual media. As of 2022, 80% of the Turkish populace used social media.

Internet journalism's advantages over traditional journalism include direct interaction between the journalist and the reader and the spread of news through user engagement. In totalitarian regimes like Türkiye's, government-controlled written, visual, and social media can transform itself into a nucleus of distortion, posing a threat to societal peace; and Türkiye media have done so.

Government Internet Trolls Spread Hate Speech

The regime, aiming to impose its policies on society and establish an infrastructure operating against the Gülen Movement and dissidents, formed a troll army that operates through media and social media platforms. This army, known as "AK-trolls" in public lore and financed by the government, swiftly orchestrated the "hi-tech lynching" of Hizmet individuals and others.

Twitter (now X) took the initial step against these AK-trolls, closing 7,340 accounts in Türkiye because their purpose was to spread AKP-oriented political propaganda and build support for Erdoğan. Monitoring, however, has declined, if not disappeared. Although the numbers are unknown, Esat Demirtaş, Provincial President of Ottoman Hearths, has claimed that he manages a troll army of 200,000 individuals in support of the regime.[18]

The hate speech, fueled by social media trolls under Erdoğan's control, amplified fabricated misinformation against Hizmet folks, even labeling them as traitors. The FETÖ hate speech campaign contributed to Hizmet's exclusion and criminalization despite the utter absence of any evidence of wrongdoing or illegal activity.

The Media as Government Consort

Given the regime's dominance over the media and the opposition's inability to respond with any effectiveness, the public does not receive fair and unbiased news coverage or even another viewpoint. Even worse, the minute any media step out of line with the government's official narrative, they become subject to pressure and censorship and tagged immediately and discredited with the "FETÖ" appellation.

An example was the 60th Golden Orange Film Festival (2023) organized by the Antalya Metropolitan Municipality. The documentary "The Decree," depicting the struggle of two civil servants dismissed by a state of emergency decree, was abruptly removed from the festival on the pretext that the judicial process of one of the individuals depicted in the film was ongoing, as if the government was intent on protecting due process rather than abusing it.

The primary reason was government pressure, undoubtedly to avoid sympathetic feelings for the dismissed civil servants and to avoid people raising any questions about the regime's actions that led to their misfortune.

Rather than deal with the debate initiated over the film's removal from the festival and risk stepping on Erdoğan's toe, the CHP (Republican People's Party) mayor, Muhittin Böcek, simply canceled the festival. Ironic this, the one time that the government wanted to protect a person's due process.

Hate Speech, Like a Virus, Transcends Borders

The government's loyalist media pool, besides proliferating hate speech in Türkiye, sometimes publishes news that explicitly targets individuals in foreign lands with a desire to foment violence against them, sort of like "we know where you are, and now others do, just in case they want to do something you deserve…."

As a result of hate policies conducted through the media, Hizmet people have been, and are, exposed to violence, both domestically and internationally. In October 2022, for example, the *Daily Sabah* pinpointed former Police Chief Murat Çetiner, who lives in Sweden, on its front page.[19] *Sabah* disclosed personal information, including his vehicle and places he frequented for shopping. Ten days later, someone shattered a window of his vehicle. Çetiner was part of the police team investigating Erdoğan, his family, and inner circle in the December 2013 corruption scandal.

As the AKP mouthpiece, *Sabah* also targeted journalists Abdullah Bozkurt, Bülent Keneş, and Levent Kenez, who reside in Sweden and have Gülen Movement affiliations. *Sabah*'s coverage, propelled by hate like the government for which it speaks, disregards personal privacy, knowingly endangering life and property. The newspaper's "Special intelligence chief" Abdurrahman Şimşek, strongly associated with the National Intelligence Organization (MİT), has targeted people residing abroad.

Ramazan Yılmazer (age 59), a person of Turkish origin and a forty-one-year resident of Germany, was assaulted in May 2022 in the city of Kamen in the North Rhine-Westphalia state. Accompanied by his daughter and son-in-law, he was attacked in the Ö.K.H. kebab shop by the new owner, who accused him of being a "terrorist." He ended up needing hospital treatment.

Ahmet Dönmez, the former Ankara correspondent of *Zaman* newspaper, which the regime shuttered, was assaulted in front of his child in Stockholm in March 2022, by reputed mafia leader İhsan Hızarcı, known to be close to Türkiye's government.

Media Hate Speech in Numbers

During the state of emergency, the regime's control over the media enabled the rapid diffusion of hate speech, communicating a unified, government-endorsed message. The carefully assembled media pool obligingly and consistently depicted the regime itself as the primary victim of the coup attempt and generated public opinion against anyone opposing or questioning the government.

The media pool, abandoning any sense of journalistic integrity, transformed itself into a production and dissemination center for hate speech against Hizmet. Data from 2015 to 2020 show the extensive hate speech use in three major newspapers: *Sabah*, with 215,610 times; *Yeni Şafak*, with 126,867; and *Hürriyet*, with 113,263.[20]

The media reflected and repeated this hate speech against Hizmet. Statistics indicate that the mainstream media used twenty-two different hate speech terms 862,632 times in mainstream media; and columnists and reporters, 53,415 times.[21]

Solidarity with Others, a nonprofit organization in Brussels, coordinated the Hate Crime Monitoring Project against Hizmet members,[22] which revealed a total of 917,061 hate expressions as of the end of 2020 on nineteen broadcasting platforms and from 473 mainstream media columnists. These expressions fell into four groups: (1) intolerance, exaggeration, loading, and distortion; (2) attacks on rights and reputation, cursing, insults, and degradation; (3) incitement to hostility, discrimination, and violence; and (4) incitement to politicide/crimes against humanity.

Hate speech sustained through social media has almost transformed into digital violence. Being the subject of this speech by organized forces on every platform where injustices are voiced results in consequences sometimes heavier than physical violence – psychological violence. Psychological violence can be long-lasting with deep emotional problems and even more personally devastating than physical violence.

The written, visual, and social media hate speech levied against Hizmet not only negatively affects Hizmet, but it also adversely impacts people who believe in a free and democratic civil society based on equality. One might see this, too, as a form of psychological violence.

International Documents on Hate Speech and Media's Role

A look at how international institutions have attempted to increase hate speech awareness and facilitate preventive measures in the media is helpful in appraising the responsibility and culpability of Türkiye's media in its proliferation of hate speech in the country.

Recommendation (97) 20 on "Hate Speech" adopted by the Committee of Ministers of the Council of Europe in October 1997 acknowledges the potentially greater and more destructive impact when expressions of intolerance are disseminated through the media, distinguishing their role in conveying information and opinions on matters of public interest as part of their mission. In other words, the media can and should report a government's hate crime campaign as news but also offer counter opinions and information. Reporting and critiquing, yes; propagating, no. Türkiye permits neither of the former.

The Committee of Ministers, seven years later, in its Declaration on Political Freedom in the Media underscored that political freedom of debate does not encompass inciting racist ideas or hatred or any form of intolerance. It also highlights principles ensuring the right to criticize political figures and public officials.[23] Erdoğan and Türkiye do not allow this either.

The Committee of Ministers went a step further in 2014 in a note to Recommendation 6 on Human Rights for Internet Users, highlighting the institutional responsibility of online service providers to combat hate speech, violence, and other content that promotes discrimination or could be considered illegal. Türkiye, on the other hand, does just the opposite, permitting and purveying hate speech.

The international community, principally Europe, has moved in the direction of establishing legal, political, and project-based principles concerning hate speech. Countries are urged to take measures against the spread of hate speech within society and its dissemination through media.

Likewise, prominent public figures should avoid hate speech. Politicians refraining from hate speech alone, though, is insufficient; they must actively combat such discourse. Türkiye has chosen to go in the opposite direction and banked on the media use of hate speech to further its politicide agenda.

Concluding Observations

Erdoğan's hate speech campaign, pushed forward through the controlled media, succeeded in turning most of the country against Hizmet. He has created great division in the country for his personal political purposes, not the public's good.

Government measures that promote the Gülen Movement's civil death have caused familial discord. Parents and children are at odds with one another. Siblings have fraught interactions. Loving relationships have unraveled badly. The same has occurred with one-time friends and business associates. Erdoğan lacked any qualms about creating disharmony in Türkiye; doing so was, and continues to be, to his political advantage.

Hizmet people are being subjected to a *de facto* "media lynching" in the written, visual, and social media controlled by the Erdoğan regime. There is no effective and functional administrative or judicial recourse against the baseless labeling, targeting, and destructive hate speech. In today's Türkiye, it is impossible to publish a correction for any false, defamatory, or hate-filled news story about a Hizmet member.

Lawsuits that are filed and rejected as being within the scope of the press' freedom of expression, no matter how slanderous, libelous, and deliberately false the story or item may be. Hizmet people, however, are imprisoned for saying something a hundred times milder and a hundred times more accurate. They have no freedom of expression.

As a final note to state the obvious, no one in the media ever raised a question about the government violating Article 77 of the Turkish Criminal Code, the crimes against humanity section of the penal code.

Endnotes

1 "Türkiye: ten years of state hostility towards the press under President Erdoğan," Reporters Without Borders (RSF) (10.08.2024), Türkiye: ten years of state hostility towards the press under President Erdoğan | RSF. *See also* Nina Ognianova, "Turkey–world's top press jailer once more," Committee to Protect Journalists (December 18, 2023), https://cpj.org/2013/12/turkey-worlds-top-press-jailer-once-more/.

2 *See* Vedat Demir, "Freedom of the Media in Turkey Under the AKP Government," in Hasan Aydin and Winston Langley (eds), *Human Rights in Turkey: Assaults on Human Dignity* (New York: Springer, 2021), pp. 51-88, https://doi.org/10.1007/978-3-030-57476-5_2.

3 Zeynep Altıok, "OHAL Bilançosu Hak İhlalleri Raporu," Cumhuriyet Halk Partisi, https://content.chp.org.tr/file/33743.pdf, pp.15-16, ["State of Emergency Balance: Report on Human Rights Violations"].

4 "Closed and Confiscated Institutions by Emergency Decree Laws," Solidarity With Others Closed institutions | OTHERS (solidaritywithothers.com). *See also* Owen Bowcott, "UK court rejects Turkish extradition request for media boss," The Guardian (28 Nov. 2018), https://www.theguardian.com/law/2018/nov/28/uk-court-rejects-turkish-extradition-request-for-media-boss. Turkey later tried unsuccessfully to extradite Ipek from England: Owen Bowcott, "UK court rejects Turkish extradition request for media boss," Guardian (28 Nov 2018). https://www.theguardian.com/law/2018/nov/28/uk-court-rejects-turkish-extradition-request-for-media-boss.

5 "Verilerle 2022 Yılında Türkiye'de İnsan Hakları İhlalleri," Human Rights Foundation of Turkey (10 Dec. 2022), https://tihv.org.tr/ozel-raporlar-ve-degerlendirmeler/verilerle-2022-yilinda-turkiyede-insan-haklari-ihlalleri/ ["Human Rights Violations in Turkey in 2022 with Data"].

6 "Erdoğan has used his control of the media to rig Türkiye's elections," Reporters Without Borders (RSF) (25.05.2023), Erdoğan has used his control of the media to rig Türkiye's elections | RSF.

7 "Turkey must stop using state advertising allocation to penalise critical media," Reporters Without Borders (RSF) (08.07.2022), Turkey must stop using state advertising allocation to penalise critical media | RSF.

8 "Closed and Confiscated Institutions by Emergency Decree Laws, Solidarity With Others, https://www.solidaritywithothers.com/closed-institutions

9 The words "shameless" (kaba) and "stone" (taş) make up the word "Kabataş," referring to the scene of the fabricated attack.

10 "Erdoğan has used his control of the media to rig Türkiye's elections," Reporters Without Borders (RSF) (5 May 2023), https://rsf.org/en/erdo%C4%9Fan-has-used-his-control-media-rig-turkiye-s-elections.

11 Proposed Law No. 7418 (23 Oct. 2022), amending the Press Law.

12 "'Etki ajanlığı' yasa teklifi komisyonda kabul edildi, gazeteciler kaygılı," BBC News Türkçe (24 Oct. 2024), 'Influence agency' bill passed in committee, opposition and journalists concerned - BBC News English

13 "Erol Önderoğlu," Sessiz Kalma (March 27, 2025), https://www.sessizkalma.org/en/defender/erol-onderoglu.

14 "Erdoğan's persecution of journalists does not stop at Türkiye's borders," Reporters Without Borders (RSF) (06.05.2023), Erdoğan's persecution of journalists does not stop at Türkiye's borders | RSF

15 "Temmuz içimde kaldı, bizim aile 50 kişiyi götürür' diyen Sevda Noyan'a

ailesinden hakaret davası," EuroNews (10/05/2020), https://tr.euronews.com/2020/05/10/15-temmuz-icimde-kald-bizim-aile-50-kisiyi-goturur-diyen-sevda-noyan-a-ailesinden-hakaret ["Insult case filed against Sevda Noyan, who said 'July 15 is stuck in my mind; our family will take 50 people.'"].

16 "Pro-Erdoğan propagandist threatens Turkish president's critics with bloodshed," Stockholm Center for Freedom (May 13, 2020), https://stockholmcf.org/pro-Erdoğan-propagandist-threatens-turkish-presidents-critics-with-bloodshed/.

17 "Sedat Peker: Onları, boyunlarından bayrak direklerine asacağız, Azrail'den memuriyet dileyin!," T24 (16 July 2017), https://t24.com.tr/haber/sedat-peker-onlari-boyunlarindan-bayrak-direklerine-asacagiz-azrailden-memuriyet-dileyin,414672 ["Sedat Peker: We will hang them from their necks to flagpoles. Ask Azrael for a civil service!"]. *See also* "Mahkeme Sedat Peker'in beraat gerekçesinde övgü dolu sözler kullandı," Evrensel (16 July 2018), https://www.evrensel.net/haber/357048/mahkeme-sedat-pekerin-beraat-gerekcesinde-ovgu-dolu-sozler-kullandi ["The court used words of praise in Sedat Peker's justification for acquittal"].

18 "Seçim hazırlığı: 200 Bin kişilik 'Ak trol' ordusu kuruldu," Yurtsever (17-10-2021), https://yurtsever.org.tr/2021/secim-hazirligi-200-bin-kisilik-ak-trol-ordusu-kuruldu-469518/ ["Election preparations: 'White troll' army of 200,000 people was established"].

19 Abdurrahman Şimşek, "Suspect involved in FETÖ plot in Türkiye spotted in Sweden," *Daily Sabah* (25 Oct. 2022), https://www.dailysabah.com/turkey/investigations/suspect-involved-in-feto-plot-in-turkiye-spotted-in-sweden. *See also* "Sweden refuses to extradite 4 people on Turkey's list, including a former police chief," Stockholm Center for Freedom (Jan. 13, 2023), https://stockholmcf.org/sweden-refuses-to-extradite-4-people-on-turkeys-list-including-a-former-police-chief/.

20 Nefret Suçu, https://nefretsucu.com/category/yayin-54.

21 "Gülen Hareketine Yönelik Nefret Söylemi [2015-2020]," Nefret Suçu, https://nefretsucu.com/istatistikler ["Hate Speech Against the Gülen Movement"].

22 Solidarity With Others, https://www.solidaritywithothers.com/. *See also* "Gülen Hareketi Mensuplarına Karşı Yürütülen Nefret Suçu İzleme Projesi," Nefret Suçu, https://nefretsucu.com/hakkimizda ["Hate Crime Monitoring Project Conducted Against Gülen Movement Members"].

23 "Declaration on freedom of political debate in the media," Committee of Ministers, Council of Europe (12 Feb. 2004), 1680505d5b (coe.int).

Chapter 7

Preaching Hate: The Diyanet

The shortness of this chapter should not underestimate the immense power of the country's religious institutions in spreading and legitimizing Erdoğan's politicide project. Given that about 96% of the nation's population professes Islam, religious leaders can have a profound impact on the country.

The Presidency of Religious Affairs (Diyanet İşleri Başkanlığı, DİB) is the government's official constitutional and legal tool for overseeing the country's Islamic faith and worship. It represents a more traditionalist Islam, reflective of conservative and religious Turks, especially in less heavily urban areas.

The scheme, developed by the country's founder, Atatürk, was to respect people's spiritual inclinations, but to keep religion nonpartisan and under control for national stability. It had worked well until Erdoğan.

The Diyanet exercises significant influence over devout Turkish Muslims, both in the country and within the diaspora. It drafts a weekly sermon and delivers it to the nation's 85,000 mosques and more than 2,000 mosques abroad that function under its management. It provides Quranic education for children; and trains and employs Türkiye's imams, who are considered civil servants. It is not lost on the Diyanet that it depends on government funding, and it responds accordingly.

For someone like Erdoğan, who publicly espouses conservative Islamic piety, if only for political reasons, the Diyanet is a perfect regime adjunct. Hizmet's more moderate and less structured approach to Islam is not in sync with the more conservative and structured version of Islam to which a sizeable segment of society ascribes and which the Diyanet serves. Erdoğan sometimes adeptly plays into that dissonance.

That the Diyanet is on course with the correct agenda is reflected in the government's financial largesse. From 2006 to 2015, its budget increased fourfold, and its staff doubled to 150,000. Its 2019 budget was estimated at $1.87 billion, far exceeding that of most government ministries. It has about a thousand branches across Türkiye and offers educational, cultural, and charitable activities in foreign countries. Diyanet TV came online in 2012 and now broadcasts around the clock.

The Diyanet headquarters is large, well-appointed, and elegant, due to Erdoğan's (actually, the taxpayers') largesse. Its wealth and holdings increased when the government turned over property that belonged to the Hizmet Movement. Even individual clerics profited nicely.[1]

Inside Türkiye

The Diyanet has sought over time to diminish popular sympathy for movements over which it has no control, especially a movement like Hizmet, which historically has provided significant services to Turkish Islamic society through education, dialogue, and community projects and which preaches moderate religious principles, practices a moral ethic, and fosters social participation across fields such as media, business, and civil society generally. Erdoğan understood and played off this antipathy. Mutual backscratching, without regard for the consequences in people's lives.

The Diyanet became a major exponent of hate speech. It has consistently targeted Hizmet in the prepared Friday sermons it distributes, symposiums, published materials, and various other hostile activities.[2] Going against Islamic principles, the Diyanet has maliciously depicted Hizmet followers as deviant or apostate, labeling them in the mosque sermons as "non-religious, hypocritical, sowers of discord, nests of mischief, traitors, exploiters, a network of treachery, coup plotters,"[3] and more.

The Diyanet has used its central offices and branches to conduct a smear campaign against Hizmet, disseminating false information and often blatant government propaganda about Hizmet's nature, goals, structure, operations, and perspectives on other movements. It candidly functions as a disinformation hub.

The rhetoric has attempted to portray the hatred against the Gülen Movement as legitimate by adorning it with religious arguments, aiming to instill the idea that hating Hizmet would lead to heavenly rewards, a message particularly targeting conservative segments of society. The Diyanet has consistently propagated hate speech and false information, labeling Hizmet adherents as violators of fundamental Islamic principles, portraying their beliefs as heretical, secretive, and dangerous, and comparing them to historically controversial groups.

The Diyanet's deviation from its role as a non-political institution and its transformation into a tool for the government's hate policies has had detrimental effects on religion and caused damage within religious congregations. Spreading hatred from mosque pulpits, as one might expect, has led to resentment, animosity, partisanship in communities, and alienation of younger people from religion generally. The minbar is not a fitting place for sermons of political hate.

Outside Türkiye

Internationally, Diyanet's overseas organizations became centers that spied on people associated with the Gülen Movement in their respective countries. Instances of surveilling, profiling, and informing on Hizmet people occurred in the Netherlands,[4] Belgium,[5] Norway, Australia, and Germany[6] after the coup attempt.[7] Diyanet Foundation officials in Europe urged reporting of Hizmet affiliates through social media platforms.

Official correspondence by Halife Keskin, former General Director of Diyanet's External Relations, reported that the Diyanet collected intelligence through religious officials in thirty-eight different countries.[8] These reprehensible actions by a religious institution, manipulated by the government (Erdoğan had attended a Diyanet-led planning meeting in August 2016), were an orchestrated boost to the spread of hate speech—by a religious entity that preaches peace, of all things.

The hate speech perpetrated among the Turkish diaspora also impeded Hizmet members' access to mosques to practice their faith because of the hate speech, alienation, and discord directed against them. And sometimes there was fear.

Final Comments

The regime's hostile policies against the Gülen Movement enlisted the official religious establishment, the Diyanet, to undermine the movement's moderate Islamic discourse and to establish its own Islamist ideology for political purposes. Just as bad, the Diyanet justified Erdoğan and supported him as he reconfigured and circumscribed democracy in Türkiye.

Various other conservative religious groups within Türkiye also joined in functioning as extensions of the Erdoğan regime and legitimizing the government's illicit actions in the eyes of society. Another example of hatred perpetrated in the name of religion. Not to ignore as well that they were participants in the government's crime against humanity under the country's criminal law.

Endnotes

1 *See, e.g.*, "Diyanet'in Fetö'den Aldığı Bina 133 Öğrenciye Ev Olacak," Diyanet (Sept. 13, 2018), https://diyanet.tv/diyanetin-fetoden-aldigi-bina-133-ogrenciye-ev-olacak ["The Building Purchased by Diyanet from Feto will Become a Home for 133 Students"]. See also "Fetö'nün El Konulan Yurdu Diyanet Vakfı'na Tahsis Edildi," Haberler (28 Aug, 2017), https://www.haberler.com/feto-nun-el-konulan-yurdu-diyanet-vakfi-na-tahsis-9976068-haberi/?m=0&redirect=false ["Fetö's Seized Dormitory Was Allocated to Diyanet Foundation"]. See also "İstanbul Müftüsünün işadamının gasp edilen evinde oturduğu ortaya çıktı," Samanyolu Haber (19 Sept. 2017), https://www.samanyoluhaber.com/istanbul-muftusunun-isadaminin-gasp-edilen-evinde-oturdugu-ortaya-cikti-haberi/1290584/ ["It was revealed that the Mufti of Istanbul lived in the usurped house of the businessman"].

2 "Avrupa camilerinde de okundu; Diyanet'in Cuma hutbesinde 'nefret söylemi,'" TR724 (12 July 2024), https://www.tr724.com/avrupa-camilerinde-de-okundu-diyanetin-cuma-hutbesinde-nefret-sucu/ ["It was also read in European mosques; 'Hate speech' in Diyanet's Friday sermon"]. See also "Diyanet pens different texts for Friday sermons in Turkey and abroad on sixth anniversary of failed coup," Turkish Minute (July 14, 2022), https://turkishminute.com/2022/07/14/net-pens-different-texts-for-friday-sermons-in-turkey-and-abroad-on-6th-anniversary-of-failed-coup/.

3 "July 15: Our Nation's Epic Victory," General Directorate of Religious Services (12.07.2024), https://dinhizmetleri.diyanet.gov.tr/Documents/July%2015;%20Our%20Nation's%20Epic%20Victory.pdf. See also "Hate speech monitoring," Solidarity With Others, https://www.solidaritywithothers.com/hatespeech (28 reports of hate speech incidents targeting Hizmet).

4 "Dutch FM to summon Turkish ambassador over Diyanet's intelligence activities, Turkish Minute (Dec. 14, 2016), https://turkishminute.com/2016/12/14/dutch-fm-summon-turkish-ambassador-diyanets-intelligence-activities/.

5 "Belgian justice minister orders close scrutiny of Diyanet mosques amid spying claims," Turkish Minute (Dec. 16, 2016), https://turkishminute.com/2016/12/16/belgian-justice-minister-orders-close-scrutiny-diyanet-mosques-amid-spying-claims/.

6 "Germany drops inquiry against Turkish imams suspected of spying on Erdoğan's behalf," Reuters (Dec. 6, 2017), https://www.reuters.com/article/world/germany-drops-inquiry-against-turkish-imams-suspected-of-spying-on-Erdoğans-beh-idUSKBN1E023B/.

7 Chip le Grand, "Ankara-supplied clerics spy on Turkish-Australian communities," Hizmet Movement (Dec. 19, 2016), https://hizmetnews.com/20881/ankara-supplied-clerics-spy-turkish-australian-communities/.

8 *Supra* n.4.

Chapter 8

The Sycophant Opposition

The Political Opposition's Hate Speech Contributions

Even though strongly disagreeing in other matters, the political opposition and dissident media have helped the Erdoğan regime cultivate its anti-Hizmet hate speech. Some opposition politicians, press members, and prominent figures, previously harboring negative sentiments toward the Gülen Movement for a variety of reasons, have not criticized the regime for overstepping boundaries but have almost adopted its hate speech—sometimes more extensively than the government itself, hopping on the bandwagon for their own reasons, oblivious to the fact that, at any time, they might be struck with the Erdoğan boomerang.

The opposition has at times used terms like "parallel structure," "coup plotters," "treacherous structure," and "FETÖ" as vehemently as the government, contributing to the barrage of hate speech against the Gülen Movement. The steady drumbeat of this hate speech by both the government and the opposition, amplified by the media, has become so normalized in Turkish society that most people began to not doubt it.

Opposition political parties, including CHP (Republican People's Party), İYİ (Good Party), Gelecek (Future Party), DEVA (Democracy and Progress Party), Zafer (Victory Party), and HDP (Peoples' Democratic Party), have all piled on the Gülen Movement in varying degrees with hate rhetoric like the regime's. They were never friends of Hizmet for a host of reasons. Philosophical disagreements ranged from Hizmet not being sufficiently religious, fundamentalist, or nationalist, on the one hand, to the movement being too religious for the secularists, on the other hand. Other reasons were also at play.

They shared a common apprehension of Hizmet's popular appeal, to their political detriment. Erdoğan was handing them a golden opportunity to jump on his bandwagon and whittle down the favor and respect that the movement enjoyed among the general population. And they leapt at it. This was their chance to gain political capital for themselves and curry favor with Erdoğan at Hizmet's expense.

Rhetoric from these parties and their leaders, attacking and condemning the Gülen Movement, augmented Erdoğan's ruthless political narrative. The opposition's bombast at times was even harsher than Erdoğan's. Their rhetoric served them both as a shield and as an attack mechanism in their struggle against the ruling government. The opposition embraced Hizmet's marginalization and demonization and helped legitimize hate speech in line with government expectations.

Between 2015 and 2020, the strong broadcast arms of the political opposition media used expressions of hate speech against the Gülen Movement nearly as much as the government-controlled media. They did the regime's work for it, giving it an illegitimate façade of legitimacy. It was a clever and cynical co-option stunt by the government, and the opposition fell for it.

If the opposition had taken a stand, highlighting hate speech and the move to politicide as contrary to international law and shared values in the Turkish Constitution, the government's policies would never have gained such traction across society. The opposition groups should have faced down the mass arrests, detentions, dismissals, and property confiscations and created a backlash. Instead, they opted to share responsibility with Erdoğan for violence, injustice, and lawlessness against those associated with the Gülen Movement.

Likewise, the opposition's frequent use of demeaning phrases like the "FETÖ project" or "FETÖ tactics," unrelated to anything Hizmet but to define any kind of illegitimate action, contributed to the popularization and unending cycle of hate speech. Using the Hizmet generalized template or punching bag to cover up an unlawful act or deflect one's own misdeeds, with which the movement had nothing to do, furthered and popularized a culture of hatred.

Erdoğan's inevitable utilization of the same hate rhetoric against his political opposition led to the late realization that supporting his rhetoric could backfire. Whenever the regime targets or attempts to discredit any opposition figure, it promptly labels them as part of FETÖ through its flagship media pool.

An illustrative instance involved *Hürriyet* newspaper columnist Nedim Şener, an emblematic figure of the media pool, branding Özgür Özel, CHP Deputy Group Chairman (later, party leader), with whom he had a tactical political disagreement, as a cryptic FETÖ member.[1] It is interesting, but not surprising, how the hate speech that the political opposition, including CHP, helped legitimize and deploy can come back to haunt, silence, and discredit them.

Şener's caveat worked with Özel. After Gülen's death in late 2024, Özel parroted the government's words, "The founder is dead, but the organization remains. No one should think that this danger has passed or is over. Everyone should be on guard against this organization."[2] This does not say much about Özel's backbone.

Riding the Erdoğan bandwagon is dangerous, even for self-defense. What he does to the Gülen Movement is an indicator of what he might (and will) do to another opposition group when it behooves him politically. It is potentially self-defeating not to defend others from an unjust debilitating hate campaign. Temporary self-pragmatism only serves the political opposition until Erdoğan decides to give a shove from the bandwagon.

Final Comments

Acceptance and adoption of the regime's hate speech by its loyal opposition helped solidify a mass-scale negative narrative directed at Hizmet. Even if one does not directly participate as an executor of hate policies, openly using similar rhetoric against the targeted group equates to complicity in hate crimes.

Benjamin Franklin's counsel at the signing of America's Declaration of Independence from the King of England is much wiser, "We must, indeed, all hang together or, most assuredly, we shall all hang separately." Pastor Martin Niemöller's famous poetic quote about the lack of opposition to the incremental rise of Nazi Germany echoes this historical reality, "First they came for [socialists, then trade unionists, and then Jews] and I did not speak out because I was not [one of them]....

Then they came for me—and there was no one left to speak for me."[3] The Niemöller litany should be taped to democracy's bathroom mirror.

Protecting civil liberties for one group, whether friend or foe, is protecting civil liberties for everyone. Once the government gets a foot in the door, the door will always open wider, step by step. This is a lesson that history has repeatedly taught, but which people have too easily repeatedly ignored, to their ultimate detriment.

Endnotes

1 "FETÖ 'parlatması' CHP'li Özgür Özel," *Hürriyet*, (Jan. 16, 2023), https://www.hurriyet.com.tr/yazarlar/nedim-sener/feto-parlatmasi-chpli-ozgur-ozel-42204470 ["FETÖ 'polishing' CHP's Özgür Özel"].

2 Michael Rubinkam, "Thousands mourn Fethullah Gülen, a Turkish spiritual leader who died in the US," Associated Press (Oct. 24, 2024), https://apnews.com/article/fethullah-gulen-turkey-dead-funeral-burial-69336b5a23988b0c-2c350a4799ff6c51.

3 "Martin Niemöller: 'First they came for…,'" Holocaust Encyclopedia, https://encyclopedia.ushmm.org/content/en/article/martin-niemoeller-first-they-came-for-the-socialists.

Chapter 9

Detention Centers and Prisons

In Türkiye, prisons and detention centers ("ceza ve tevkifevi") serve different purposes legally and theoretically. Prisons are primarily for the execution of sentences after conviction and focus on punishment, while detention centers are for pre-arrest and pre-trial detention until acquittal or conviction. In practice, they are not necessarily separate facilities but more of a legal distinction within the same facility. Pre-arrest centers are usually in police stations and are called "nezarethane ("custody rooms").

Türkiye has always had a deservedly bad reputation for its prisons. The country's prison population has grown significantly over the past two decades. Roughly 58,000 people were incarcerated in 2000. The country now holds more than 300,000 prisoners, a five-fold increase. Hizmet-related incarcerations, in the range of 50,000, account for a significant share of the expanded numbers.

Erdoğan's anti-Hizmet campaign to detain and imprison individuals comes with a sizeable fiscal note. Using the prisoner number of 50,000, the cost to the country and taxpayers would be in the range of $100 million yearly, apart from the cost of having to build new facilities for the expanded number of prisoners overall. That is a good deal of the people's money to support a man's ruthless, personal, political agenda.

Independent monitoring bodies have documented systemic and widespread torture and ill-treatment, including psychological techniques. Fundamental rights recognized by national law are not respected. Officials treat prisoners' rights as privileges and arbitrarily withdraw them from "non-compliant" prisoners. Authorities obstruct access to lawyers, attorney and family confidentiality, and the right to appeal. Arbitrary sanctions are frequently imposed, and prisoners filing complaints against miscreant jailers may be subject to reprisals.[1]

Medical care inside prisons and detention centers was never good, significantly inferior to that of the general population, which itself is not particularly good. It would be safe to call it notorious; it has been the subject of human rights reports. It suffered drastically with the Erdoğan healthcare clampdown, as discussed earlier, expelling nearly 4,000 Hizmet healthcare professionals.[2] Prison healthcare is wholly inadequate regarding women-specific medical treatment.

Clean drinking water, nutritious food, and hygienic conditions are deficient. Rodents and insects infest facilities. Elderly people and those with disabilities, who are unable to care for themselves, do not receive the support they need. Conditions are particularly severe for those sentenced to aggravated life imprisonment. They are socially isolated (solitary confinement) and restricted in their activities and communication with the outside world.

Originally, the regime immediately detained or arrested more than 40,000 individuals on coup-related charges. The authorities opened the prison doors to 38,000 common criminals, including drug dealers, and released them to make room for journalists, teachers, attorneys, judges, police officers, state bureaucrats, and union leaders whom the government wanted to marginalize.

Prisons filled beyond capacity in the weeks after the coup attempt. Detainees slept in the communal spaces of jails, often without any bedding. The authorities also used sports arenas to house the flood of prisoners. Öztürk Türkdoğan, the president of the Human Rights Association in Türkiye criticized the government: "This is a serious case of bad treatment, and the prisoners are suffering from serious health concerns as a result."[3]

At the same time, Türkiye severely curtailed the rights of prisoners overall. A state of emergency decree restricted visits by lawyers and family members and allowed the state to record conversations between prisoners and their lawyers and, sometimes, an official was present for those discussions. "This leads to fear of repercussions, especially in reporting torture and mistreatment," Türkdoğan pointed out. Even after the state of emergency ended, the attorney-client privacy right has not been completely restored for "terrorism" offenses. An official can be present or the court can see the documents exchanged between counsel and client.[4]

Arbitrary and inhumane actions routinely occurred in detention centers and prisons. Systematic ill-treatment, torture, and strip searches became routine prison practices. Judges responded to victims' claims for relief not by punishing the perpetrators but by allowing and legitimizing their conduct. A culture of impunity prevailed and continues to prevail.[5]

A harbinger of bad things to come was Erdoğan's revamping and weakening the country's board that monitored penal institutions for human rights violations.[6] He dismissed all current board members and put in place a new procedure for appointing board members. The new system with less independent and more malleable appointees favored the government and mirrored the regime's jaded perspective on human rights.

After the failed coup and then during and after the state of emergency, a growing number of people have been sentenced under the legal pretext of the 1991 Anti-Terror Law, primarily outspoken critics of the government, political opponents, activists, journalists, lawyers, and Kurdish advocates.[7]

A majority were associated with Hizmet. More than one-tenth of the prison population falls into this category, most of whom bear the Gülen Movement accusation. Just to note again that Turkish courts had acquitted Gülen of charges under the 1991 Anti-Terror Law, although the government continued to use it to persecute and prosecute Hizmet or Hizmet-associated people, an incongruity the government saw fit no to explain for obvious reasons.

Setting the Stage

Then-Minister of Economy Nihat Zeybekçi minced no hate speech words at a rally two weeks after the thwarted coup about organized mistreatment and violence against Hizmet detainees and prisoners, using astonishingly vitriolic language, let alone for a government minister:

> But here's the thing: as some say, "We wish we were dead to be free." We will punish them in such a way that, execution aside, they will

> beg to die to be free. We will make them beg. We will shove them into such holes and make them serve their sentences there such that they will never see God's sun again while they breathe. They will not see the sun. They will never hear another human voice. They will beg for us to kill them. They will beg for us to kill them. And, as our President said, "Whatever the nation says, that will be."' That is what my heart and conscience tell me. But do not forget this: even if you execute all of them, my heart will not be satisfied.[8]

Zeybekçi, a close friend of Erdoğan with whom he spends summer holidays, joined the cabinet after its reshuffle because of the December 2013 corruption scandal.

Türkiye has rejected international pressure and scrutiny regarding allegations of systematic ill-treatment of Gülen Movement members, and even torture, which is prohibited by Türkiye's constitution. The country has nullified all the gains achieved during the now-defunct European Union accession process and turned itself into an oppressive state. The courts have all ignored petitions filed by incarcerated Hizmet people over human rights violations. Instead, the judiciary has covered them up and, worse, legally justified systematic hate crimes in prison.

Torture

Türkiye only recently and reluctantly officially banned torture, although credible human rights reports suggest that it still goes on as an "unofficial" practice. Were it not for international law and pressure, the hate-motivated actions targeting Hizmet members would be even more disastrous and despicable, a thought difficult to fathom in the reality that has played out.

Numerous reported cases involved Hizmet people suffering torture and ill-treatment in prisons and other undisclosed locations, with their whereabouts remaining unknown for months.

Various international organizations highlighted an increase in torture and ill-treatment following the state of emergency declaration. These include Amnesty International and Human Rights Watch. Although the exact number of victims is unknown, figures in the reports portrayed widespread torture and ill-treatment.

Amnesty International reports for years have detailed cases of torture and mistreatment against thousands of Hizmet associates or suspected associates during detentions and arrests following the coup attempt.[9] The reports highlighted grotesque violations of fundamental rights.

Amnesty found reliable evidence of people arrested after the coup attempt being subjected to beatings and torture.[10] The 2016 Human Rights Watch report, "Blank Check: Türkiye's Post-Coup Suspension of Safeguards Against Torture,"[11] outlined how torture was legitimized under the ruse of the abysmal coup attempt.

Similarly, Amnesty's 2020/21 report emphasized the continued use of torture and ill-treatment. Among these cases was Gökhan Türkmen, one of seven individuals who disappeared in 2019 after being accused of Hizmet affiliation. According to the report, he had been subjected to torture and other ill-treatment during his 271 days of enforced disappearance.[12]

The Human Rights Foundation of Türkiye reported that 5,268 individuals claimed to have experienced torture in 2017. It noted eleven cases of enforced disappearances, mostly in Ankara, with four individuals being released later and one committing suicide. A year later, another case of enforced disappearance occurred. Many Hizmet members are still missing and believed to be imprisoned in secret detention centers.[13]

According to Türkiye's Human Rights Association, at least 980 individuals faced torture and other ill-treatment in detention centers in the first eleven months of 2022. Additionally, 310 prisoners lodged complaints about torture and ill-treatment in prisons.[14] Torture and maltreatment became commonplace during and after the state of emergency, intending to harm dedicated public servants imprisoned solely for affiliation with the Gülen Movement.

Torture is a severe violation of human rights, a crime for which there is no statute of limitations (time limit within which to prosecute the crime). State of emergency decrees extended legal impunity to torturers. Even after the state of emergency, the culture of impunity for torture continues, implicitly endorsed by the state, even though torture is one of the crimes against humanity proscribed by Article 77 of the Turkish Penal Code.

The judiciary has played a major role in perpetuating impunity and shielding torturers from accountability. The lack of a statute of limitations may come back to haunt judges, as well as the torture inflictors, when justice prevails years down the line. They are joint purveyors of torture.

Personal Stories of Torture and Violence in Detention Centers and Prisons

Gökhan Açıkkollu, Teacher Who Died

After Being Tortured in Detention

Gökhan Açıkkollu, a history teacher at Ümraniye Atatürk Vocational and Technical Anatolian High School, was taken into custody from his home in July 2016 by Istanbul counterterrorism police for suspected Hizmet affiliation. He was subjected to physical and psychological torture during his thirteen-day detention at the Vatan Police Station and deprived of his diabetes medication.

Twice, the police took Açıkkollu to the hospital for health crises but returned him to detention both times. Video footage of his deteriorating condition and death showed him in a cell designed for one person but occupied by five. He called for help, but the officers ignored his plea. He struggled on his bed before passing away at age forty-two from a heart attack.[15]

Following his death, Açıkkollu's body was initially withheld from his family and an attempt was made to bury him in a "traitors' cemetery." Imams affiliated with the Diyanet refused to conduct funeral prayers, calling him a "traitor." Eventually, his family transported his body in their personal vehicle for hours to Büyüköz Mahallesi. The mosque's imam there also refused to lead the funeral prayers. A local resident helped conduct burial prayers.[16]

The public prosecutor refused to pursue the family's complaint about Açıkkollu's death. His wife sought relief from the United Nations Human Rights Committee regarding violations of her husband's rights. The Committee ruled in her favor in November 2022 and identified violations concerning torture and ill-treatment resulting in her husband's death.[17]

The committee findings are representative of the legion of violations in similar cases: Türkiye's Constitutional Court would not provide relief for the detention and death of her husband; the state's declaration of derogation, following the state of emergency, could not suspend basic safeguards against arbitrary detention concerning her husband's arrest; the state failed to promptly, impartially, and comprehensively investigate the allegations that her husband suffered physical and psychological trauma in custody; and the state did not take the necessary precautions to protect her husband from torture and ill-treatment; and, ultimately, the state did not do a comprehensive and impartial investigation after his death.

What is more bizarre and reprehensively ironic is that a Turkish court found Açıkkollu innocent one-and-a-half years later and reinstated him to his job.[18] This sad coda speaks to the injustice afoot.

The Cancer-Stricken Former Judge

Sincan F1 Prison has been holding Judge Mustafa Başer since early May 2015. Despite being eligible for probationary release for more than a year and being diagnosed with recurring bladder cancer three times, he has been denied this lawful right based on alleged Hizmet affiliation. He underwent major surgery, which made him eligible for conditional medical release as of September 2022. The government, however, has denied him this right.[19]

While the regime has granted probationary and conditional release to thousands of inmates in similar situations, it has refused Judge Başer this humane right. The primary reason behind this maltreatment was in retaliation for his judicial decision to release sixty police officers associated with the December 2013 corruption scandal, which implicated government ministers. The government had retaliated against the officers and arrested them. The judge was arrested days after releasing the officers.

Judge Başer is being unlawfully held in solitary confinement and being left to die out of revenge and hatred. Parliament member Ömer Faruk Gergerlioğlu of the Peoples' Democratic Party (HDP) from Kocaeli submitted a parliamentary question regarding this issue, but it fell on deaf ears.

Gergerlioğlu is a stalwart advocate, defending the rights of prisoners and people purged after the coup attempt and of the rights of Kurds. He lost his public hospital job as a doctor because of an emergency decree. An outspoken parliament member against the government, he was stripped of his immunity by the AKP majority and imprisoned in April 2021. Two months later, the Constitutional Court restored him to parliament.

Other Judges

Similarly, a former member of the Council of Judges and Prosecutors (HSK), Judge Teoman Gökçe, suffered a heart attack in prison and died because of the lack of timely intervention.[20]

Likewise, Judge Mustafa Erdoğan from the Court of Cassation, while receiving treatment in the hospital for a brain tumor, was arrested in February 2017 by the Antalya Criminal Peace Court without any stated grounds for the warrant. The judge, who underwent major surgery, spent six months in a prison ward of the hospital with half of his body paralyzed.

Pleas for his release by his lawyers and his family were fruitless. Nor could he meet with his family. An application to the Constitutional Court for a health release was rejected because "the detainee was not in any danger." His illness progressed, and he was moved to intensive care in August 2017, but still not allowed to see his family. His consciousness faded, and, finally, he was released. He went into a coma and died four days later.[21]

Death in the "White Plastic Chair"

The government's hate-driven practices have left severely ill people to die in prison. One distressing incident is the death of deputy police inspector Mustafa Kabakçıoğlu, who was dismissed from duty and later arrested on FETÖ charges. He passed away in August 2020 in Gümüşhane Prison, slumped in a white plastic chair.

Kabakçıoğlu had been diagnosed with diabetes three years earlier while in prison, and his health continued to deteriorate thereafter. He outlined his ailments to the prison doctor: "I have been regularly taking the medicines you provided, but I believe they have side effects. I have swelling in the left side of my mouth and in my left leg and have difficulty speaking. My arm is numb. I experience numbness below the waist and have no functioning below the waist."[22]

Despite the doctor's recommendation for urgent hospitalization, Kabakçıoğlu was not taken to the hospital. Nor was he taken when he reported acute discomfort on three different days immediately before he died.[23] This visual image of him—head slumped backward, nails discolored, hands on his legs—graphically portrays the ultimate consequence faced by Hizmet prisoners. Kabakçıoğlu's death after four years in custody is not solely due to his illness but to policies imposed on a particular group of people, purportedly aimed at rooting out "evil."[24]

Years later, an AKP parliament member would brag, "... we do not give them the right to live in Türkiye."[25] Indeed, not only are Gülen Movement people abandoned to civil death in Turkish society, but ill detainees are deliberately left to perish in prison.

Halime Gülsu: A Compassionate Teacher

Another lamentable death is that of English teacher Halime Gülsu, allegedly associated with Hizmet. She was arrested in March 2018, accused of selling stuffed meatballs to aid families sorely affected by emergency decrees. She had a form of chronic Lupus and passed away a month later in Tarsus Closed Women's Prison because of being denied medication and medical attention, which she detailed in a letter to the Prime Ministry Communication Center just days before her death.[26]

Halime Gülsu was unlawfully jailed for doing something utterly humane and compassionate. How can a country be so meanspirited to abandon her unto death for being merciful to a family in need of food?

Sick Prisoners Abandoned to Their Fate

Thousands of arrested individuals fell ill due to deplorable prison conditions and pressure.[27] The state, which bears the responsibility of safeguarding the right to life, engaged in practices that lead to people's deaths within prison walls.[28] Those detained are deliberately abandoned to perish amid abysmal prison conditions and deficient medical services.

A singular example in this context was the country's Forensic Medicine Institute 2022 report for an emergency decree victim and paralyzed teacher Şerife Sulukan that, despite an 89% disability and the need for assistance in most daily activities, she could still "remain in prison."[29]

Businessman With Hizmet Links Dies in Prison

Ill-treatment continues into current times, as exemplified by the fate of Fahrettin İşgüder, a 73-year-old businessman, sentenced to more than six years in prison for alleged Gülen Movement links. He died in mid-July 2024 after being hospitalized when he collapsed because of prison heat and overcrowding.[30]

That İşgüder was arrested in 2024, two-and-a-half months before his death, reflects the ongoing persecution of Hizmet. He was accused of attending religious sermons organized by Hizmet and going on pilgrimage with members who were dismissed from their jobs by government decrees during the purges following the botched coup.

Torture, Sexual Harassment, and Ill Treatment: Mersin and Ankara Police

Prisons and detention centers were not the only locations where authorities inflicted pain and suffering on Hizmet-associated people, but also at police stations.

In early 2018, eighty women, including high school and university students, were subjected to torture and maltreatment at the Mersin police station. Police from the Smuggling and Organized Crime Directorate detained them for "helping Gülenist families in need of food and resources." One detainee was a mother with her two-month-old infant, who was held in custody for four days. Another was a 15-year-old high school student.[31]

In May 2019, HDP parliament member Gergerlioğlu used his Twitter account to alert the public about alleged ill-treatment and torture within Ankara police headquarters of a hundred individuals, including former employees of the Ministry of Foreign Affairs, dismissed between

2016 and 2018 under emergency decrees for suspected Gülen Movement affiliation.

The Ankara Bar Association's Human Rights Center published five separate detailed reports prepared January-April 2022, based on discussions with the alleged victims.[32] Five detainees interviewed by the center claimed to have been tortured by police. In August, nevertheless, the Ankara Chief Public Prosecutor decided there was insufficient evidence to initiate an investigation, a point reiterated unfavorably in the U.S. Secretary of State's 2020 Türkiye report.

In January, the Human Rights Center reported on its inquiries into complaints from individuals detained by Ankara police for being Hizmet members and found they faced torture, insults, threats, and sexual assault. The findings, substantiated by records, described appalling mistreatment and torture, confessions under intimidation, severe beatings, kicking, strip-searches during interviews accompanied by insults and threats, and terrorization of naked prisoners about inserting objects into the rectum and soaking them with cold water.

The center's February report concerned an individual detained by Ankara police, again on suspicion of Hizmet affiliation, who suffered torture, insults, threats, and sexual assault. Details revealed through interviews and records include forced confessions under threats, severe beatings, kicks to various parts of the body, forced nudity, striking the genital area with a broomstick, and threats of inserting an olive oil bottle into the rectum.

Similarly, in March, the Human Rights Center reported on its investigations of the mistreatment of an individual arrested by Ankara police for Hizmet association. This inquiry also addressed allegations of torture, brutal beatings, threats, and sexual assault. The findings sustained the allegations of continuing mistreatment and torture.[33]

These reports and cases demonstrate that Ankara police, connected with the national Directorate of Security's Counterterrorism Branch, perpetrated grotesque, inhumane treatment and torture because of the detainees' (one of whom was a woman) alleged Hizmet relationship.

Even worse, a variety of reports show that torture incidents have become normalized within detention facilities and prisons because of the impunity granted through the emergency decrees. Public officials, who are legally bound to treat everyone equally, nevertheless engage in illegal acts, especially torture, which is a crime against humanity under Turkish Penal Code Article 77.

Article 77 also proscribes intentional injury or inhuman treatment. The same provisions are in the international law charters to which has obligated itself.

Strip Searches, Men and Women

Harassing and humiliating illegal strip searches became routine—especially against alleged Hizmet members and former public officials in detention facilities and prisons during the state of emergency. This became public when parliament member Gergerlioğlu discussed interviews with victims who shared their stories. The facilities and the Ministry of Interior hastily denied allegations of widespread abuse, claiming there were only isolated incidents.[34]

The Constitutional Court, which had previously issued decisions finding strip-search violations, notably refrained from finding any violations in investigations concerning alleged Hizmet members during the state of emergency. In fact, in one ruling, the court decided that "… the act of strip-search cannot solely be considered a violation of Article 17 [Personal Inviolability] in the Bill of Rights of the Turkish Constitution…."[35] thus legitimizing this personally degrading practice.

Degrading strip searches are not limited to detainees and prisoners. Visitors, especially women and children, have been subjected to this demeaning treatment without legitimate reason. Arbitrary strip searches have been done even in buildings where retinal scans are used as security for entry.

In February 2021, during operations targeting Hizmet members, thirty female students detained at Uşak police headquarters underwent humiliating strip searches.[36] Prosecutors dismissed their criminal complaints against the policy regarding these incidents, consistent with the pattern of impunity allowed by the judiciary.

Following the revelation of these events, AKP Group Deputy Chair Özlem Zengin issued statements blaming and shaming the women detained.[37] Uşak Governor Funda Kocabıyık took extraordinary efforts to cover up the incident, associating the victims directly with terrorist organizations to deflect attention from herself. She was responsible for overseeing the police department involved in the incident.

Another incident of this degrading practice involved female volunteers with the Furkan Movement in Konya, an anti-AKP Islamist organization. In June 2022, the victims announced to the media that they had been subjected to strip searches while in custody.[38]

Special Prison Uniforms for Hizmet

The government introduced a mandate that individuals accused of terrorism-related offenses wear a standardized uniform when leaving prisons for court hearings or any other external movement from prison (*e.g.*, hospital visits). This was tantamount to wearing a "terrorist" label on their backs and portraying the individual to the public as guilty, despite the lack of a definitive conviction.

The regulation was not for prison safety, order, or the detainee's safety. Rather, it aimed to expose these individuals to the public, devalue them, and make them targets. Thus, a detainee going to the hospital for emergency care in a beige jumpsuit will be recognized as "FETÖ" and be treated accordingly.[39] The uniform policy has a second prong: to generate government support from coup attempt victims and their families. Erdoğan bluntly laid out the intent of this regulation in his July 15, 2017, National Unity and Democracy Day speech:

> .... let's also bring these [FETÖ suspects] to court in a uniform, just like in a Guantanamo uniform. ... From now on, FETÖ coup plotters and terrorists will not be able to show up to trials with airs of arrogance, fancied up .... This uniform will be a dark almond color. There will be two types: one will be a jumpsuit, and the other will be a jacket and trousers. Coup plotters will wear jumpsuits, and the others, meaning terrorists, will wear jackets and trousers. They will no longer dress as they wish. This way, they will be presented to the world, and this is how they will put on their show from now on.[40]

National Unity and Democracy Day occurs on the anniversary date of the abortive coup. The government's post-coup actions, though, did nothing but undermine national unity and weaken democracy. George Orwell would be impressed with how a government can proclaim those aspirations as it becomes ever more totalitarian and authoritarian. A sad oxymoron.

Requiring unique uniforms for those accused of terrorism-related charges targets Hizmet-associated individuals in prison. It is a discriminatory practice and intended as such, like the infamous Yellow Star of Hitler's era. Public statements by Erdoğan and others, along with displaying such uniforms during rallies in front of Silivri and Sincan prisons where trials take place is crass hate speech propaganda with a nod toward possible violence.

The European Court of Human Rights has ruled that forcing detainees to attend trials wearing the same attire as convicts would violate the right to a fair trial and that a uniform, depending on what it was, might constitute humiliating treatment. In the *Jiga/Romania* case,[41] the ECtHR emphasized this very point. Individuals awaiting trial in specific clothing might be perceived as "guilty" in the public eye, thereby violating the presumption of innocence—and, depending on the circumstances, these clothes could be humiliating for both the public and the detainee.

Under both Turkish Constitution Article 38 and ECHR Article 6/2, the beige jumpsuit rule for individuals accused, but not convicted, of terrorism violates the presumption of innocence. Further, it imposed a disproportionate sanction of a three-month ban on visitations for individuals refusing to wear the uniform, which would qualify as ill-treatment under Turkish Constitution Article 17 and ECHR Article 3.

Pro-government media outlets played up the regulation as "uniforms for FETÖ suspects." Hizmet was the target. Murder or sexual assault suspects attend trials wearing their desired attire.

Although certain provincial prosecutors, notably in Diyarbakır, required use of the uniforms, strong national and international public reaction has stalled the practice. It smells too much like an odious Nazi practice.

Other Systematic Discriminatory Practices

During the state of emergency, systematic and deliberate discriminatory practices against Hizmet people persistently applied within prisons and still do.

Correctional administrators deviated from standard practices to degrade, intimidate, and coerce Hizmet-related individuals into confessions and deny them the same rights and privileges afforded regular inmates. This included: restricted written correspondence, phone usage, and visitation rights; isolation; limitations on visits with lawyers and families; mandatory uniform shaving in corridors under surveillance cameras; prohibition of sitting beside visitors during open visits; denial of collective cultural, social, and sports activities, vocational training, educational courses; internet access for educational purposes; and prohibition on possessing radios.

State of Emergency Decree 667 stipulated that only a spouse, blood relative to the second degree, or legal guardian could visit a detainee. It also restricted communication to a phone call every fifteen days and limited visits to ten minutes with these specific individuals. Many prisons, particularly Silivri and Bakırköy, prohibited Hizmet individuals from corresponding with their families until after the two-year state of emergency.

Hizmet-associated prisoners were often located hundreds of miles from their families, obviously to hinder interaction with relatives.

These intentionally discriminatory practices eventually became standard practice, which local courts, and even the Constitutional Court, legitimized instead of safeguarding individual rights.

Whitewashing by the Constitutional Court

The Constitutional Court was of no avail in curtailing the discriminatory practices in detention centers and prisons, rejecting appeals with little analysis other than they were not arbitrary or capricious in light of the coup attempt and state of emergency, granting unrestricted discretion to facility administrators.[42] It mattered not if the Hizmet-associated people felt the brunt of discriminatory administrative decisions.

A state of emergency is the very time when the courts must be most active in carefully circumscribing government power. Türkiye's judiciary failed the test.

Concluding Summary

One does not incarcerate non-violent public servants, judges, and teachers, with health problems, knowing the likelihood of their demise, without another agenda at hand. Politicide, in this case.

Endnotes

1 "Türkiye: prisons in 2024," Prison Insider (April 18, 2024), https://www.prison-insider.com/en/articles/turkiye-prisons-in-2024#:~:text=Conditions%20of%20detention%20are%20most,a%20form%20of%20perpetual%20torture.

2 "Dismissal of Public Servants by Emergency Decree Laws & HSYK/HSK Decisions," Solidarity with Others, https://www.solidaritywithothers.com/dismissal-by-decree-laws-and-hsk.

3 "2017 İnsan Hakları İhlalleri Raporu: OHAL Altında Geçen Bir Yıl," İnsan Hakları Derneği, İnsan Hakları Derneği (Human Rights Association) (6 April 2018), https://www.ihd.org.tr/2017-insan-haklari-ihlalleri-raporu-ohal-altinda-gecen-bir-yil/, İET:12/08/2023 ["2017 Human rights Violations Report: A Year Under the State of Emergency"].

4 Article 20, Directive on the Visiting of Convicts and Detainees, "Hükümlü Ve Tutuklularin Ziyaret Edilmeleri Hakkinda Yönetmelik," Mevzuat Information System (17.06.2005), https://www.mevzuat.gov.tr/mevzuat?MevzuatNo=8345&MevzuatTur=7&MevzuatTertip=5.

5 *See* "Concluding observations on the fifth periodic report of Türkiye," Convention against Torture and Other Cruel, Inhuman or Degrading Treatment or Punishment, United Nations High Commissioner for Human Rights (14 Aug. 2024), https://tbinternet.ohchr.org/_layouts/15/treatybodyexternal/Download.aspx?symbolno=CAT%2FC%2FTUR%2FCO%2F5&Lang=en.

6 Article 3, Decree No. 673.

7 *See* Emre Turkut and Thomas Phillips, "Non-Discrimination, Minority Rights and Self-Determination: Turkey's Post-Coup State of Emergency and the Position of Turkey's Kurds," in Hasan Aydin and Winston Langley (eds), *Human Rights in Turkey: Assaults on Human Dignity* (New York: Springer, 2021), pp. 109–129, https://doi.org/10.1007/978-3-030-57476-5_5.

8 "Bakan Zeybekci: Bunlara öyle bir ceza vereceğiz ki…." Hürriyet (Aug. 01, 2016), https://www.hurriyet.com.tr/gundem/bakan-zeybekci-bunlara-oyle-bir-ceza-verecegiz-ki-40177470 ["Minister Zeybekci: We will punish them in such a way that..."].

9 *See, e.g.,* "Amnesty International Report 2017/18: The state of the world's human rights," Amnesty International (Feb. 22, 2018), Amnesty International Annual Report 2017/18 - Amnesty International (Turkey, pp. 367-372). *See also* "Amnesty International Report 2016/17: The state of the world's human rights," Amnesty International (Feb. 22, 2017), Amnesty International Report 2016/17: The state of the world's human rights - Amnesty International (Turkey, pp. 367-371).

10 "Turkey: Independent monitors must be allowed to access detainees amid torture allegations," Amnesty International (June 24, 2016), https://www.amnesty.org/en/latest/press-release/2016/07/turkey-independent-monitors-must-be-allowed-to-access-detainees-amid-torture-allegations/.

11 "A Blank Check: Turkey's Post-Coup Suspension of Safeguards Against Torture," Human Rights Watch (24 Oct. 2016), https://www.refworld.org/reference/countryrep/hrw/2016/en/113368.

12 "Amnesty International Report 2020/21: The state of the world's human rights," Amnesty International (2021), https://www.amnesty.org/en/documents/pol10/3202/2021/en/ (p.65).

13 "Ankara Bar exposes new torture cases which the former admin hid from public," Arrested Lawyers Initiative (5 Jan. 2023), https://arrestedlawyers.org/2023/01/05/ankara-bar-exposes-new-torture-cases-which-the-former-admin-hid-from-public/.

14 "2020 Country Reports on Human Rights Practices: Turkey," U.S. Department of State, https://www.state.gov/reports/2020-country-reports-on-human-rights-practices/turkey/.

15 "Gökhan Açıkkollu'nun ölümü işkenceyle ilintili,'" Aktif Haber (March 12, 2018), https://aktifhaber.com/iskence/gokhan-acikkollunun-olumu-iskenceyle-ilintili-h113645.html ["Gökhan Açıkkollu's death is related to torture"].

16 "Gözaltında ölen öğretmene imam da, mezar da vermediler," Yeni Asya (07 Aug. 2016), https://www.yeniasya.com.tr/gundem/gozaltinda-olen-ogretmene-imam-da-mezar-da-vermediler_406193 ["They did not give an imam or a grave to the teacher who died in custody"].

17 "Views adopted by the Committee under Article 5(4) of the Optional Protocol, concerning Communication No. 3730/2020," United Nations (Human Rights Committee) (20 Feb. 2023), https://ccprcentre.org/files/decisions/G2301281_(1).pdf; Güneş, Gökhan, "United Nations Committee on Human Rights Decision About Gökhan Açikollu," Justice Square, https://www.justicesquare.com/english/united-nations-committee-on-human-rights-decision-about-gokhan-acikollu/; "UN committee faults Türkiye in case of teacher who died in custody after arrest over Gülen links," Turkish Minute (Dec. 1, 2022), https://turkishminute.committee-faults-turkey-in-case-of-teacher-who-died-in-custody-after-arrest-over-gulen-links/. *See also* "Amnesty slammed for ignoring plight of Gülen movement members in new report," Turkish Minute (April 24, 2024), https://www.turkishminute.com/2024/04/24/amnesty-slammed-for-ignored-plight-gulen-movement-member-in-new-report/.

18 "Turkish teacher Gökhan Açıkkollu, tortured to death under police custody, reinstated to his job (!)," Stockholm Center for Freedom (Feb. 27, 2018), https://stockholmcf.org/turkish-teacher-gokhan-acikkollu-tortured-to-death-under-police-custody-reinstated-to-his-job/.

19 "Cezaevinde hastalığı 3. kez nüksetti: Başer'in oğlu yetkilileri hukuku uygulamaya çağırdı," Samanyoulu Haber (11 January 2023), https://www.shaber3.com/cezaevinde-hastaligi-3-kez-nuksetti-baser-in-oglu-yetkilileri-hukuku-uygulamaya-cagirdi-haberi/1404643/ ["His illness recurred for the third time in prison: Başer's son called on the authorities to enforce the law"].

20 "Photographs of former judge who died in prison cell shed light on poor conditions," Turkish Minute (Dec. 29, 2021), https://www.turkishminute.com/2021/12/29/photographs-of-former-judge-who-died-in-prison-cell-shed-light-on-poor-conditions/.

21 "Supreme court member dies in hospital after release from prison," Turkish Minute (Aug. 22, 2017), https://turkishminute.com/2017/08/22/supreme-court-member-dies-in-hospital-after-release-from-prison/.

22 "Photographs of deputy police inspector who died in prison quarantine show criminal neglect," Stockholm Center for Freedom (Oct. 14, 2020), https://stockholmcf.org/photographs-of-deputy-police-inspector-who-died-in-prison-quarantine-show-criminal-neglect/.

23 "Mustafa Kabakçıoğlu: KHK'lı eski polisin ölümü cezaevinde ihmal iddialarını gündeme getirdi?," BBC (15 Oct. 2020), https://www.bbc.com/turkce/haberler-turkiye-54561319/ ["Mustafa Kabakçıoğlu: Why did the death of the former police officer with a statutory decree bring up allegations of negligence in prison?"]. *See also* "KHK'lı polisin karantina hücresinden cenazesi çıktı: Plastik sandalyede ölüm," Arti Gerçek (Oct. 14, 2020), https://artigercek.com/guncel/khk-li-polisin-karantina-hucresinden-cenazesi-cikti-plastik-sandalyede-olum-141301h ["The corpse of a police officer with a statutory decree was

released from his quarantine cell: Death in a plastic chair"]. *See also* "Public outcry for police officer's death in Erdoğan's 'execution chamber,'" PoliTurco (Oct. 15, 2020), https://politurco.com/public-outcry-for-police-officers-death-in-Erdoğans-execution-chamber.html.

24 "Hate Crimes Against the Gülen Movement in Turkey," Justice Square (29 Feb. 2024), https://justicesquare.org/wp-content/uploads/2024/03/STATEMENT-HATE-CRIMES-AGAINST-GULEN-MOVEMENT-IN-TURKEY.pdf. (para. 28).

25 *Id.* (para. 29).

26 "Book tells story of teacher who died in Turkish prison due to lack of medication," Turkish Minute (Dec. 15, 2022), https://www.turkishminute.com/2022/12/15/ook-tells-story-of-teacher-who-died-in-turkish-prison-due-to-lack-of-medication/. *See also* "Cezaevinde göz göre göre bir ölüm daha: Halime Gülsu öğretmen vefat etti," TR724 (28 April 2018), https://www.tr724.com/cezaevinde-goz-gore-gore-bir-olum-daha-halime-gulsu-vefat-etti/ ["Another apparent death in prison: Teacher Halime Gülsu passed away"].

27 *See, e.g.*, "84-year-old Nusret Muğla dies after contracting COVID-19 in prison," Stockholm Center for Freedom (Feb. 14 2022), https://stockholmcf.org/84-year-old-nusret-mugla-dies-after-contracting-covid-19-in-prison/.

28 *See* Alper Keten, "Human Rights Violations and Medicolegal Approach," in Hasan Aydin and Winston Langley (eds), *Human Rights in Turkey: Assaults on Human Dignity* (New York: Springer, 2021), pp. 293–316, https://doi.org/10.1007/978-3-030-57476-5_13.

29 "Felçli ve yüzde 89 engelli öğretmen Şerife Sulukan cezaevinde nöbet geçirdi," Bold Medya (14/06/2022), https://www.boldmedya.com/2022/06/02/felcli-ve-yuzde-89-engelli-ogretmen-serife-sulukan-cezaevinde-nobet-gecirdi/ ["Paralyzed and 89 percent disabled teacher Şerife Sulukan had a seizure in prison"]. *See also* "Paralyzed former teacher arrested to serve sentence for conviction of Gülen links," Turkish Minute (May 5, 2022), https://www.turkishminute.com/2022/05/05/paralyzed-former-teacher-arrested-to-serve-sentence-for-conviction-of-gulen-links/; *and see* Voice of Women Platform (@VoiceOfWomenW), "Physically disabled Physics Teacher Şerife Sulukan was arrested in 2022 although she hasn't committed any crimes. Sulukan, who also suffers from heart, epilepsy, and paralysis, cannot meet her needs alone. She must be released for her health," x.com (Feb 28, 2024), https://twitter.com/VoiceOfWomenW/status/1762903534276616564.

30 "Businessman jailed over Gülen links dies due to excessive heat and overcrowding in Turkish prison," Stockholm Center for Freedom (July 23, 2024), https://stockholmcf.org/businessman-jailed-over-gulen-links-dies-due-to-excessive-heat-and-overcrowding-in-turkish-prison/.

31 "80 women reportedly subjected to inhumane treatment at Mersin police station, Turkish Minute (Feb. 26, 2018), 80 women reportedly subjected to inhumane treatment at Mersin police station - Turkish Minute.

32 "Ankara Birotunda tartışmalara neden olan işkence raporları yayınlandı," Yeni Yaşam (2 Jan. 023), Controversial reports of torture in Ankara Bar Association have been published – Yeni Yaşam Newspaper | New Life (yeniyasamgazetesi6.com)

33 "Ankara İl Emiliya Modorluğu Terörle Mücadele Şubesi İşkence İddialari Raporu," Ankara Barosu (Ankara Bar Association) (06.03.2022), https://ankarabarosu.org.tr/upload/diger/raporlar/04.04.2022_tarihli_ihm_rapor1.pdf ["Ankara Provincial Emi'liytr Modorship Anti-Terrorism Branch Report and Torture Allegations"].

34 "Strip-search is an ongoing practice in Turkish prisons, opposition deputy says,"

Stockholm Center for Freedom (Dec. 7, 2022), https://stockholmcf.org/strip-search-is-an-ongoing-practice-in-turkish-prisons-opposition-deputy-says/.

35 Article 17, Turkish Constitution ("…. The physical integrity of the individual shall not be violated except under medical necessity and in cases prescribed by law…. No one shall be subjected to torture or ill-treatment; no one shall be subjected to penalty or treatment incompatible with human dignity.").

36 "Uşak'taki çıplak aramaya dair suç duyurusu ortaya çıktı," Cumhuriyet (28.02.2021), https://www.cumhuriyet.com.tr/haber/usaktaki-ciplak-aramaya-dair-suc-duyurusu-ortaya-cikti-1817119 ["Criminal complaint about strip search in Uşak revealed"].

37 *See* "Strip search of women in Turkey used for humiliation, witness testimonies show," Stockholm Center for Freedom (Sept. 17, 2020), https://stockholmcf.org/strip-search-of-women-in-turkey-used-for-humiliation-witness-testimonies-show/; "Students strip-searched, maltreated during ECtHR president's Turkey visit," Turkish Minute (Sept. 8, 2020); https://www.turkishminute.com/2020/09/08/students-strip-searched-maltreated-during-ecthr-presidents-turkey-visit/.

38 "Furkan gönüllüsü kadın karakolda dayatılan 'çıplak aramayı' anlattı: 'Savcının talimatı var,'" Bold Medya (13/06/2022, https://www.boldmedya.com/2022/06/13/furkan-gonullusu-kadin-karakolda-dayatilan-ciplak-aramayi-anlatti-savcinin-talimati-var/ ["Furkan volunteer woman talked about the 'strip search' imposed at the police station: 'The prosecutor has an instruction.'"]. *See also* "Uşak Valisi'nin 'çıplak arama' yanıtı: FETÖ ve PKK aynı amaç için birleşti," Gazete Duva R (17 Dec. 2020), https://www.gazeteduvar.com.tr/usak-valisinin-ciplak-arama-yaniti-feto-ve-pkk-ayni-amac-icin-birlesti-haber-1507595 ["Uşak Governor's 'naked search' response: FETÖ and PKK united for the same purpose"].

39 Ayça Söylemez, "Guantanamo Turuncusundan "Badem Kurusu"na: Tek Tip Kıyafet Ne Anlama Geliyor?" Bianet (7 Aug. 2017), https://bianet.org/haber/guantanamo-turuncusundan-badem-kurusu-na-tek-tip-kiyafet-ne-anlama-geliyor-188921 ["From Guantanamo Orange to "Dried Almonds": What Does Uniform Clothing Mean?"].

40 "Erdoğan 'tek tip kıyafet'i anlattı: Darbeciler tulum giyecek, teröristler ceket pantolon," Diken (05/08/2017), https://www.diken.com.tr/Erdoğan-tek-tip-kiyafeti-anlatti-darbeciler-tulum-giyecek-teroristler-ceket-pantolon/ ["Erdoğan talked about 'uniform clothing': Coup plotters will wear overalls, terrorists will wear jackets and trousers"].

41 *Jiga c. Roumanie* (No: 14352/04), European Court of Human Rights (16 March 2010), https://hudoc.echr.coe.int/eng#{%22fulltext%22:[%22Dan%20Jiga%22],%22itemid%22:[%22001-97687%22]}.

42 *Müjdat Gürbüz* (No: 2017/36529), Constitutional Court (23/5/2018), https://kararlarbilgibankasi.anayasa.gov.tr/BB/2017/36529. *See also* Te Bilisim, "Hapisteki gazeteciler: Kitap ve mektup yasağı psikolojik işkence," Politik Yol (04.12.2016), "https://www.politikyol.com/hapisteki-gazeteciler-kitap-ve-mektup-yasagi-psikolojik-iskenc ["Journalists in prison: Ban on books and letters is psychological torture"]. For a personal account of imprisonment after the coup attempt, see Ismail Albayrak, *A Contemporary Turkish Prison Diary: Reflections on the Writings of Said Nursi and Aleksander Solzhenitsyn* (Springer Singapore, 2024), https://link.springer.com/book/10.1007/978-981-97-1564-0.

Chapter 10

Suicide Victims and Psychological Pressure

One certain consequence of the regime's hate-driven campaign against people associated with Hizmet was the severe psychological violence and damage it wreaked on them and their families. It continues to this day. This was one of the goals and known anticipated outcomes of Erdoğan's politicide agenda.

The users of degrading hate-speech rhetoric deliberately subjected Hizmet-related individuals to psychological cruelty. They knew that the regime's long-term, pressure-cooker atmosphere was conducive to suicide for some, especially among those for whom the tension was intensely severe. People have different capacities to withstand a psychological onslaught, and some may be weighed down under the burden of other anxieties.

People, young and old, suffered from being publicly marginalized, ostracized, devalued, falsely associated with crime, and accused of betraying their country. They were forced to live under the immense strain of escalating psychological anxiety. The intense societal and political stress generated by Erdoğan's assault predictably resulted in an alarming number of suicides,[1] not that Erdoğan was bothered by the consequences of his running roughshod over people.

As might be expected, there are countless accounts of family division, exacerbated by the regime's hate speech propaganda prowess. Parents and children no longer talk. Siblings have stopped communicating with each other. Former loving relationships have frayed badly if not breaking altogether. The same is true of one-time friends. Individuals' support systems and bonds were torn asunder. Withstanding the power of the government is no easy task, and having to do so alone, without bending, is impossibly daunting. The psychological pressure is intense and can be overbearing.

Women who had nothing to do with the spoiled coup attempt were victimized for their alleged ties with the Gülen Movement. They suffered all kinds of human rights abuses including arrests (often during pregnancy or postpartum period), detention, harassment, intimidation, job dismissals, threats, ostracism, the inability to find employment, economic difficulties, illness, psychological problems, forced separation from loved ones, and torture. The personal consequences included miscarriage, suicide, and death. Women often experienced victimization with their children.[2]

Many Hizmet members have suffered mental breakdowns due to the unfair treatment they have endured, worsened by harsh prison conditions, resulting in illnesses. However, their requests for treatment have been ignored by those in power, leading to the deaths of hundreds due to lack of medical attention.[3] The systematic lack of action by state officials, affecting not just one but hundreds of individuals, demonstrates that this outcome is a widespread and systematic consequence of hate policies.[4]

With the state of emergency following the bungled coup, the situation became more destructive. According to a 2017 report, "Suicides During the State of Emergency," by Veli Ağbaba, a Republican People's Party (CHP) parliament member, within the first nine months of the state of emergency, thirty-five individuals committed suicide: seventeen police officers, four soldiers, four teachers, two correctional officers, a guidance counselor, a district governor, a mosque imam, a prosecutor, an engineer, a student, a doctor, and a dentist. Seven suicides occurred in prison, and one in a detention facility.[5]

The Heavy Toll on Children

The Ağbaba report did not include the suicides of family members of those directly targeted by the regime (such as people discharged from their jobs). The true number of young people and children who lost their lives due to severe psychological trauma will never be known. The following are some sad instances of this.

A year later, in 2018, the Confederation of Progressive Trade Unions of Türkiye (DİSK) published its own assessment, "The Effects of the State of Emergency and the Presidential Regime on Labor: The State of Emergency and the Presidency Are Harmful to Labor," linking the number of suicides by persons dismissed, detained, arrested, and by their relatives as one of the tragic outcomes of the state of emergency.[6]

As of late 2024, ninety-seven individuals associated with Hizmet have died by suicide due to the allegations related to their Hizmet affiliation.[7] Despite eight years passing since the state of emergency, incidents of suicide and death persist. Particularly alarming is the frequency of suicide among family members, young adults, and children due to the severe societal hatred and discriminatory treatment they face from the state. Extreme isolation, marginalization, and ostracization have contributed to psychological breakdowns and suicides.

There have been notable suicide cases. For instance, Bahadır Odabaşı, a sixteen-year-old youth whose father, a teacher, was dismissed by an emergency decree and later arrested in 2016 in Diyarbakır, died by jumping from the 10th floor of his apartment building in January 2022.[8]

Similarly, Nahit Emre Güney, the son of Haşim Güney, a former member of the Council of State sentenced to ten years in prison on charges related to Hizmet, jumped to his death from Istanbul's Galata Tower in October 2022. For his son's funeral, the regime's hate practices were such that Haşim Güney had to attend in handcuffs,[9] something unreservedly despicable.

Another suicide involved Ayşe D., who visited her father, a detained sergeant dismissed by decree, with her mother and brother at Buca Kırıklar Prison in July 2023. After returning home, Ayşe D. left a letter on her desk and went to the Nergis railway station in İzmir, where she committed suicide. She left these words behind: "It was nobody's fault, but I hold the right of retaliation against the government and everyone who ever voted for them. I do not believe in heaven or hell; I do not want to. Let it end when I die. I do not want my conscience or my soul or my fourth dimension to continue to exist."[10]

The state of emergency impact extends beyond the increase in suicidal tendencies. It has resulted in a catalog of psychological consequences. The injustices suffered during this period have led to increased tensions among victims and their families, a rise in divorce rates, unexpected and untimely deaths due to excessive stress and pressure, resurgences of illnesses, and the emergence of additional medical and psychological problems.[11]

An in-depth 2022 report of the Crossborder Jurists Association lays out in statistics and personal histories the psychological toll of the state of emergency and its aftermath on victims and their families as of that time.[12]

The 55-page document notes that the crude death rate and the suicide rate among Hizmet-associated victims and their families were both much higher than Türkiye's average. For families of emergency decree victims, the suicide rate was 30-35 times higher than the suicide average for the general population; and the crude mortality rate was at least twice as high as the general average.

As one might expect, children, who are the main subject of the report, experienced a range of severe psychological issues. They became depressed and experienced severe depression due to their inability to express themselves, being ignored, and being subjected to mobbing and peer bullying at home and school. Some had suicide ideation; and children, ages 12-14, had attempted suicide.

Most children reported negative experiences like quitting sports, dropping out of school, gaining excessive weight, becoming withdrawn, withdrawing from their friends, and starting smoking. Many suffered from psychiatric trauma and illnesses and needed medication and psychological support, but did not receive it.

Some children witnessed the suicide of their parents. Several parents interviewed indicated that they seriously considered suicide but did not pursue it out of not wanting to abandon their children. Far too many innocent young lives became needless victims of a despot's politically fabricated "war" to which they were in no way party.

Final Comment

Sometimes, as in this case, the statistics are far too cut and dry to relay the pain and suffering underneath. Then, too, the enormity of the statistics points to the enormity of the pain and suffering.

Endnotes

1 "OHAL'in İki Yılının ve Başkanlık Rejiminin Çalışma Hayatına Etkileri OHAL ve Başkanlık Emeğe Zararlıdır," Devrimci İşçi Konfederasyonları (DİSK) (21 July 2018), http://arastirma.disk.org.tr/wp-content/uploads/2020/08/OHAL-2-Y%C4%B1l-ve-Ba%C5%9Fkanl%C4%B1k-Rejimi-Yeni-Rapor-TASLAK-SON.pdf ["The Effects of Two Years of the State of Emergency and the Presidential Regime on Working Life: The State of Emergency and the Presidency are Harmful to Labor"]. *See also* "Deaths Caused by Rights Violations on and after July 15, 2016," Solidarity with Others, https://www.solidaritywithothers.com/deaths.

2 *See* Ömer Faruk Gergerlioğlu, "Imprisoned Women and Children in Turkey: Human Rights Violations Under the State of Emergency," in Hasan Aydin and Winston Langley (eds), Human Rights in Turkey: Assaults on Human Dignity (New York: Springer, 2021), pp. 411–434, https://doi.org/10.1007/978-3-030-57476-5_18.

3 *Supra* n. 1, "Deaths Caused by Rights Violations."

4 *Id.*

5 "OHAL öldürüyor: Sayı 35'e yükseldi," Cumhuriyet (29.04.2017), https://www.cumhuriyet.com.tr/haber/ohal-olduruyor-sayi-35e-yukseldi-730232 ["State of Emergency deaths: The number increased to 35"].

6 *Supra* n. 1.

7 *Id.* "Deaths Caused by Rights Violations."

8 Gönül Morkoç, "16 yaşında intihar eden Bahadır'ın yürek burkan dramı," Tigris Haber (19 Jan. 2022), https://www.tigrishaber.com/16-yasinda-intihar-eden-bahadirin-yurek-burkan-drami-76129h.htm ["The heartbreaking drama of Bahadır, who committed suicide at the age of 16"].

9 "Galata Kulesi'nde canına kıyan Nahit Emre'nin yakınları: Bir gecede lojmandan çıkarıldılar gidecek evleri yoktu," Bold Medya (15/10/2022), https://boldmedya.com/2022/10/15/galata-kulesinde-canina-kiyan-nahit-emrenin-yakinlari-bir-gecede-lojmandan-cikardilar-gidecek-evleri-yoktu/ ["Relatives of Nahit Emre, who killed himself from the Galata Tower: They were evicted from their lodging overnight and had no home to go to"].

10 "Cezaevinde babasını ziyaret ettikten sonra canına kıyan 18 yaşındaki Ayşe: 'Bir kez olsun bunlara oy veren herkese hakkım haramdır,'" TR724 (28 July 2023), https://www.tr724.com/cezaevinde-babasini-ziyaret-ettikten-sonra-canina-kiyan-18-yasindaki-ayse-bir-kez-olsun-bunlara-oy-veren-herkese-hakkim-haramdir/ ["Eighteen-year-old Ayşe, who took her own life after visiting her father in prison: 'My rights are forbidden by anyone who votes for them even once'"].

11 *Supra* n. 2.

12 Mustafa Doğan, "Turkey Child Rights Report (The "KHK" Children- The Little Victims of Turkey's State of Emergency Laws)," Crossborder Jurists Association (Sept. 2022), https://justicesquare.org/wp-content/uploads/2023/09/CBJ-TÜRKIYE-CHILD-RIGHTS-REPORT.pdf.

Chapter 11

Wholesale Undoing of Legal Rights

Immunity for Unlawful and Inhumane Practices

During the state of emergency, those who conducted operations against Hizmet executed unlawful orders, engaged in torture, mistreatment, and degrading actions, and acted inhumanely. The emergency decrees shielded them from repercussions. Subsequently, this immunity was extended to civilians.

State of emergency decrees, also known as decrees having the force of law, are issued by the Council of Ministers, chaired by the President, and are not subject to review by the Constitutional Court. Many of the decrees were consequential and dramatically altered Türkiye's legal landscape. The decrees on immunity are an example.

Under Decrees 667 and 668 (27 July 27, 2016), officials who made decisions and took actions consistent with their duties during the state of emergency were absolved of legal, administrative, financial, and penal repercussions. Subsequent parliamentary legislation confirmed similar immunity provisions.

While Decree 667 bestowed immunity solely regarding "duties," Decree 668 granted immunity to any official's "actions" during this period. This was to protect those who engaged in torture, mistreatment, and inhumane acts, as well as officials who added individuals to expulsion lists without reasonable cause. This latter provision protected officials who added people to the purge lists for personally malicious reasons, even if doing so unjustly deprived someone of their livelihood. The fact that this immunity shield was provided indicates that malevolently adding people to the purge lists was not an uncommon practice, which is the case.

Similarly, Article 52 of Decree 690 absolved members of the Inquiry Commission on State of Emergency Measures of all liability related to their decisions and actions within the scope of their duties. This provision aimed to protect commission members who made discretionary decisions aligned with the will of the Erdoğan regime but not aligned with the standards of legality or justice. There was no other purpose behind providing immunity to a commission established to address injustices. Nor was there any review of its manifestly unjust decisions. The commission was a travesty.

As if this was not enough, Article 121 of Decree 696 accorded immunity to civilians intervening in the events surrounding the attempted coup. This raises a serious question. If people took to the streets for legitimate self-defense and to oppose the coup, why did they need this protective shield? This decree aimed at protecting armed individuals who, on the night of the coup, slaughtered and lynched surrendered military cadets and soldiers who were not involved in the coup attempt.

These armed civilians, whose rapid deployment and access to heavy weaponry remain shrouded in mystery, are considered elements of illegal paramilitary groups. It is also believed that the unregistered firearms distributed on the night of July 15 were allocated to these groups.[1] This remains shrouded in mystery because the conclusions of the parliamentary investigation of the coup attempt were never made public, and the unreleased report has disappeared.

The Venice Commission expressed concerns regarding the decrees that exempted state institutions and officials from accountability for their actions during the state of emergency. For the commission, these provisions sent a dangerous message of criminal immunity. The decrees directly permitted or commanded actions that, under the Turkish Penal Code, could be considered "crimes," or, at the very least, ensured that those committing crimes while fulfilling their duties would not be held accountable.[2]

Public prosecutors have cited these overarching immunity provisions as grounds for dismissing investigations into torture, assault, mistreatment, and similar claims against both public officials and civilians committed within the framework of hate policies. The was no accountability for lawlessness.

Special Laws for Hizmet: Investigation and Prosecution Procedures

In the immediate aftermath of the fizzled coup attempt, the Erdoğan regime moved swiftly to revamp provisions of the country's criminal procedure laws that hindered it from achieving its desired outcome of rapidly eradicating Hizmet. Decrees 667 and 668 introduced new "Investigation and Prosecution Procedures" tailored to suppressing Hizmet.[3]

The fundamental principle in a state governed by the rule of law is to protect citizens with objective and general rules. The principle of the generality of laws requires that laws be designed to apply to incidents and individuals in identical circumstances. Any rule established solely for private interests or to benefit or target specific individuals or a group and devoid of public interest contradicts the principle of the rule of law, as previous decisions of the Turkish Constitutional Court explicitly recognized and emphasized before coming under Erdoğan's sway.

Laws should be of a general nature, foreseeing objective legal situations for everyone in the same legal circumstances, without discrimination or targeting someone specifically. Nor may laws target people or groups because of their political or social inclinations or lack thereof. Law may only penalize a person's direct breach of the social order. The state of emergency decrees in Türkiye targeting pre-identified individuals and affinity groups contravene the universal legal principles of the generality of laws and equality before the law. Rather, they sketched a detailed roadmap for applying hostile law to Hizmet.

Enemy Criminal Law Regulations

The Erdoğan regime's legal approach against Hizmet meets the definition of an "enemy criminal law," proposed by German criminal law expert Professor Günther Jacobs. This legal framework does not recognize targeted individuals or groups as "citizens" with fundamental rights.

Instead, this framework regards them as "enemies" to be suppressed or eliminated, stripping them of their rights within the sphere of criminal law. Enemy criminal law lacks legitimacy because it is at odds with fundamental human rights and universal legal principles. It is an inherent form of discrimination and goes hand-in-hand with a politicide agenda.

Countries that adopt enemy criminal law find their legal systems gradually eroding over time, shifting from the understanding of the rule of law to accepting the supremacy of power of the regime. In implementing its brand of enemy criminal law through state of emergency decrees, the Erdoğan government does not regard individuals associated with Hizmet as "citizens" entitled to the basic rights enjoined by the citizenry at large. Instead, it treats them as "enemies" to be oppressed or eradicated.

Because the Turkish Constitution prohibits imposing the death sentence as the ultimate penalty, the Erdoğan regime devised an alternative aggressive and ruthless enforcement process to target Hizmet people illegally and achieve their politicide.

Prejudicial Revisions to the Code of Criminal Procedure

The Turkish Constitution's state of emergency provision neither anticipates nor supports wholesale revamping of statutory law during a state of emergency, which, by definition, is to be short, temporary, and protective of the status quo with measures limited by necessity and proportionality. The goal is immediate return to status quo. Any other path is contrary to the constitutional purpose of a state of emergency.

Nevertheless, the Erdoğan agenda was to radically revamp Turkish criminal law protections and drastically lessen them for citizens, on the one hand, and to augment the power of the state, on the other.

In short, Erdoğan set out to, and did, change the balance of power that the Code of Criminal Procedure (CMK) strove to achieve between the state and the people and to tip that scale in the government's favor. "Tip" might be an understatement; it is more like using the regime's thumb to push down the balance of justice against the people in civil society. And, of course, he did this behind the noxious and stinging smokescreen of hate speech.

Decrees 667 and 668 introduced provisions to facilitate the prosecution and persecution of Hizmet and, in the process, nullified existing protections and hampered or eliminated everyone's most basic rights in a criminal justice context. Rather than being necessary and proportionate measures demanded by the state of emergency, these decrees retracted, restricted, and narrowed the people's fundamental rights and freedoms. These changes did not just affect Hizmet, but they curtailed the rights of everyone in the country.

The supine judiciary, already refashioned in Erdoğan's image and no longer an independent equal branch of government, sanctioned this comprehensive implementation of hostile law, which although allegedly geared to suppress Hizmet, likewise was intended to encompass any individual or group that lifted a finger of opposition against the regime's excesses, misdirection, or corruption.

These actions, undermining fundamental principles such as the right to a fair trial, the presumption of innocence and benefit of doubt for the accused, protection against retroactive criminality and punishment, legal certainty, and access to counsel are products of a discriminatory state policy executed to eradicate Hizmet, but detrimentally impacting everyone.

Article 2 of Decrees 667 and 668 explicitly and exclusively address measures related to the "Fethullahist Terrorist Organization (FETÖ/PDY)." Considering the potential international negative repercussions from such biased provisions, Decree 689 amended Decree 670, adding "or other terrorist organizations" following the phrase "Fethullahist Terrorist organization (FETÖ/PDY)."

Consequently, these provisions, openly discriminatory and targeting Hizmet, were updated, legalizing sanctions imposed on all opposition figures and groups retroactively, to soften the rancor of international public opinion and human rights organizations. Although the government was trying to signal that its operations were not solely directed at Hizmet, there was no hiding the amendment's potential of ensnaring even more regime opponents within its net. It was a win-win for the regime's capriciousness.

Laws Changed by State of Emergency Decrees

One of the government's most draconian steps was to stage-manage emergency decrees to make dramatic changes to the Code of Criminal Procedure, forty-one new provisions altogether. Those forty-one amendments radically tipped the "balance of justice" against accused persons then and, in the future, thus enhancing government power. They tied the accused's hands behind their back, figuratively speaking.

These provisions abolished guarantees previously granted to suspects and defendants under the Code of Criminal Procedure. Crucial requirements of the right to a fair trial, particularly the right to a defense, were unabashedly contrary to Article 6 of the European Convention on Human Rights. Those provisions were strengthened and codified in 2004 as Türkiye was trying to come more in sync with Europe's system of rights and move toward EU admission.

The regime finessed the smoke screen of a national emergency to permanently strip away citizens' rights and enhance government power. The regime cynically manipulated the anti-Hizmet hate campaign to camouflage its sinister agenda that it would never have been able to accomplish in "non-emergency" times. It was reversing individuals' rights that had come into being during the time of Türkiye's European Union accession aspirations.

The government's objective was to ensure continuation of discriminatory and unfair practices regarding investigations and prosecutions after the state of emergency concluded. This was a stunning regression of civil liberties and a far distance from other countries' practices under the European Convention on Human Rights.

The fundamental investigation and prosecution protections that had remained in effect since the coups of the 1960s and 1980s and which were not to be annulled were overridden by the state of emergency decrees. Specific investigative and prosecutorial provisions targeting Hizmet became part of, and perverted, the legal system.

Türkiye, even in its struggle against various armed groups such as the Kurdistan Workers' Party (PKK) and Hezbollah, had never implemented such procedures. While there certainly were shortcomings and breaches of the law, the government conducted operations against those armed groups within the framework of the law. Erdoğan's decision to obliterate Hizmet created a process guided not by laws but by the government's machinations, sanctioned by judicial bodies that the regime had restructured to do its will.

The following summary list describes some of the drastic alterations of the Code of Criminal Procedure, which the government used against Hizmet and anyone opposing it and which it will use in the years to come against anyone whom the regime targets for political reasons. This was a carefully planned strategy to tip the balance of government power against people's rights.

Decrees No. 667 and No. 668 made the following changes to Turkish criminal law procedures during the two-year state of emergency. Most of the regulations mentioned here were enacted into law by parliament, sometimes with modification.[4]

- Detention periods were extended from five to thirty days.
- Prosecutors were empowered to issue arrest warrants on their own without court approval.
- Requests for release were decided based on case files, alongside the review of detention, in periods of no more than thirty days.
- Searches of residences, workplaces, and non-public areas were authorized with a written order from the prosecutor without court approval. (Military premises can still be searched after the state of emergency by order of the prosecutor.)
- The seizure of assets was allowed without prior obtaining reports on the value of assets from institutions, such as the Banking Regulation and Supervision Agency, the Capital Markets Board, the Financial Crimes Investigation Board, the Treasury Undersecretariat, and the Public Oversight, Accounting, and Auditing Standards Authority, was allowed, as stipulated in Article 128 of Law No. 5271. Maintaining photos of the confiscated property was not required.
- Searches and seizures of lawyers' offices were authorized based on the written order of the prosecutor or, in urgent cases, by law enforcement officers without the prosecutor's authority. Judicial procedure or order was no longer required.
- Regarding searches of computers and digital material, imaging was no longer required before seizing the hard drive. Nor was any prior judicial procedure required. (A modified version of this with judicial

oversight was passed by parliament that is applicable after the state of emergency.)

- A suspect's right to meet with their counsel was restricted for up to five days upon the prosecutor's decision. (Even after the restriction period returned to twenty-four hours after the state of emergency, some jurisdictions still apply the five-day restriction.)
- Recordings between individuals and their counsel in prison in front of staff were allowed. (This has become permitted by law, even after the state of emergency.)
- The prosecutor could request the peace criminal judge to prohibit any specific lawyer from assuming the role of defense counsel in a case if the lawyer was being investigated for being a member of a terrorist organization. That effectively narrowed representation by attorneys who were under investigation for Hizmet affiliation or whom the prosecutor suddenly decided should be under investigation to make the defendant's case more difficult.
- Suspects were limited to up to three lawyers during investigations, interrogations, or trials. (Parliament passed this into law and is still applicable.)
- Prosecutors could summarize the indictment (formal accusation) instead of reading it aloud in court. (The Constitutional Court overturned this provision and required that the indictment be read in open court.)
- People could be arrested, their assets seized, their homes searched, their phones tapped, and be physically monitored if there is suspicion they will flee.

Limiting Attorneys Representing Organizations

One major change was to choke off effective defense rights and defense assistance. For instance, as to investigations and prosecutions regarding organizational activities, the new code provision limited the number of attorneys representing organizations who could be present during trials to three.[5] Parliament passed this into law.

Organizational trials are extremely complex, and it would not be unusual to involve a team of more than three defense lawyers. Notably, there is no such restriction on the size of the prosecution teams. By limiting the number of attorneys, the government impedes comprehensive trial preparation and presentation, makes it more ineffective, and thus has a better chance of prevailing on the terms it wants.

This was an important amendment because the government was seizing so many Hizmet-related organizations (schools, media, and the like) and summarily confiscating assets. This is not an effort at fairness or justice, but a crass play to empower the state against individuals and associations it seeks to prosecute.

Undermining Individuals' Legal Representation

Another revision (Article 216, Turkish Code of Criminal Procedure) stipulated that, in cases where the law recognizes mandatory legal representation, "if the defender [attorney] leaves the hearing without a legitimate excuse or fails to appear for the hearing, the hearing can proceed."[6]

This alteration allowed individuals to be tried and convicted in absentia without the court having to hear their defense. The result is hardly a fair trial.

This aimed to eliminate the necessity of lawyers' presence at hearings, a subterfuge to undercut attorney representation. It invested judges with enormous discretion, easily abused, to decide when and how to hold a hearing without a lawyer present. The purpose of criminal procedure law is to narrow the state's discretion, not expand it, to minimize injustice. Türkiye turned around and went in the opposite direction with the expected consequences.

Another provision (Article 148) specified that "the absence of the mandatory defender at the time of the verdict will not impede the pronouncement of the verdict." Eliminating the requirement for defense counsel's presence at pronouncement of the verdict also places defendants at a disadvantage in effectively utilizing their right to appeal.

Restricting Access to the Prosecutor's File

One of the most important aspects of criminal defense is knowing what kind of evidence is in a prosecutor's files. This is imperative for preparing to properly represent a defendant. An emergency decree allowed prosecutors to impose restrictions on an attorney's ability to review case files before trial and make copies of documents in the prosecutor's file, if not imposing the restriction could endanger the criminal investigation.[7]

This reversed the standard practice and undermined the accused's rights. It is absurd. What prosecutor would not like to restrict a defense attorney's access to the government's files? The real agenda was to prevent the defense from obtaining the "evidence" that MİT (National Intelligence Organization) submitted to the court because they knew such evidence, typically surreptitiously collected, would never stand scrutiny in a proper evidentiary proceeding held before trial.

Access to case file contents and evidence is crucial for the defense attorney, especially in challenging alleged protective security measures and preparing appeals. Access to the file might also reveal evidence favorable to the accused that the prosecutor would not want to divulge in case it jeopardized the prosecution.

Some necessary security measures may be restrictive of certain fundamental rights and freedoms of the individual to ensure that criminal proceedings are conducted safely, but those are to be the rare exception, not the general rule.

Even worse, originally the prosecutor had to have a criminal peace judge impose the restrictions on defense counsel. The change allowed the prosecutor to do it with a judge's authorization.[8] This rule had no purpose other than to make it impossible or unlikely that defense counsel could effectively challenge baseless arrests and charges. The law was modified after the state of emergency so that again only a judge can restrict access to the prosecutor's file.

Fugitives and Living in Foreign Countries

Although the criminal procedure code already had provisions for declaring individuals "fugitives," they were complex and lengthy. Decree 668 created a group fugitive status that applied to anyone associated with Hizmet, enacting a streamlined government "branding" operation.

Additionally, Decree 680 allows for Turkish citizens under investigation or prosecution who reside in foreign countries to be stripped of their citizenship if they did not return to Türkiye within three months following a "Return Home" notice published in the government's Official Gazette.

Well-founded fear of unwarranted apprehension and detention if they did return to Türkiye led to many people losing their citizenship rights (such as voting, among others). Hizmet people were caught in a Catch-22 deprivation of their fundamental rights. Parliament has since made this law.

Objecting to Release from Detention

Decree 696, amending the Code of Criminal Procedure, stipulated that objections could be raised against all decisions regarding the release of suspects or defendants from detention. The amendment granted the prosecutor the authority, which was previously lacking, to object to court decisions ordering the release of suspects or defendants, making release more problematic, whether on bond or after acquittal.

It was essentially an immediate collateral appeal from an acquittal. Prosecutors typically opposed release decisions in trials related to Hizmet. The practice was commonplace and kept people incarcerated who should have been released. It was a form of double jeopardy.

An illustrative example involved the trial of a former Brigadier General, who was dismissed from the Armed Forces and sentenced to aggravated life imprisonment for alleged involvement in the coup attempt. The Court of Cassation (appeals) acquitted him and ordered his release in January 2020. Following fierce criticism from Erdoğan, the prosecutor hastily objected to the release decision, ensuring his re-arrest and reassignment to judges in another region for trial, not those who acquitted him.[9] The judges who acquitted him were assigned to different provinces; they were punished in other words.

Blocking Injunctions (Suspensions)

Decree 667, Article 10 and Decree 668, Article 38 prohibited judicial suspensions (like injunctions) in cases brought due to decisions and actions taken by officials within the scope of emergency decrees, even where such decisions and actions were blatantly against the law.

Consequently, administrative courts were prevented from issuing judicial suspensions against actions taken by the government, even if those actions were patently unlawful. This, in turn, made the judicial review of the regime problematic, if even possible. Credit to the attorneys who did their best against such odds.

Denying Due Process to Judges

Two of the professional groups experiencing the highest rates of arrest, judges and prosecutors, were unconstitutionally assigned to specially chosen courts for trial by state of emergency decrees, contrary to the principle of the natural judge (a fair, independent trial and appellate tribunal). ECHR Article 6.1 ("Right to a fair trial"): "everyone is entitled to a fair and public hearing within a reasonable time by an independent and impartial tribunal established by law." Specially chosen judges by HSK at this time in the country's history will hardly be fair and impartial.

International Response

The Council of Europe's 2016 Türkiye Report[10] criticized the extension of detention periods for specific crimes without bringing the suspect before a judge, contrary to ECtHR precedent, and highlighted severe human rights violations, including widespread allegations of torture and ill-treatment during extensive detentions and arrests following the coup attempt, which, without concrete evidence, was ascribed to Hizmet.

The report expressed concerns about the vague criteria and weak evidence used to establish links to Hizmet, creating a perception of "aiding and abetting" crime, lack of transparency in determining association with Hizmet, and emphasized the substantial risks of discriminatory justice and political interference in cases despite clear constitutional and legislative provisions.[11]

The report also emphasized the insufficient implementation of the principle of non-discrimination in the legal and practical framework and remaining serious concerns regarding human rights violations.[12]

The suspension of important procedural safeguards during the state of emergency gave rise to serious concerns: an independent judiciary needed to conduct lawful examinations of accusations of abuse of power or criminal allegations, including procedural guarantees, particularly the presumption of innocence, the principle of individual criminal responsibility, legal certainty, the right to defense, the right to a fair trial, equality of arms (balanced procedural rights), and the right to appeal, along with transparent procedures based on evidence.[13]

The Turkish government abrogated these fundamental rights against Hizmet members and those allegedly associated with them.

These violations served as part and parcel of the comprehensive and systematic discriminatory practices pursued to eradicate Hizmet.

The government at the same time intended to, and did, weaken the rights of all citizens. It was a double axe blow—a simultaneous action against Hizmet and tilting the criminal justice system in the government's favor. Hizmet was made the "fall guy" to blanket over the regime's system-rigging.

Endnotes

1 Müyesser Yıldız, "İşte 15 Temmuz'un kayıp silahları," ODATV (19 January 2021), https://www.odatv.com/yazarlar/muyesser-yildiz/iste-15-temmuzun-kayip-silahlari-200442 ["Here are the lost weapons of July 15"].

2 "Critics Say Turkey's New Emergency Decree Could Incite Vigilante Groups," Voice of America (December 25, 2017), https://www.voanews.com/a/critics-say-turkish-new-emergency-decree-could-incite-vigilante-groups/4178637.html. *See also* "Turkey: Opinion on Emergency Decree Laws Nos. 667-676 Adopted Following the Failed Coup of July 15, 2016," European Commission for Democracy Through Law (Venice Commission) (9-10 Dec. 2016), https://www.venice.coe.int/webforms/documents/default.aspx?pdffile=CDL-AD(2016)037-e.

3 "Olağanüstü Hal Uygulamalari," İnsan Hakları Ortak Platformu (23 February 2017), https://www.ihop.org.tr/wp-content/uploads/2017/02/OHAL-%C5%9Eubat2017-raporu.pdf ["State of Emergency Applications"], pp.10-12.

4 During the state of emergency, thirty-two decrees were issued based on the authorisation granted by Article 121 of the Constitution, and the state of emergency commission convened in only one of the thirty-two decrees. Thirty-one decrees were not discussed and were sent directly to the parliament. Five of the twelve decrees issued in 2016 (Nos. 667, 668, 669, 671, and 674) were discussed and enacted into law in 2016, three months after they were published in the Official Gazette. The other seven decrees (Nos. 670, 672, 673, 675, 676, 677, and 678) were discussed and enacted in 2018, fourteen to sixteen months after being published in the Official Gazette. The eighteen decrees issued in 2017 (Nos. 679-696) were discussed and enacted by parliament in 2018, thirteen months after being published in the Official Gazette. Most of the state of emergency decrees mentioned here were enacted into law. Apparently, there was not much parliamentary scrutiny. The decrees were effective immediately.

5 Article 1, Decree No. 676 (4/12/2004), amending Code of Criminal Procedure (CMK) Article 149.2.

6 Article 5, Decree No. 676, appended to the Code of Criminal Procedure.

7 Article 3.1, Decree No. 668.

8 Decree No. 668, CMK Article 153.2.

9 "Eski Korgeneral İyidil'e beraate HSK'dan müdahale," Sabah (16.1.2020), https://www.sabah.com.tr/gundem/2020/01/16/eski-korgeneral-iyidile-beraate-hsk-dan-mudahale ["Acquittal of Former Major General İyidil by Intervention of the Supreme Council of Judges and Prosecutors (HSK)"].

10 "Commission Staff Working Document, Turkey 2016 Report, Accompanying the document Communication from the Commission to the European Parliament, the Council, the European Economic and Social Committee and the Committee of the Regions," European Commission, Brussels (9.11.2016), https://neighbourhood-enlargement.ec.europa.eu/document/download/e703a769-bf7f-46d1-8a13-6a836683e838_en?filename=20161109_report_turkey.pdf.

11 *Id.* p.17.

12 *Id.* p.24.

13 *Id.* p.25.

Chapter 12

Abductions and Violence in Foreign Lands

Türkiye has a history of the government kidnapping political opponents. It stopped in 1999 when the country had European Union aspirations. Since the failed coup, however, history is repeating itself. At least sixteen domestic abductions are known to have taken place, mostly of Gülen Movement followers, as of 2018,[1] but also Kurdistan Workers' Party (PKK) supporters.

Pursuit by Erdoğan: Renditions and Kidnappings in Other Countries

Government kidnapping, however, after the coup attempt, went one step further and expanded outside Türkiye's borders, and rapidly accelerated. Indeed, Erdoğan, in an October 2017 address to AKP members, publicly proclaimed his intent to "hunt down" every Hizmet person abroad whom he labeled as a member of a "traitors' front": "Neither in the East nor in the West is a single member of this organization comfortable as before, nor will they be."[2]

The United Nations Committee Against Torture, which has heard and decided cases in this regard, takes the position that Türkiye's abductions, renditions, and kidnappings in other countries violate Article 3 of the European Convention on Human Rights, prohibiting torture, inhuman, or degrading treatment or punishment.[3]

Reports put the number at least 144 individuals as of 2023 whom Türkiye extrajudicially abducted from other countries or within Türkiye, subjecting them to torture and ill-treatment in prisons and secret locations, with their whereabouts unknown for months.[4] This goes hand in glove with Erdoğan's politicide agenda.

According to official statements by its interior ministry, Turkey has sent 800 extradition requests to 105 countries since the coup attempt, and more than 110 alleged members of the movement have been brought back to Türkiye, one way or the other, as part of the government's global campaign.

Türkiye's transnational repression is standard authoritarian practice to silence political dissent abroad. Autocratic leaders tend to engage in extraterritorial repression after they have contained domestic opposition and gained effective control over the media. They then go after their opponents abroad whom they increasingly view as a threat. This describes Erdoğan, although part of his motivation is punitive retribution, borne out of personal hatred and spite for the Gülen Movement.

The regime has pursued the forcible returns of individuals in at least thirty-one countries in the Americas, Europe, the Middle East, Africa, and Asia. Most people were involved in Hizmet schools or development projects in that country long before the attempted coup rupture. The campaign relies heavily on renditions, whereby Türkiye and its intelligence agency (MİT) covertly persuade another country to hand over persons without judicial process or "with a slight fig leaf of legality."[5]

The United Nations Working Group on Enforced or Involuntary Disappearances has issued three reports on what its second report calls the "systematic practice of State-sponsored extraterritorial abductions and forced returns of Turkish nationals from numerous States to Turkey."[6]

Freedom House cataloged fifty-eight renditions between 2014-2021, which it believed was an undercount.[7] Since 2016, at least 110 individuals, most accused of having Hizmet ties, have been forcefully brought back to Türkiye from at least seventeen countries, including Azerbaijan, Gabon, Kenya, Kosovo, Kyrgyzstan, Malaysia, Moldova, Myanmar, Pakistan, and Saudi Arabia. *The Washington Post* puts the number at more than 118 MİT-orchestrated "renditions," naming MİT as "one of the most aggressive practitioners" of extra-legal operations.[8]

Most abductions have been in Africa and the Balkans. A political crisis erupted in Kosovo after six Turkish nationals were captured there in 2018. Kosovo's interior minister and intelligence chief were both sacked as a result.[9] Türkiye abducted Fethullah Gülen's nephew Selahaddin Gülen in May 2021 when he went to Kenya to marry. He was teaching in the United

States. His capture is described in the subsequent chapter about the Gülen family.

A Hizmet Pak Turk Schools leader, Mesut Kaçmaz, his wife, and their daughters were caught up in a harrowing and chilling tale of cruelty in September 2017. They were abducted from their home in Lahore at midnight (a MİT agent supervised a dozen Pakistani police) and held for seventeen days in a secret location. They were then put on a private aircraft for Türkiye. He was tortured on the plane, and his wife and daughters threatened with rape. He eventually served eleven months in prison; and his wife, more than six months. After his release from prison, they were able to flee the country.[10]

The Kaçmaz saga of tribulation was not unique; but, as four United Nations rapporteurs reported, it followed the standard script of Türkiye's practice of abducting dissidents abroad.[11] Several extra-territorial abductions resulted in forcible disappearances. Victims were tortured and disappeared upon their return to Türkiye.[12] A weak international response has emboldened the Turkish government to kidnap its "enemies" abroad without little pushback by other governments against its covert operations.

A 2018 plot to abduct a businessman in Switzerland was foiled, even though Western democratic nations are considered safe havens for Turkish political exiles. The Freedom House report described Türkiye's "campaign of transnational repression" as "remarkable for its intensity, its geographic reach, and the suddenness with which it escalated."[13]

Nor has Erdoğan tried to hide the kidnapping operation. He bragged about it in a speech after the abduction of six teachers from Kosovo in March 2018, "Wherever they may go, we will wrap them up and bring them here."[14] The government has not denied reports, including an inquiry from the United Nations, that it has abducted more than one hundred people.

So great is Erdoğan's antipathy toward the Gülen Movement that he has traveled personally to other countries to convince (or bully) them to shut down Hizmet schools and projects, to the harm of children and young people in those countries who benefited from the schools and local persons employed by them. If he can go one step further and have Hizmet folks yanked back to Türkiye, he will make that play, as he did in Pakistan. It is difficult to get a grip on the depth of his callousness toward others' well-being.

Besides its extrajudicial violations, Türkiye also has gained unfavorable notoriety for manipulating Interpol's Red Notice mechanism to ask other countries to honor its criminal warrants for a list of a thousand Hizmet folks, to arrest and deport them to Türkiye. It has become an international conundrum on how to limit Türkiye's Interpol usage so that it cannot be manipulated as a tool of political oppression.[15]

Interpol facilitates worldwide crime control. It is the globe's largest international police organization with 196 member countries. Interpol is dedicated to fighting crime, not expediting political persecution, and struggles to navigate that boundary with Türkiye's government.

Renditions were still going on in late 2024, even of people under United Nations protection.[16] Extraterritorial abductions and renditions of Turkish dissidents abroad take a heavy toll on the victims and the diaspora populations in general. Besides illegally depriving the victims of their fundamental rights to life, liberty, due process, and security, these extrajudicial activities spread fear and mistrust within the diaspora. Creating an atmosphere of apprehension within Turkish foreign communities is a cynical tool to deter those who fled Türkiye from criticizing the regime.

One last note. For Turkish Hizmet refugees in North American and European countries whose governments protect them from summary extradition, the regime implemented a different punitive form of transnational repression: freezing their assets in Türkiye and making them inaccessible under the non-credible pretext of preventing terrorist financing.[17] This was not only for personal retaliation but also to blunt international reproach of Erdoğan by Turks forced into exile. Those allied with the Kurdish rights movement and political leftists were also victims.

Final Comment

If there was ever even the slightest doubt as to Erdoğan's politicide agenda, his pursuit of Hizmet people in other lands and kidnapping them while deliberately avoiding due process and international law should tamp that down. He was ruthless to Hizmet people inside Türkiye and outside and continues to be so.

Endnotes

1 Rachel Goldberg, "Kidnapped, Escaped, and Survived to Tell the Tale: How Erdoğan's Regime Tried to Make Us Disappear," Haaretz (Dec 11, 2018), Kidnapped, Escaped, and Survived to Tell the Tale: How Erdoğan's Regime Tried to Make Us Disappear - Turkey - Haaretz.com.

2 Nate Schenkkan, "The Remarkable Scale of Turkey's 'Global Purge': How It Became a Threat to the Rule of Law Everywhere," Foreign Affairs (Jan. 29, 2018), How Turkey's Crackdown on Gulenists Threatens the Rule of Law Abroad | Foreign Affairs.

3 *See* decisions by the United Nations Committee against Torture: *Turhan v. Sweden* (CAT 1109/2021); *A and B v. Azerbaijan* (CAT 2018;18); *X and Y v. Switzerland* (CAT 1081/2021); *Ferhat Recep Tayyip Erdoğan v. Morocco* (CAT 827/2018); Mustafa Onder *v. Morocco* (CAT 845/2018); *Elmas Ayden v. Morocco* (CAT 846/2017); and *Ismet Bakay v. Morocco*, (CAT 826/2017).

4 "'Global purge': 144 abductions conducted by the Turkish government in Turkey and abroad," Advocates of Silenced Turkey (June 23, 2021), https://silencedTürkiye.org/global-purge-1-144-abductions-conducted-by-the-turkish-government-in-Türkiye-and-abroad. *See also* "Beyond Turkey's Borders: Unveiling Global Purge, Transnational Repression, Abductions," Advocates of Silenced Turkey (May 26, 2023), https://silencedTürkiye.org/beyond-Türkiyes-borders-unveiling-global-purge-transnational-repression-abductions; *and see* "Erdoğan's Long Arms: Abductions in Turkey and Abroad," Advocates of Silenced Türkiye (Sept. 8, 2020), https://silencedTürkiye.org/Erdoğans-long-arms-abductions-in-Türkiye-and-abroad.

5 *Id. See also* "Türkiye's Transnational Repression: Abduction, Rendition and Forcible Return of Erdoğan Critics," Stockholm Center for Freedom (Oct. 21, 2021), Türkiye's Transnational Repression: Abduction, Rendition and Forcible Return of Erdoğan Critics - Stockholm Center for Freedom (stockholmcf.org).

6 United Nations Working Group on Enforced or Involuntary Disappearances: A/HRC/42/40, para. 56 (July 2019); AL/TUR 5/2020 (May 2020); A/HRC/51/31, para. 78 (Sept. 2022). The second report: "To date, at least 100 individuals suspected of involvement with the Gülen/Hizmet movement are reported to have been subjected to arbitrary arrests and detention, enforced disappearance and torture, as part of covert operations reportedly organised or abetted by the Government of Turkey in coordination with authorities of several States." The third report notes that Turkey's pretext for such "transfers" is that it is "an effective means to combat terrorism."

7 "Turkey: Transnational Repression: Origin Country Case Study," Freedom House (2021), https://freedomhouse.org/report/transnational-repression/turkey.

8 Greg Miller, "Turkey exploits post-9/11 counterterrorism model to target critics in exile," *Washington Post* (Dec. 15, 2024), https://www.washingtonpost.com/world/2024/12/09/turkey-us-terrorism-war-exiles-repression/

9 "Nephew of Fethullah Gulen seized and brought back to Turkey," BBC (31 May 2021), https://www.bbc.com/news/world-europe-57304094.

10 "Kaçmaz couple abducted from Pakistan heard as witnesses at the Turkey Tribunal," PakTurkFile (21 Sept. 2021), https://pakturkfile.org/en/2021/09/21/kacmaz-couple-abducted-from-pakistan-heard-as-witnesses-at-the-turkey-tribunal/. *See also* Engin Yigit, *Dreams Interrupted: Backdrop of the PakTurk Schools Crisis in Pakistan, The Ordeals of the Turkish Teachers* (AST Publishing 2023).

11 Matthew Amlôt "Turkey signed secret agreements with countries to abduct dissi-

dents from abroad: UN," Al Arabiya English (12 July 2020), Turkey signed secret agreements with countries to abduct dissidents from abroad: UN (alarabiya.net).

12 Serdar San, "Turkish spies are abducting Erdoğan's political opponents abroad," openDemocracy (16 June 2012), https://www.opendemocracy.net/en/author/serdar-san/.

13 *Supra* n.3.

14 "Erdoğan'dan Macron'a: Haddini ve boyunu aşan beyan," Anadolu Ajansı (30.03.2018), https://www.aa.com.tr/tr/gunun-basliklari/Erdoğan-dan-macrona-haddini-ve-boyunu-asan-beyan/1103477 ["Erdoğan to Macron: A statement that goes beyond its limits and height."].

15 Sam Meacham, "Weaponizing the Police: Interpol as a Tool of Authoritarianism," Harvard International Review (11 Apr. 2022), https://hir.harvard.edu/weaponizing-the-police-authoritarian-abuse-of-interpol/. *See also* Elmas Topcu, "Turkey using Interpol to track dissidents," Deutsche Wells (11/07/2019), https://www.dw.com/en/Türkiye-using-interpol-to-track-down-dissidents/a-51159723; *and see* "Turkey's Abuse of INTERPOL: How Erdoğan Weaponized the International Criminal Police Organization for Transnational Repression," Stockholm Center for Freedom (Aug. 24, 2021), https://stockholmcf.org/turkeys-abuse-of-interpol-how-Erdoğan-weaponized-the-international-criminal-police-organization-for-transnational-repression/.

16 "Turkish citizens under UN protection feared to have been kidnapped by Turkish intelligence in Kenya," Turkish Minute (Oct. 18, 2024), https://www.turkishminute.com/2024/10/18/turkish-citizens-under-un-protection-feared-to-have-been-kidnapped-by-turkish-intelligence-in-kenya/.

17 "Türkiye's Transnational Repression: Abuse of asset freezing mechanisms under the pretext of prevention of terrorist financing," Stockholm Center for Freedom (May 13, 2023), Türkiye's Transnational Repression: Abuse of asset freezing mechanisms under the pretext of prevention of terrorist financing - Stockholm Center for Freedom (stockholmcf.org).

Chapter 13

Continuing Oppression of Hizmet

After the flopped coup, a tsunami of methodical mass detentions and arrests occurred against Hizmet and others opposed to the government's direction, which ripped away people's fundamental rights as a matter of state policy. Judicial bodies morphed into extensions of the regime and imposed severe penalties against people, attempting to legitimize the state's illegal conduct. Those detained and arrested were left to a civil death, whether in prison or outside. Politicide.

A prime tactic during this period was ginning up hate speech and crimes leading to Hizmet's marginalization and politics. The regime's drumbeat of hate found an echo in the general society.

This chapter presents an overview of the deprivation of state benefits, denial of public services, and overall discriminatory treatment. It does not intend to be comprehensive, but to point a finger at critical areas in this discussion for which the relevant studies can provide ample information. Individuals targeted by hate policies faced insults, threats, physical harm, property damage, and restrictions on their freedom in general society, including:

- Summary dismissal from employment and unlawful termination
- Denial of access to banking, health, or other public services
- Restricted access to public places of worship
- Denial of probation or parole rights despite meeting the conditions for such
- Denial of employment for those ordered to be reinstated to their positions by the inquiry review commission or court decisions,

after their original dismissal by decree, because the relevant institution refused to honor the reinstatement order

- Refusing to hire Hizmet-associated individuals
- Unjust and malicious inspections and administrative fines imposed by municipalities or other public institutions, preventing a person who is an employer or tradesman from conducting business
- Arson or vandalism of workplaces and individual property and assets
- Rejection of job applications because of the applicant's prior occupation in institutions closed by decrees, graduation from such institutions, or being personally dismissed by decree
- Confiscation of property or failure to conduct sales and transfers despite the lifting of a judicial seizure decision
- Labeling and targeting individuals in general society for their affiliation with Hizmet through derogatory names or nicknames in written, visual, and social media
- Earned pensions for resigned parliament members associated with Hizmet were not paid but were escheated to the state[1]
- Harassment and bullying, both in the workplace and in public (through mail, email, phone, messages, graffiti, and other similar actions)[2]

The following are but some examples from thousands illustrating the government's ongoing oppression of Hizmet to cause the movement's civil death. These are not isolated droplets of water but drops drawn from a torrent.

Confiscation of Passports and Collection of Personal Data

One particularly brutish Erdoğan measure, which could only be ascribed to hatred and politicide, was the Decree 667 provision that confiscated, restricted, or annulled the passports and travel documents of persons terminated from employment and those of their families. The regime's objective was punitive: to prevent those associated with the Gülen Movement from seeking refuge outside the country, curtail their ability to regroup abroad, and make it difficult to support themselves and their family at home.

Curtailing their freedom to travel or work abroad subjected thousands of professionals and terminated government workers to civil death at home where they could not make a proper living and faced daily insufferable recriminations from the general populace.[3] It made no difference to the regime that it was bound to the European Convention on Human Rights and its guarantee that people could freely emigrate as they chose.

Academics, doctors, teachers, engineers, and others, unjustly discharged from employment inside Türkiye, were denied the right to travel abroad to continue their vocational livelihoods. Even individuals without ongoing investigations or prosecutions against them had their passports canceled and faced severe hardships as a result. Those affected had no way to challenge the decision to invalidate their passport or travel document. They were denied even a semblance of due process along with other basic rights.

Erdoğan publicly disclosed, even bragged, in July 2018 that, as of then, the government had restricted the passports of 181,500 individuals.[4] Altogether, that figure has since escalated to more than 234,410 canceled passports.

This unlawful practice also had the goal of keeping those who had managed to escape from disseminating grievances abroad lest speaking out would subject family and friends to retaliation at home and prevent them from having any future chance of exiting the country, not an unlikely event, as people learned the hard way.

The regime did not care that this violated international law any more than the other violations it was perpetrating. As of 2018, more than 17,000 people had managed to escape to Europe and seek asylum. Others fled to Canada and the United States and received asylum there.

Erdoğan's totalitarian gambit also has driven young people and professionals unrelated to Hizmet out of the country, causing a "brain drain" that will damage Türkiye's economy and civil society far into the future.[5] But he cares not so long he holds power.

Escaping the Erdoğan Regime: Death in the Evros/Meriç River and Aegean Sea

The personal pressures during this period were immense and almost unimaginable. Sadly, there were suicides and deaths. People suddenly had no way to provide for their families and had to depend on the clandestine generosity of friends and relatives, who put themselves at risk of jail as collaborators just for being compassionate and even fulfilling a religious duty.

Because of the travel ban, oppression at home, and the real possibility of going to prison, many attempted to flee Türkiye through illegal routes because they had no alternative. One of the more common exit sites was the water passage to Greece. The price to hire a smuggler's flimsy ramshackle boat was high; but alternatives were sparse, if not non-existent. Dozens perished in the dark of the night in the waters of the Evros (Meriç) River and Aegean Sea, trying to escape.[6]

One tragic example of this was when Murat Akçabay, facing search warrants for alleged Hizmet affiliation, and his family attempted to flee to Greece in the middle of a July 2018 night. Their boat sank in the Meriç River. His wife and three children drowned. Despicably adding insult to this tragedy, Hilal Kaplan, a prominent media voice and hate speech espouser, tweeted that the children would have grown up anyway to become terrorists. One cannot find a cruder or crueler statement to underscore the nadir of hatred and loss of humanity in the country.

Another heart-rending tragedy involved a young judge, Fatma Işık, dismissed from her post and arrested for alleged Hizmet ties, despite her sterling reputation as impartially serving in her judicial capacity. To escape the pressures and potential re-arrest, she and her husband decided to leave for Greece. Their attempt ended disastrously when they capsized in the Aegean Sea, and their four-month-old baby and three-year-old son drowned in the cold dark water. The couple buried their young sons on the island of Chios.

Yet another tragedy was of former prosecutor İbrahim Gündüz and his wife Nurdan Şenocak Gündüz. After being summarily dismissed from his job and spending time in detention, he and his wife decided to escape. While attempting to cross the Aegean Sea toward Kos Island, their speed boat capsized near the island in early December 2021; and they both perished in the cold churning water.

Dreadful calamities like these shattered the lives of too many families, who, along with their children, embarked on such perilous journeys and risked their lives because they knew they no longer had lives worth living in their own country. Such was the ugliness of the hatred that led others to put themselves in death's way.[7]

Nor did getting to Greece's shores guarantee a safe harbor. As of January 2023, Greece had pushed back more than 35,000 people, including many accused of Hizmet affiliation.[8] That stunning figure alone offers an insight into the depth and scope of Erdoğan's push toward politicide.

Family Punishment and Retribution

Family or kin punishment is a practice by authoritarian regimes of penalizing or holding immediate family members accountable for the offenses or actions of a relative. Modern democratic societies reject the practice. Collective punishment has occurred in various forms throughout history across different societies. Its earlier appearance was as tribal or clan retributive justice. Roman law moved away from that custom to the legal principle of individual guilt and punishment rather than collective penalties. Liability for what you do, not for who you are. And no punishment for what a relative does.

Current authoritarian regimes like China, North Korea, Iran, and Venezuela practice family punishment. The Nazis were cruel practitioners of kin punishment or *Sippenhaft*. The Chinese government's persecution of Uighur Muslims entails extensive family retributions to suppress religious and ethnic identity. Other countries also stand accused of collective punishment.

Even though prohibited by Article 38 of the Turkish Constitution, the Erdoğan regime has utilized family punishment since the July 15 abortive coup as a broader scheme of "guilt by association." It has levied family punishment to extort individuals residing outside of Türkiye into returning to the country, to prevent family members of dissidents from holding public office, to suppress dissent abroad, or simply to take vengeance.[9]

The regime's family punishment has been extensive and gratuitously punitive. It has included imprisoning spouses of police chiefs involved in anti-corruption investigations of Erdoğan's government and his family, jailing the fathers of former NBA basketball star Enes Kanter Freedom and former football star Hakan Şükür, imprisoning the spouse of exiled journalist Bülent Korucu, revoking the passports of family members associated with Hizmet and dissident groups (such as the wife of exiled journalist Can Dündar, mentioned earlier, who exposed illegal arms transfers to Syria by Turkish intelligence operatives), and summarily confiscating family properties of individuals accused of "terrorism."

Branding and Segregating: Türkiye's Hate Policies and Nazi Germany

History amply demonstrates that totalitarian governments develop processes of segregating and marginalizing those in disfavor with the ruling elites. As with the Erdoğan regime, these negative processes are often incremental, step-by-step, slight in the beginning but building at an oppressive and treacherous crescendo. Once the government got its foot in the door, there was no stopping it from eventually flinging the door wide open.

Various analogs to Hizmet's situation come from Nazi Germany's racial laws that separated German Jews ("German subjects") from non-Jewish Germans ("Germanic origin"). The nationalist pretext was to protect and preserve Germans' "racial ancestry." The political reality was different. The German state, in chaos and unrest, desperately needed a scapegoat and invoked venomous racialized hate speech and crimes that became central to its intensive crusade against German Jews, stripping them of their humanity, culture, and wealth.

The 1935 Nuremberg Race Laws announced the system of segregating and marginalizing German Jews, who had assimilated into broader society and lived integrated lives. Initially, Jews had only a few rights revoked. Then followed the prohibition of marriage between Jews and Germans and laws divesting German Jews of civil rights. A 1938 law required Jews to adopt a second name, a Jewish name. Then, their identity documents and passports were collected, their "Jewish names" added, and then stamped with a bold black "J," making it impossible for them to conceal their Jewish identities in official documents.

Because the paper measures were insufficient for government purposes to publicly identify Jews, it implemented new measures to ensure immediate public identification of Jews without time-consuming paper identification checks. Thus, a law in 1941 mandated that Jews wear a yellow Star of David inscribed with "Jew" on a black background on their chests in territory under German control. The Nazis revitalized a centuries-long practice by medieval bishops and caliphs of marking Jews with an identifying badge.

This ensured the visual surveillance of German Jews in all aspects of life, making it easy to spot and humiliate them. Because of the anti-Jewish propaganda, the compulsory yellow star served both to stigmatize and debase Jews and as a tool for segregating and controlling them. People were physically abused on the spot and even subjected to torture. Although assorted colors were used in the inhumane concentration camps for other disfavored individuals and political opponents, the yellow Star of David became the symbol of the Nazi's genocidal terror.

In a somewhat similar vein and with the same purpose, the Turkish government's process of isolating and targeting Hizmet, which began with the December 2013 corruption scandal, forcibly introduced a catalog of hate speech terms into the national discourse, culminating in the widespread use of "FETÖ" ("Fethullah Terrorist Organization"), a symbolic acronym, portraying Hizmet as a terrorist organization, inimical to the homeland, and stripping Hizmet-associated individuals of their humanity. Politicide was the objective.

The Erdoğan regime and its supporting actors used "FETÖ" extensively to defame, stigmatize, denigrate, incite hostility, encourage violence against, segregate, and humiliate Hizmet members and supporters. So poisonous did they make that acronym that they gratuitously lobbed it against non-Hizmet opponents to denigrate and weaken them—a cynical "divide and conquer" tactic.

Erdoğan did try to get special jail suits for Hizmet prisoners, which would have been another form of branding. It faced a backlash and is now on hold. The effort, though, reflects his mindset.

There are also other branding and segregating parallels to the tactics of the Nazi state, as follow.

"Codes 36/37" Branding

After the coup fiasco, Erdoğan spun decrees and investigations into motion and oversaw massive summary terminations of people from their life professions because they belonged to, or had connection with, the Gülen movement. This not only suddenly ripped away their livelihood but hindered them from continuing their regular social and economic lives and ensnared them in the state's perpetual control and its surveillance web.

Türkiye's Social Security Institution (SSI), which manages a variety of workers' insurance programs, old-age benefits, and other societal projects, within two weeks of the coup debacle, implemented a branding system regarding individuals whose workplaces were closed or whom emergency decrees had dismissed from public service.[10] The new rules required inserting Codes 36 or 37 in the section of individuals' records that lists reasons for employment dismissal.

Code 36 indicated "closure of the workplace by emergency decree." Code 37 denoted "dismissed from public duty by emergency decree." This regulation, which became permanent, set up a nationwide banning mechanism and a computerized way to track Hizmet people through official records. Hizmet individuals were recipients of Code 36 and Code 37. That is the way the regime devised it.

The tagged individuals also ended up in databases of the Turkish Employment Agency (ISKUR), which further effectuated the banning scheme. That had disastrous consequences for discharged people seeking new employment, relegating them to "professional annihilation." The regime cared not at all for their families' well-being.

It was bad enough that state of emergency decrees had abruptly discharged a multitude of public servants, including teachers, police officers, judges, prosecutors, and others on mere allegations of affiliation, linkage, or connection with Hizmet. But affixing "Code 37" to their records after termination, further impeded their social and economic lives, while under the malicious watchful eye of the Erdoğan state.

This SSI banning tag was a concerted effort to exclude a specific group of people from society, Hizmet. The codes reached into every facet and sector of Turkish society and even affected people's pensions. Civil death, politicide, was the ultimate objective.

Subsequent potential employers, as might be expected, refused to employ applicants discharged by emergency decrees when faced with Codes 36 or 37 on their records. Knowing the regime's intense game plan, no employers wanted to incur its displeasure. They needed to keep their economic boat afloat without being hit by a government torpedo. Sometimes employers hired workers "under the table," but those employees had no rights or protections. It was at least something, though, with which they could feed their families.

Individuals had to accept any jobs they could find, no matter how menial, just to survive. They even looked for jobs "off the books" so the regime could not track them and disemploy them again. People who had dedicated their lives as professionals in building civil society suddenly found themselves sweeping streets, doing construction work, providing private transportation, gardening, and so on.

Here is unfortunately a not-unusual example. A.S., a police officer of twenty-three years' experience dismissed by a decree without any concrete justification, started working as a school bus driver and, after serving as a driver in Ankara for a good while, moved to Kayseri with his family. Wanting to continue the same job there, he applied for a work permit at the Kayseri Metropolitan Municipality. Despite submitting all the required documents, the municipality refused to issue an eligibility certificate, stating, "You are restricted."[11]

This analogous "Yellow Star" coding process not only deprived decent, hardworking people of the ability to sustain their livelihoods and support their families. It also wantonly and punitively wreaked severe social and psychological consequences on them and violated their right to privacy. Branding individuals and banning them had no legitimate purpose. It served only to make life miserable for them and their families, which, of course, is the government's averred objective. Hatred in action.

The nationwide government practice of profiling and tracking individuals should send up a bright warning flare into the human rights sky. The Erdoğan regime has done its utmost to subjugate Hizmet for sheer political reasons, to continue unhindered on the path to autocratic rule. Erdoğan will tread on anyone as relentlessly as necessary for his gain. The needs of the country are not before his eyes.

Another Branding Measure: Annotated Diplomas

The regime's perverse banning vengeance infected people's lives in another way. The government not only closed down Hizmet educational institutions and foundations but also penalized the students whose only goal was to improve their lives. The tactic manifested itself in the government-prescribed method of transferring the academic documents and records of graduates and students enrolled in associate and undergraduate programs of closed higher education institutions to the student's new university assigned by the Council of Higher Education.[12] This adversely affected students' ability to obtain scholarships.

Universities to which the council transferred them eventually issued diplomas to the students, but the courses that students completed at their previous universities were marked on diploma supplements and transcripts. Despite the official statement that only their previous universities would be named in transcripts without specific mention that the university had been closed, diplomas with such notations were routinely issued to students of an institution to which the council had assigned them. This same kind of profiling also occurred when temporary graduation documents were issued to students who had attended a banned educational institution.

These annotated academic documents imposed a lifetime burden on young people whose only goal was to secure an education and advance in life and had taken advantage of the Hizmet-offered opportunity. Many were poor youth or from low-income families. These marks on their diplomas encumbered their future. Prospective public and private employers will consider this record; and students who attended or graduated from a closed university have suffered, and will likely suffer, adverse employment consequences as a result.

Private Sector: Employment and Daily Life

Discrimination against Hizmet-associated individuals was state policy within public institutions. The Erdoğan regime did its best to exert sustained pressure on the private sector to adopt similar discriminatory and marginalizing policies, particularly in employment, banking, and healthcare. This book has noted assorted studies that have examined this in detail.[13] What follows is a brief summary.

The proliferation of hate speech against the Gülen Movement, legitimized within a political framework and coupled with growing societal acceptance, has propelled discrimination, harassment, threats, physical violence, and severe human rights violations since the December 2013 scandal and ramped up more fiercely after the coup attempt. It continues to this day, not only violating individuals' rights to be free from violence but also putting their lives, property, and material and psychological well-being at risk.

Adverse Financial Consequences

Again, the anecdotes in this section are by no means a complete list of financial repercussions against those associated with the Gülen Movement but only illustrative examples. Reasonably complete lists are available, and they are lengthy. Some appear or are cited here and in other sections of this book.

Seizure of Assets: $40 Billion Worth

Following the attempted coup, the government used state of emergency decrees to summarily shut down 1,748 foundations and associations, ranging from health and educational facilities to media outlets, and seized their assets, estimated in the range of $40 billion.[14]

One might wonder how much a motive for seizing this wealth played into "shutting down" the Hizmet Movement. It certainly must have been a lucrative consideration. The second matter to wonder about is where did the wealth go? How much of it made its way into private hands? Given the history of the Erdoğan government, this is hardly an unreasonable question.

Besides the seized property, bank accounts and assets of thousands of individuals connected with these institutions and entities were frozen on unsubstantiated grounds without due process, marking a violation of their property rights. Freezing an account blocks the use of its funds or assets until the government seizes the funds as proceeds of crime. There is no way to measure the total amount of those funds that the government seized from these indivduals other than note that it was stunningly substantial.

In 2021, five years later, the regime froze the financial assets of more than 1,150 people and published their names in the government's Official Gazette after amending the terrorist financing law in 2020 to make it broader and certain to reach the assets of anyone allegedly affiliated with the Hizmet Movement.[15] More wealth unjustly confiscated. The same question again: where did it end up? There are no financial accountability tally sheets. Transparency is not a hallmark of the Erdoğan regime.

As Chapter 16 more fully discusses, Article 122 of the Penal Code (under the Hatred and Discrimination subsection) does proscribe four general classes of crime committed with a hate motive. A person who obstructs the sale, transfer, lease of movable or immovable property, the utilization of certain services, employment recruitment, or ordinary economic activities of an individual due to hatred based on … political opinion, philosophical belief, religion … or sect, faces imprisonment from one to three years.[16]

Turkish officials have certainly breached Article 122 in this context; neither they nor the courts have paid deference to Article 122.

Interfering with Attorney-Client Relationship

In 2023, Levent Mazılıgüney, a well-respected Ankara attorney, received a modest fee from a client categorized as "grey" on the Ministry of Interior's "Wanted for Terrorism" list,[17] a move criticized by legal experts for Türkiye's illegal manipulation of the list against Hizmet people by labeling them as terrorists.

Grey-listing refers to a country under increased monitoring by the Financial Action Task Force, the global money laundering and terrorist financing watchdog. This was ironic since FATF in 2021 had placed Türkiye itself on its "grey list" of countries that require special scrutiny over concerns about money laundering and terrorist financing. FATF did not remove Türkiye from the list until mid-2024.

The $1,300 fee to Mazılıgüney was for legal services he rendered for a client abroad. A bank in the client's resident country transferred the money. After deducting the transfer fee, the remaining $1,268 was credited to Mazılıgüney's account at Deniz Bank. When he attempted to withdraw the funds, he discovered the bank had frozen his account. The bank's FATF unit imposed the block due to "financing terrorism."

Besides the bank violating United Nations protocols against penalizing attorneys for the clients whom they represent, the process discouraged lawyers from providing legal assistance for fear of non-payment of fees, interfering with the attorney-client relationship.[18]

Denial of Bank Accounts and Credit Card Applications

People dismissed by state of emergency decrees were automatically listed on systems accessed by banks besides government entities, which prevented them from using banks. Not only did the government arbitrarily deprive people and their families of access to their financial resources, but those whose names appeared on the published lists found no recourse from private banking institutions. Even if the banks were not swayed by the merit of the government's actions toward Hizmet dissidents, they wanted no risk.

Individuals dismissed by emergency decrees were prevented from opening accounts in state and private banks and from acquiring credit cards.[19] Others faced negative credit scores and found that, as an alleged "terrorist" or "terrorism financier," the regime had shared their personal information with international financial risk intelligence databases used by financial institutions in breach of data protection laws and standards, which made their lives even more difficult. Those machinations prevented them from opening bank accounts, obtaining credit cards, and taking out loans.

A concrete example. When the regime shuttered a nonprofit association in Diyarbakır for alleged Hizmet connections, one of its directors faced charges of "membership in a terrorist organization." The court found her guilty, but suspended her sentence, conditioned on no criminal activity for five years. She then went to work at a private company. Her employer required her to open a salary account at Türkiye İş Bankası. However, the bank denied the application because of the closure of the organization where she had held a position. She was on the "restricted list." She had to have the account because her employer required it, and she needed the job since the 2023 Maraş earthquake had badly damaged her home. After intense negotiation, the bank agreed to cash her paychecks but not give her access to an account.[20]

Exclusion from Tax Amnesty Arrangements

In 2023, Türkiye passed a tax amnesty and restructuring law but excluded individuals under investigation or prosecution for their Hizmet affiliation.[21] People who owed back taxes, administrative fines, student loans, traffic fines, or social security premiums before December 31, 2022, could pay off the amount due in forty-eight equal instalments.

The Hizmet exclusion, which affected tens of thousands of people deprived them and their families of tax benefits under a measure benefiting all of society and hurt those who had lost employment under Erdoğan's decrees. This is yet another example of Hizmet's continued marginalization and Erdoğan's persistent oppression six years after the coup debacle, designed to financially harm people. It is another of his orchestrated pivots rewarding people who support him and punishing those who do not.

Private and Public Services: Discrimination and Denial of Access

Individuals employed by institutions closed by state of emergency decrees or dismissed because of Hizmet connections have faced discrimination such as prosecutorial restrictions, Social Security codes, and "restricted identity numbers." Being on a restricted list prevents people from accessing private and public services. The banned individuals are identified by their marked or branded identity cards.

Government Retaliation Against Earthquake Survivors

—Earthquake Survivor Not Admitted to Temporary Dormitory

Well-documented cases arose from the regime's denial of assistance to Hizmet-associated people affected by the major earthquake that struck on February 6, 2023, in Kahramanmaraş. The following are typical and not stand-alone events.

The family home of a teacher dismissed from work by decree, underwent severe damage from the earthquake and was uninhabitable. Needing shelter, he and his family applied for accommodation at government-run dormitories (Kredi ve Yurtlar Kurumu, or KYK) that normally serve college students, but then temporarily opened to earthquake victims. After attempting to settle in dormitories in Kırıkkale, then being redirected to Sivas and Konya due to full occupancy, they tried to stay in the Sultan İkinci Kılıçarslan dormitory in Niğde, not far from their home.[22]

Before traveling to Niğde, the former teacher contacted dormitory management and was informed that space was available for his family. Upon arrival and after having communicated with dorm personnel throughout the day and completed registration procedures, he and his family underwent police record checks and were denied entry. Dorm officials cited the reason for denial was that the teacher was laid off by an emergency decree.

Despite being earthquake victims and homeless, the family was refused shelter. The ugly face of hatred revealed its merciless side even toward families who lost everything in a natural calamity.

—Scholarships Denied to Earthquake Survivors Dismissed by Emergency Decree

Following the earthquake, TÜBİTAK, the Scientific and Technological Research Council of Türkiye, announced its intention to provide scholarships to college students in the earthquake-affected region. TÜBİTAK is the country's leading agency for funding and conducting research. However, it barred individuals dismissed by emergency decrees from the scholarships.

—Bank Loan Rejection for Earthquake Victims

Also, after the Kahramanmaraş earthquake, former Prosecutor Vedat Demir, who had to relocate from Hatay to Ankara with his family, applied for a bank loan for earthquake victims at the Türkiye Vakıflar Bank Ankara College Branch. However, the bank rejected his loan application, citing his spouse's dismissal by emergency decree as the reason.

Denying Individuals Medical and Social Services

One of the most heartless implications of hate policies is their impact on vulnerable individuals in need of care and assistance. As an example, Aslı Kır, who was ill and elderly, needed care. Her daughter Emine Özlü looked after her. The family received public homecare aid while living in Giresun.

However, after moving to Ortahisar in Trabzon, her home care assistance ended because her husband, Ali Özlü, had been dismissed from his teaching position by a state of emergency decree. The Ortahisar District Governorship sent her a letter to this effect in November 2017. Even after the Inquiry Commission on State of Emergency Measures reinstated the disability aid, the governorship again denied the assistance on the same pretext. A further instance of refusing to follow court orders.

Another example is the plight of a mother of two children and the wife of a police officer who was dismissed and detained by decree. Economically destitute and psychologically prone to suicide, as confirmed by a doctor's report, local social services denied her assistance. Neighbors acquainted with the family's situation made a plea for help to the social services department.

Two representatives visited the family, saw no food in the house, and were quite disturbed by the mother's psychological state. When one of them asked the supervisor if they could provide aid, the response was a blunt "No!"

The other reminded the supervisor that they had granted an allowance to the wife of an ISIS member the previous week. The supervisor replied, "We can assist an ISIS member but not those dismissed by decree!"[23] There is no way to describe this deprivation of help to the mother and her children. It verges on condemning them to social death and is a crime against humanity.

These two anecdotes are among others that demonstrate the consistent pattern of discriminatory, inhumane, and illegal actions aimed at isolating Hizmet-associated people from public and private institutions—and ultimately, from all social life.

Denial of Police Assistance

Emine Özdemir Kara, a schoolteacher dismissed by decree in 2016, faced a distressing situation in Eskişehir. She was ostracized and targeted with slanderous and demeaning remarks like "terrorist" and "traitor to the nation" and endured physical assaults from neighbors and fellow tenants. She and her brother sought help from the authorities but to no avail. Pro-Kurdish HDP lawmaker Gergerlioğlu highlighted these events in 2022 in parliament.

Other Mean-Spirited Decrees

Public servants in law enforcement who retired before the state of emergency had their ranks revoked by decree,[24] something from which retirees were protected before rule by decree took effect. There was no process. This deprived retirees of their economic, financial, and social rights, restricted them from using their former titles, and effectively blocked them from establishing, or working for, private security companies. Their weapons permits were canceled, too, further impeding any "off the record" security employment.

One particularly spiteful and callous move was to strip away medals people had earned for exceptional achievements or valiant heroism for their country.[25] Other than the National Security Council simply saying so without a shred of evidence, humiliatingly revoking hard-earned and well-deserved patriotic medals had absolutely nothing to do with the nation's immediate security. Indeed, given these persons' outstanding service to Türkiye, one would think the National Security Council would have operated with the assumption of these individuals' loyalty and integrity. Spiteful hatred can only be the motivator.

Another malicious measure denied public servants bonuses they earned under the country's Anti-Smuggling Law.[26] This prevented officers, engaged in combating smuggling, from receiving the legally-entitled remuneration or bonuses for successful efforts. Another malevolent slap in the face of those who diligently serve their country.

Graveyard of Traitors: A Crime Against Human Dignity

Immediately following the failed coup, not only the living but also those who passed away were subjected to the regime's hate rhetoric. One striking example was the "Traitors' Cemetery" in Istanbul.

Within five days of the attempt, the Istanbul Metropolitan Municipality Council unanimously decided to establish a "Traitors' Cemetery" for those allegedly involved in the attempt and later died. They located the cemetery in the Tepeören neighborhood in Tuzla, where an animal shelter previously existed.

Declaring people to be coup plotters and unceremoniously interring them in a "Traitors' Cemetery" without any trial or confirmation of their involvement was not only disrespectful toward the deceased but deeply hurt their families. It was another propaganda tool to escalate public hatred against those accused of the coup.

Notably, several soldiers, initially identified as coup plotters, were later recognized as martyrs rather than plotters, thus restoring their honor. Such an unprincipled rush to judgment brought unnecessary grief to the families besides what they were already suffering.

After a public backlash, Mayor Kadir Topbaş announced the cemetery's disbanding on the premise that designating a place specifically for "traitors" would evoke curses from passersby. He revealed that, after discussions with Mehmet Görmez, President of the Diyanet, the government agency for religious affairs, they decided to remove the sign because of its negative impact on the families of the deceased. But the bodies remained in the same undignified location, as if people would not know.

It was a strained decision by two leaders. political and religious: how to keep doing something unprincipled while saying they were being principled. That the religious leader acquiesced rather than insisting on a respectful burial is telling about his interplay with Erdoğan's politics.

Although traitors' cemeteries were not officially established, mosque imams in different regions of the country refused to conduct funeral prayers and denied permission to bury individuals in regular cemeteries.

For instance, as mentioned earlier, Gökhan Açıkkollu, a 42-year-old history teacher in Istanbul, who fell ill while in custody after the coup attempt and died, was refused burial in Istanbul and had to be buried in the village of Büyüköz, Konya. Even there, the mosque imam refused to lead his funeral prayer. A local resident showed the compassion that the imam lacked and led the prayer.

Neither the Turkish Constitution nor the European Convention on Human Rights (ECHR) specifically delineate the right to respectful burial and the right of individuals' loved ones to conduct burials and funeral rites. However, the European Court of Human Rights has decided that ECHR Article 8, which protects the right to respect private and family life, posits that everyone has the right to be buried with dignity following their family's traditions so they can perform their moral duties, mourn, and commemorate the deceased person, as well as according the individual a resting place. This right, in the court's view, is so inherently natural and indisputable that it requires no written guarantee by law.[27]

Other accounts in this book detail incidents of denying burial prayers at the direction of the Diyanet. Neither the state nor its religious arm should ever violate anyone's right to a dignified funeral rite and burial, regardless of the reason. The denial of funeral rites against deceased Hizmet people revealed that the regime's hate campaign extended even into death, which is hypocritical for a government that prides itself on its religious tenor.

One more item underlining the Diyanet's game playing with Erdoğan. It changed the name of the mosque in Erzurum Province, originally named after Gülen's father, Ramiz Efendi, to Sultan Alparslan Mosque.

Summary

Unfortunately, there are no shortage of examples, stories, and anecdotes that various sources have well documented. They number in the thousands, illustrating the Erdoğan regime's ongoing oppression of Hizmet to cause the movement's politicide. The reports that record this information do not, and cannot, describe the depth of pain and suffering inflicted so heartlessly on so many people.

Endnotes

1 Atakan Irmak, "Brazen demand from fugitive FETÖ member in the US: He wants salary from Turkey," Sabah (3.7.20220), https://www.sabah.com.tr/dunya/abdde-ki-firari-fetocuden-piskin-talep-emekli-maasi-talebinde-bulundu-6060516.

2 Kemal Ucar (@crkml), "Sayın QNB Finansbank yetkilileri; Bir doktorun kredi kartı başvurusunu KHK'lı olduğu için mi reddettiniz!? Sizin insanlığınıza da izlediğiniz politikalara da," x.com (Apr 1, 2023), https://twitter.com/crkml/status/1642138046102401024?t=Bgf8FMEY7d-BayZMftN8wg&s=09 ["Dear QNB Finansbank officials; Did you reject a doctor's credit card application because he had a statutory decree? It depends on your humanity and the policies you follow."].

3 Similarly, Article 22 of Law No. 3463, amending the Passport Law, stipulated that "persons deemed to pose a general security risk by the Ministry of Interior would not be granted a passport or travel document." Consequently, the passports of thousands of individuals, including their spouses and children, were annotated or canceled.

4 "OHAL sona erdi: İki yıllık sürecin bilançosu," BBC Türkçe (17 July 2018), https://www.bbc.com/turkce/haberler-turkiye-44799489 ["The state of emergency has ended: The balance sheet of the two-year period"].

5 "Turkey's brain drain keeps worsening," Taipei Times (Nov 10, 2023), https://www.taipeitimes.com/News/world/archives/2023/11/10/2003808975. *See also* Jason Corcoran, "Erdoğan victory set to trigger a new Turkish brain drain," IntelliNews (May 24, 2023), https://www.intellinews.com/Erdoğan-victory-set-to-trigger-a-new-turkish-brain-drain-279497/; *and* Zeliha Ozdogan, "The Effects of Democratic Regression on Turkish Economy and the Brain Drain," in Hasan Aydin and Winston Langley (eds), *Human Rights in Turkey: Assaults on Human Dignity* (New York: Springer, 2021), pp. 365–382, https://doi.org/10.1007/978-3-030-57476-5_16.

6 *See also* "Turkish educator Halil Dinç passes away in Greece after fleeing persecution in Turkey," Stockholm Center for Freedom (Aug. 17, 2018), https://stockholmcf.org/turkish-educator-halil-dinc-passes-away-in-greece-after-fleeing-persecution-in-turkey/.

7 *See* Sophia Pandya, Brenda Oliden, and Ibrahim Aytac Anli, "Shunned and Purged: Turkey's Crackdown on the Hizmet (Gülen) Movement," in Hasan Aydin and Winston Langley (eds), *Human Rights in Turkey: Assaults on Human Dignity* (New York: Springer, 2021), pp. 199-225, https://doi.org/10.1007/978-3-030-57476-5_10.

8 "Pushbacks of Turkish asylum seekers from Greece to Turkey: Violation of the principle of non-refoulement," Stockholm Center for Freedom (Jan. 20, 2023), Pushbacks of Turkish asylum seekers from Greece to Turkey: Violation of the principle of non-refoulement - Stockholm Center for Freedom (stockholmcf.org).

9 "Family Punishment in Turkey: How Erdoğan's Uses the Nazi Practice of Sippenhaft," Stockholm Center for Freedom (July 2024), https://stockholmcf.org/wp-content/uploads/2024/07/Family-Punishment-in-Turkey.pdf.

10 Circular No. 2016-20 (1 Sept. 2016), finalized by the Circular No. 2019/9 (24 April 2019).

11 "AKP'li belediye KHK'lıya servis şoförlüğü belgesi vermedi," Davul (19 Feb. 2022), https://gazetedavul.com/gundem/akpli-belediye-khkliya-servis-soforlugu-belgesi-vermedi-34790.html, ["AKP-run municipality did not issue a shuttle driver's license to a person subject to statutory decree"].

12 Article 2, para. 4, Decree No. 667.

13 *See, e.g.*, "Persecution & Genocide Committees," Advocates of Silenced Türkiye, Persecution & Genocide Committees - Advocates of Silenced Turkey.

14 Yasir Gökce, Hakan Kaplankaya, Harun Resit Halisoglu, Mehmet Bozkaya, "Persecutory Confiscation Amounting to Crimes Against Humanity: Case Of The Gülen Group," Institude (Nov. 2023), https://institude.ams3.cdn.digitaloceanspaces.com/Persecutory_Confiscation_Amounting_to_Crimes_Against_Humanity_Case_Of_the_Gulen_Group.pdf.

15 Article 7, para. 3, Law on the Prevention of Financing Terrorism (Law No. 6415) (2013), amended by Law on the Prevention of Financing of Proliferation of Weapons of Mass Destruction (Law No. 7262) (2020).

16 Article 122, Turkish Penal Code (Law No. 5237), revised by Law No. 6529 (2 March 2014).

17 "Arananlar," İçişleri Bakanlığı, Terör Arananlar (Ministry of Internal Affairs, Terrorism Wanted), https://www.terorarananlar.pol.tr/tarananlar, ["Wanted"]. *See also* "Müvekkili 'gri liste'ye alınan avukatın hesabına bloke konuldu," Gazete Duva R (10 March 2023), https://www.gazeteduvar.com.tr/muvekkili-gri-listeye-alinan-avukatin-hesabina-bloke-konuldu-haber-1607592 ["The account of the lawyer whose client was included in the 'grey list' was blocked"].

18 "Basic Principles on the Role of Lawyers," United Nations Human Rights Instruments (07 Sept. 1990), https://www.ohchr.org/en/instruments-mechanisms/instruments/basic-principles-role-lawyers (*see* Articles 16, 18).

19 Kemal Uçar (@crkml), "Sayın Akbank Yetkilileri; KHK'lı bir savcının başvurusunu aşağıdaki gerekçeyle reddetmişsiniz… Gerçekten merak ediyorum; eski bir savcı ve yeni bir avukat olan meslektaşımız, sizin hangi kriterinize uymuyor? İnşallah avukatlara muhtaç kalırsınız," x.com (April 1, 2023), https://twitter.com/crkml/status/1642265215323496448?t=PRs4cC0AgkOeev-LK53yRw&s=09 ["Dear Akbank Officials; You rejected the application of a prosecutor with a decree law for the following reason… I'm really curious; Which of your criteria does our colleague, a former prosecutor and a new lawyer, not meet? I hope you will need lawyers."]. *See also* Kemal Uçar (@crkml), "Sayın Vakıfbank yetkilileri! Aşağıda, sizin müşterinize yolladığınız mailin ekran görüntüsü ve müşterinin bana yazdığı DM var. Bu iğrenç mail gerçekse insanlık suçu işliyorsunuz!" x.com (Apr 10, 2023), https://x.com/crkml/status/1645510689551679490 ["Dear Vakıfbank officials! Below is the screenshot of the email you sent to your customer and the DM the customer wrote to me. If this disgusting e-mail is real, you are committing a crime against humanity!"].

20 "KHK'lı depremzede, İş Bankası'nda hesap bile açamadı," Kronos38 (02 March 2023), https://kronos38.news/tr/khkli-depremzede-is-bankasinda-hesap-bile-acamadi/ ["Earthquake survivor with statutory decree could not even open an account at İşbank"].

21 "Turkey's post-coup purge victims not allowed to benefit from tax amnesty," Stockholm Center for Freedom (March 14, 2023), https://stockholmcf.org/turkeys-post-coup-purge-victims-not-allowed-to-benefit-from-tax-amnesty/. *See also* "Bu kadarı da 'pes' dedirtti! KHK'lılar vergi affından da yararlanamayacak," Aktif Haber (March 14, 2023), https://aktifhaber.com/gundem/bu-kadari-da-pes-dedirtti-khklilar-vergi-affindan-da-yararlanamayacak.html ["This much made me say 'give up'! People with decree laws will not be able to benefit from tax amnesty"].

22 "Depremzedeye GBT: KHK'li olduğu için yurda alınmadı," Gazete DuvaR (08 March 2023), https://www.gazeteduvar.com.tr/depremzedeye-gbt-khkli-oldu-

gu-icin-yurda-alinmadi-haber-1607142 ["GBT to the earthquake victim: Not allowed into the dormitory because he had a statutory decree"].

23 "IŞİD'liye maaş, KHK'lıya ağaç kökü!," TR724 (25 November 2019), https://www.tr724.com/isidliye-maas-khkliya-agac-koku/,%20 ["Salary for ISIS members, tree roots for those with Decree Law!"].

24 Decree No. 679 and subsequent decrees.

25 Decree No. 692 revoked medals awarded under the Medal and Orders Law No. 2933.

26 Decree No. 679 denied public servants bonuses earned under Anti-Smuggling Law No. 5607.

27 "Adalet Bakanlığı Daire Başkanı, 15 Temmuz gecesi nefret saçmış: Başlarını ve ellerini kesip, kan kusturacağız!," TR724 (22 Nov. 2021), https://www.tr724.com/adalet-bakanligi-daire-baskani-15-temmuz-gecesi-nefret-sacmis-baslari-ni-ve-ellerini-kesip-kan-kusturacagiz/ ["The Head of Department of the Ministry of Justice spread hatred on the night of July 15: We will cut off their heads and hands and make them vomit blood!"].

Chapter 14

Shifting Daily Discourse Against Hizmet

Redefining Patriotism

Authoritarian regimes strive mightily to reframe national discourse, even to the point of creating a vocabulary of pejorative expressions and inventing false facts. Hate speech is a perfect vehicle for this enterprise, and Erdoğan unfortunately showed mastery at it. Nor did the political opposition rise to the occasion. Had it done so early on, Türkiye would be on a far different arc.

A striking example of how Erdoğan commandeered the stage is the "July 15 Democracy and National Unity Day," inaugurated by the regime as a patriotic anniversary of the failed coup. In reality, the remembrance, which the state vigorously promotes, is a day of hate propaganda, scorn, and humiliation directed at the Gülen Movement and all the good and faithful people who had served their country until Erdoğan decided to sacrifice them mercilessly on his altar of power and expediency. One can only imagine their pain at the shame heaped upon them, patriots to the core.

The regime likewise imposed its hate-laden agenda on elementary school textbooks and activities. Children must grow up hearing the drumming of the government's hate speech. Their schools have become ahistorical indoctrination foci, teaching students lies and how to hate—hardly a worthy educational enterprise in civil society. The country would profit better from academic lessons about democracy and morality in high places. The students are future leaders. Corrupting their learning does not benefit Türkiye's future but only makes it bleaker.

The Ministry of National Education (MEB) issues directives to all educational institutions and conducts training programs for educators and supervisors, which propagate hate speech. MEB-produced booklets like "July 15 Democracy Victory and in Memory of Martyrs," with Erdoğan's foreword, are raw regime indoctrination. Time and resources would be better spent on teaching the art of critical thinking, which is needed for civil society.

Incidents have occurred in schools in this disinformation context. One example is that, when Atatürk University Rector, Dr. Ömer Çomaklı, visited Yarımca Primary School on Teachers' Day, a primary school student identified himself as "Fethullah," to which the rector replied, "Immediately tell your father to remove that name from you."[1] This response showcases how elementary school children are exposed to a policy of hate by people claiming to be academic leaders.

It would be more historically accurate to designate July 15 as the day the government began tearing down democracy, rather than shoring it up, and undermining national unity, rather than creating solidarity. Erdoğan's "July 15 Democracy and National Unity Day" signals his own dystopian Newspeak, worthy of George Orwell's *Nineteen Eighty-Four.*

"FETÖ" in Daily Derogatory Vocabulary, as Accusation and Defense

Human experience shows us how easily derisive hate speech can seep into common, everyday social speech. Even if illogically expressed, it still damages those tarnished by its use and belies the bigotry in the speaker's mind.

This happened with "FETÖ," which became part and parcel of everyday hate speech vocabulary. People use it as a magical term or a defense mechanism to dissociate themselves from unlawful conduct or problems that they caused.

Particularly noteworthy is how AKP routinely brandishes "FETÖ" to defame people, while the political opposition, with the very same rhetoric, accuses AKP of being linked to FETÖ. The pervasive use of this poisonous term cuts across political factions and spreads hatred within their respective ordinary citizen voter bases.

Also noteworthy is a December 2022 interview on Swedish state television with İbrahim Kalın, presidential spokesperson for Erdoğan (and later National Intelligence Organization (MİT) director). He responded sharply and defensively to a question about whether Türkiye was becoming a cocaine trade hub and if foreign criminals felt comfortable doing business in Türkiye. He dodged the question, obviously because it struck home, and blew out a smoke screen that worked for him in Türkiye, but not in Sweden, "...these are FETÖ words; these are PKK words...."[2]

Kalın's response was the regime's well-honed, rote tact of insidiously invoking Hizmet to cloud over its failings and embarrassment—of shouting "FETÖ" to deflect scrutiny and avoid taking responsibility. Constantly reiterated hate speech blankets a multitude of regime failures, unlawfulness, and crimes, and facilitates witch hunts against all opponents. It also deflects attention from the government's shattering of democracy, the rule of law, and justice.

One striking example: A hospital in Istanbul (Sultan Süleyman Training and Research Hospital) failed to report to authorities 115 underage girls who were pregnant (39 of whom were Syrian nationals). According to the regulations enforced by Turkish Health Ministry, hospitals are required to notify the police in cases where the pregnant girl is younger than eighteen years old, while cases involving children below fifteen years of age automatically qualify as "sexual abuse."[3]

The Deputy Chief Medical Officer defended himself at his criminal trial as follows: "I believe this case against me is a conspiracy orchestrated by the FETÖ terrorist organization. I am innocent." What the motivation might have been to cause his dereliction of duty or how it was done is opaque, of course. He just wanted to dodge responsibility for his criminal negligence.

Turkish professor and human rights activist Dr. Baskın Oran, in 2017, cited and summarized some of the following select examples of widespread hate-driven demonization of the Gülen Movement.[4] Oran is an expert on ethnicities and nationalism in Türkiye and the National Liaison Officer for Türkiye to the Council of Europe's Commission against Racism and Intolerance.

During a sensational criminal trial in Istanbul, Atalay Filiz, who murdered a father and son while robbing them of 120,000 Turkish Lira (TL) ($3,060) as they left the land registry office, at first tried to claim they were killed by FETÖ members. In court, he shifted his story and claimed that one of the men he killed was a FETÖ member, stating, "Our people demand the execution of traitors. In a way, I fulfilled the wishes of our people."[5] He also killed his landlord. A brutal serial killer, he is now serving three life terms in prison.[6]

In June 2017, Çankırı Chief Public Prosecutor Hüsnü Aldemir asserted that FETÖ "was a complete Jewish organization," which drew condemnation from the country's small Jewish community for inciting hate speech.[7]

Islamists and Erdoğan's wider voter base portray Jewish people as a source of all evil, even though their total population is fewer than 20,000 persons. This is not just anti-Israel or anti-Zionist sentiment, but animosity toward every Jewish person. The loathing is as entrenched as it is irrational and bigoted. Connecting any person or organization with Jews is a way of fomenting hatred toward them and reinforcing hatred of Jewish people.[8]

In March 2017, Professors Ali Aydın Yavuz and Melek Nur Yavuz, his wife, at Akdeniz University Faculty of Medicine, Department of Radiation Oncology, filed a 29-page denunciation with the Antalya Chief Public Prosecutor, accusing fifteen prominent colleagues of being FETÖ members and seeking their dismissal. Some of the accused professors are renowned for their worldwide facial and arm transplant surgeries. The Yavuz couple was unsuccessful when the university faculty pushed back. They lost their jobs for "unfounded allegations"[9]

During the trial of Fadıl Akgündüz, known as Jet Fadıl, for defrauding 349 individuals in real estate projects, a complainant ran into him in Mecca for Hajj and confronted him about being conned out of 900,000 TL ($22,000) (and his wife out of 100,000 TL, $2,500). Akgündüz blamed the "parallel structure," another dysphemism for the Gülen Movement.

The court where Akgündüz was on trial eventually released him in 2016. He had been in prison earlier in 2002-2004 on another matter. He blamed his legal problems on the Gezi Park unrest and the December 2013 scandal.[10] Unable to admit to his own criminal activity, he tried to scapegoat the Gülen Movement. That is how lame his defense was and how willing he was to blame innocent people.

When he lost a civil case over the purchase of a private airplane, İbrahim Tatlıses, Turkish Folk Music artist and AKP supporter, who has a bit of a shady character about him publicly, claimed to have been a "FETÖ victim" because he attended the patriotic post-coup Yenikapı Rally in August 2016, organized by Erdoğan. He accused the police of negligence in handling a shooting incident in which he was nearly killed in March 2011 and demanded that they be punished for their FETÖ membership.[11] Violence of a dubious nature often swirled about Tatlıses.

Singer Nihat Doğan claimed he was the first person in 2016 to mention FETÖ regarding the death of Turkish American actor Defne Joy Foster, who died at the home of Ahmet Altan's son, Kerem, in 2021. He suggested that FETÖ might have killed her,[12] although the autopsy faulted cardiac arrest. The widespread suspicion was that Doğan, adept at using the media, was trying to shore up a sputtering career.

When people found out that the municipality of Kayseri was killing puppies in its animal shelter and more than eight hundred dogs supposedly in its care were missing and probably killed, the authorities, instead of explaining the situation and accepting responsibility, accused the media of trying to damage the unity of the nation that became stronger after the coup attempt by diverting attention to the killing of the dogs. They thought mentioning July 15th would help silence criticism and let them sweep the matter under the carpet.

As these anecdotes show, the two-step dance of invoking July 15 and blaming others, typically the Gülen Movement, became a whetted political tact.[13]

Sometimes people tried to remake history in absurd ways to pile blame onto Hizmet. CHP parliament member and journalist Tuncay Özkan, for example, tried to attribute Türkiye's 1997 "post-modern coup" "to police directors affiliated with FETÖ" instead of the generals who issued the "soft coup" ultimatum that eventually brought down the government: "If you ask me, it was Fethullah Gülen and his followers who brought down the Erbakan government on 28 February."[14]

That Özkan's revisionist facts made no sense, timeline-wise, nineteen years later, was beside the point; he wanted to heap more rocks on Hizmet's shoulders. Political reasons, no doubt.

Former AKP Metropolitan Mayor of Ankara Melih Gökçek accused M. Rıfat Hisarcıklıoğlu of collaborating with FETÖ members when he defeated his son Osman Gökçek in the 2016 Chamber of Commerce elections.[15] Hisarcıklıoğlu was president of the Union of Chambers and Commodity Exchanges of Türkiye. Gökçek wanted to extend his political power through his son's election, which was not the majority's wish. He was not known for dispassionate logic or unwillingness to jump on the FETÖ bandwagon.

A Germencik Courthouse clerk filed a criminal complaint in 2016 against a colleague as a FETÖ member after she rejected his marriage proposal.[16] The seriousness and irrationality of this incident is how FETÖ has been weaponized in such a widespread fashion that one person can use it to bully another and make another's life miserable.

In July 2017, B.K., who operated a four-story guesthouse in a historic building in Şanlıurfa's Haşimiye Square, blamed "FETÖ municipal managers" for the demolition of an illegally constructed floor.[17] He had added a floor of glass and wood to the terrace of the historic building without permission.

When the municipality demolished this addition in line with the opinion of the Directorate of Preservation of Historical and Cultural Assets, B.K. hung a banner, "The destruction of this building is the work of FETÖ-affiliated municipal officials. When will you liberate the management of this city from FETÖ? The people can no longer tolerate oppression, torture, and exploitation. Our esteemed President [Erdoğan]: the bones of our martyrs ache [their deaths were in vain]," in reference to the demolished floor. A total self-absolving non-sequitur

Oğuz Bulut, a prominent far-right ultranationalist and former president of the Sivas Ülkü Ocakları (Grey Wolves' Hearths), was caught in August 2017 sexually abusing an alleged 15-year-old boy. He was rumored to be close to Sedat Peker, a criminal enterprise boss with whom he shared a cell in prison. Fearing the implications as a boss of having been a roommate with a gay man, Peker, who appears earlier in this book, attacked people who talked about it as Hizmet members, almost all of whom, he falsely charged, were gay (using a derogatory anti-gay word in Turkish, which also means a person one cannot trust).[18]

In testimony before the July 15 Coup Attempt Commission in December 2016, Kerem Kınık, President of the Turkish Red Crescent, said FETÖ members had attempted to infiltrate the Red Crescent but failed to do so because the internal election processes for its seven hundred branches assured a slow transfer of leadership.

Not only did he present no proof, but he also offered no logic why Hizmet would want to take over the Red Crescent. He gratuitously commented that it was "one of the very few organizations that [Hizmet] could not infiltrate." He was pandering to what the commission wanted to hear.

Later, in February 2023, Kınık claimed that Hizmet had destroyed the Red Crescent civil defense mechanism, attempting to dodge responsibility for his own incompetence, as he was transferred to another position.[19]

Onetime Ankara Metropolitan Mayor Melih Gökçek made weird statements about the coup night of July 15 on Hakan Çelik's program on CNN Türk. Gökçek argued that Fethullah Gülen did many events, especially the coup attempt, with jinns [demons]: "He does this with demons. He gave me something in gold and a jawshan [prayer book]. He does these things with demons." When Çelik asked him, "Do you really believe this?" Gökçek replied, "I do. I have experienced similar things myself..."[20]

A woman passenger traveling on an intercity bus asked the bus driver to stop for her to pray. He rudely refused. A video of the incident spread on social media. Galip Öztürk, the owner of Metro Tourism and an ardent Erdoğan supporter, tweeted, "The FETÖ treasonous scum who filmed and posted the altercation between our driver and one of our passengers! Our company has terminated the captain's contract. I ask for prayers from my fellow countrymen to be safe from the evil of FETÖ scum!"[21] There is no logic to his comment other than not wanting to stray from currying Erdoğan's favor.

The politics of hatred has provided a common and cheap avenue to attribute every negativity to Hizmet. Similar situations occurred during the 2023 elections. The common propaganda point for both AKP and the opposition centered around "FETÖ." AKP says the opposition parties are driving Hizmet's objectives and thus have Hizmet support. CHP says there has never been an investigation as to whether there are Hizmet members within AKP. During an election campaign, if one candidate is accused of wrongdoing by an opponent, the candidate blames Hizmet to shirk personal responsibility.

In an era where even those who sympathize with Hizmet are punished, someone needs to speak up, and shout out, "What's going on? You have been purging and imprisoning them for years, sending them into exile, and now that all your people fill the positions and ranks of power, you keep accusing each other of being associated with FETÖ. Don't you see the utter stupidity of this and how badly it wounds our country?"

Due to the widespread occurrence and normalization of cases exemplified in this chapter, many "victims" are attempting to publicize their situations through social media or with the help of their lawyers. They continue their lies at others' expense.

Signage of Hate

Türkiye's hate politics have motivated local public and private entities to engage in practices targeting Hizmet.

One strange incident involved road signs constructed along the roadside in Sakarya's Ferizli District Municipality, displaying a picture of Fethullah Gülen alongside a traffic monster with the inscription "Caution, FETÖ might emerge." Mayor Ahmet Soğuk conceded that the municipality had installed the signs in areas of frequent accidents.[22] Not only was this malevolent and hateful, but it was incredibly stupid and dangerous to construct a distraction in places of frequent accidents.

Ordinary citizens, influenced by these practices of public entities, adopted similar offensive conduct. For instance, a barber affixed a sign on the window, "FETÖ Members Not Allowed." The public discourse of hate, starting from state institutions, has rendered Hizmet members targets of ridicule and marginalization in every aspect of society.

Book Burnings and Banning

Throughout history, authoritarian regimes have banned and destroyed books that disturb or challenge the autocrat's official narrative. Book burnings abounded. Türkiye and Erdoğan are no exception.

As of August 2019, more than 301,000 books have been removed from Turkish schools and libraries and destroyed, according to Turkey's Ministry of Education, that show any link to Fethullah Gülen. The figure was first reported by the newspaper *Hürriyet*, with images of books being seized and burned published by online news outlet Kronos38.

According to the website Turkey Purge, in 2016 a math book was banned for featuring Gülen's initials in a question reading "from point F to point G." In December 2016, Turkish newspaper *BirGün* reported that 1.8m textbooks had been destroyed and reprinted for containing the "objectionable" word "Pennsylvania," where Gülen lived in exile.[23] This, too, evidences the politicide program against Hizmet, to eradicate its memory and presence..

Other Anti-Gülen Measures

In Türkiye, vehicle registration plates have a combination of letters and numbers. In 2014, the combination "FG" was due in the registration sequence. Because of the letters' association with Fethullah Gülen, the General Directorate of Security invalidated all "FG" license plates issued in 2014 and thereafter. They were replaced with alternative license plates so that one never sees a plate with "FG" together.

The name of the village, Korucuk in Erzurum Province, where Fethullah Gülen was from, was changed to Şehit Burak Karakoç Village. There was an attempt to set fire to the house where he was born. Further, as noted earlier, the Presidency of Religious Affairs, the Diyanet. changed the name of the mosque in Erzurum Province, originally named after Gülen's father, Ramiz Efendi, to Sultan Alparslan Mosque. Streets named Gülen in Ankara have also been renamed.

Such was the institutionalization and socialization of anti-Hizmet rhetoric in Türkiye.

Endnotes

1 "Fethullah isimli öğrenciye rektörden 'adını değiştir' tepkisi," Sabah TV (24.11.2016), https://www.sabah.com.tr/video/turkiye/fethullah-isimli-ogrenciye-rektorden-adini-degistir-tepkisi ["'Change your name' reaction from the rector to the student named Fethullah"].

2 "O soru gerilimi yükseltti, söyleşi yarıda kesildi! İbrahim Kalın'dan İsveç televizyonunda gündem yaratan tepki," Mynet (02.12.2022), https://www.mynet.com/o-soru-gerilimi-yukseltti-soylesi-yarida-kesildi-ibrahim-kalin-dan-isvec-televizyonunda-gundem-yaratan-tepki-110107075744 ["That question increased the tension and the interview was interrupted! A trending reaction from İbrahim Kalın on Swedish television"]. ("Türkiye, kokain ticareti için bir merkez haline geldi mi ve yabancı suçlular Türkiye'de rahat hissediyorlar mı?" ["Has Turkey become a hub for cocaine trafficking and do foreign criminals feel comfortable in Turkey?"]).

3 "115 underage pregnant girls treated in İstanbul hospital not notified to Turkish authorities," Stockholm Center for Freedom (Jan 17, 2018), https://stockholmcf.org/115-underage-pregnant-girls-treated-in-istanbul-hospital-not-notified-to-turkish-authorities/

4 Baskın Oran, "PKK'lidir ve FETÖ'cüdür' söylemi de olmasa AKP ne yaparmış?" T24 (20 Oct. 2017), https://t24.com.tr/yazarlar/baskin-oran/pkklidir-ve-feto-cudur-soylemi-de-olmasa-akp-ne-yaparmis,18336 ["What would the AKP do if there was no discourse of 'he is from PKK and FETÖ'?"].

5 "Atalay Filiz de 'FETÖ'ye sığındı: Halk idam istiyor, ben halkın talebini yerine getirdim," Diken (09/03/2017), https://www.diken.com.tr/atalay-filiz-de-fetoye-sigindi-halk-idam-istiyor-ben-halkin-talebini-yerine-getirdim/ ["Atalay Filiz also took refuge in 'FETO': The people want execution, I fulfilled the people's demand"]. *See also* "128 bin liralık gasp yaptı, kendini böyle savundu: Sanki cinayet işledik, FETÖ'cü müyüz!," T24 (04 March 2017), https://t24.com.tr/haber/128-bin-liralik-gasp-yapti-kendini-boyle-savundu-sanki-cinayet-isledik-fetocu-muyuz,391996 ["He extorted 128 thousand liras, he defended himself like this: It's like we committed murder, are we FETÖ members!"].

6 "Serial killer Atalay Filiz gets another life sentence," Daily Sabah (Dec 02, 2017), https://www.dailysabah.com/investigations/2017/12/02/serial-killer-atalay-filiz-gets-another-life-sentence.

7 "Başsavcı: FETÖ tam bir Yahudi örgütlenmesi," Gazete Duva R (18 June 2017), https://www.gazeteduvar.com.tr/gundem/2017/06/18/bassavci-feto-tam-bir-yahudi-orgutlenmesi ["Chief Public Prosecutor: FETÖ is a pure Jewish organization."].

8 Uzay Bulut, "Turkey: A "Jewish Terrorist Organization" Behind the Attempted Coup?," Provicence (Dec. 27, 2017), https://providencemag.com/2017/12/turkey-jewish-terrorist-organization-attempted-coup-feto/. *See also* "How Israel's Mossad links with Riyadh, FETÖ to target Turkey," Daily Sabah (April 21, 2020), https://www.dailysabah.com/politics/news-analysis/how-israels-mossad-links-with-riyadh-feto-to-target-turkey; https://www.hurriyetdailynews.com/turkish-intelligence-agency-report-describes-massive-global-gulenist-organization--113634.

9 "Akdeniz Üniversitesi'ni karıştıran suç duyurusu… Suçlama: FETÖ," Cumhuriyet (07.05.2017), https://www.cumhuriyet.com.tr/haber/akdeniz-universitesi-ni-karistiran-suc-duyurusu-suclama-feto-735431 ["Criminal complaint involving Akdeniz University… Accusation: FETÖ"]. *See also* "AÜ Rektörlüğü: İddialar

mesnetsiz," Hürriyet (May 08, 2017), https://www.hurriyet.com.tr/yerel-haberler/antalya/au-rektorlugu-iddialar-mesnetsiz-40450668 ["AU Rector's Office: The allegations are baseless."].

10 "Alacaklısına hacda yakalanan 'Jet Fadıl': 'Paralel yapı' yüzünden," Diken (05/07/2017), https://www.diken.com.tr/alacaklisina-hacda-yakalanan-jet-fadil-paralel-yapi-yuzunden/ ['Jet Fadl,' caught on pilgrimage by creditor: It's because of the 'parallel structure.']. *See also* "Jet Fadıl'dan kendisini Hac'da yakalayan mağdura: Paralel yapı yüzünden," Cumhuriyet (05/07/2017), https://www.cumhuriyet.com.tr/haber/jet-fadildan-kendisini-hacda-yakalayan-magdura-paralel-yapi-yuzunden-774644 ["From Jet Fadıl to the victim who caught him during Hajj: It's because of the parallel structure"].

11 "İbrahim Tatlıses: Ben de FETÖ gazisiyim," Haber Turk (01.11.2016), https://www.haberturk.com/magazin/fiskos/haber/1317882-ibrahim-tatlises-ben-de-feto-gazisiyim/5. ["İbrahim Tatlıses: I am also an anti-FETÖ veteran"]. *See also* "Turkish singer Ibrahim Tatlises shot in head in attack," BBC (15 March 2011), https://www.bbc.com/news/world-europe-12730390.

12 "Nihat Doğan'dan şok iddia: Defne Joy Foster'ı FETÖ öldürdü!," aHBR (31.08.2016), https://www.ahaber.com.tr/magazin/2016/08/31/nihat-dogan-dan-sok-iddia-defne-joy-fosteri-feto-oldurdu ["Shocking claim from Nihat Doğan: FETÖ killed Defne Joy Foster!"].

13 "Kayseri Belediyesi, köpek katliamı iddialarını 'FETÖ'ye bağladı!," T24 (02 Oct. 2016), https://t24.com.tr/haber/kayseri-belediyesi-kopek-katliami-iddialarini-fetoye-bagladi,362852 ["Kayseri Municipality attributed dog massacre allegations to 'FETO'!"].

14 "Tuncay Özkan: 28 Şubat'ta Erbakan hükümetini deviren Fethullah Gülen ve adamlarıdır," T24 (09 Oct. 2016), https://t24.com.tr/haber/tuncay-ozkan-28-subatta-erbakan-hukumetini-deviren-fethullah-gulen-ve-adamlaridir,363922. ["Tuncay Özkan: It was Fethullah Gülen and his men who overthrew the Erbakan government on February 28"].

15 "Oğlu seçimi kaybedince Gökçek hedef tahtasına oturttu: Hisarcıklıoğlu'na 'FETÖ' suçlaması," Cumhuriyet (26.12.2016), https://www.cumhuriyet.com.tr/haber/oglu-secimi-kaybedince-gokcek-hedef-tahtasina-oturttu-hisarciklioglu-na-feto-suclamasi-650833 ["When his son lost the election, Gökçek put him in the crosshairs: 'FETÖ accusation against Hisarcıklıoğlu"].

16 "Evlilik teklifini reddeden kadını 'FETÖ'cü diye ihbar etti!," T24 (27 Dec. 2016), https://t24.com.tr/haber/evlilik-teklifini-reddeden-kadini-fetocu-diye-ihbar-etti,379589 ["He reported the woman who rejected his marriage proposal as a 'FETÖ member!"].

17 "Kaçak kat inşaatı yıkılan şahıs, pankart asıp belediyeyi 'FETÖ'cülükle' suçladı," T24 (17 July 2017), https://t24.com.tr/haber/kacak-kat-insaati-yikilan-sahis-pankart-asip-belediyeyi-fetoculukle-sucladi,414841 ["The person whose illegal floor construction was demolished hung a banner and accused the municipality of 'FETÖism'"].

18 "Sedat Peker: LGBT'yi Fethullah Gülen kurdu," T24 (21 August 2017), https://t24.com.tr/haber/sedat-peker-lgbtyi-fethullah-gulen-kurdu,422802 ["Sedat Peker: Fethullah Gülen founded LGBT"].

19 "Kerem Kınık: Olağanüstü durumlarda Cumhurbaşkanı bütün cep telefonlarına bağlanabilsin," Haber Turk (22.12.2016), https://www.haberturk.com/gundem/haber/1339836-kerem-kinik-olaganustu-durumlarda-cumhurbaskani-butun-cep-telefonlarina-baglanabilsin ["Kerem Kınık: In case of emergency, the President should be able to connect to all mobile phones"]. *See also* "Kızılay

Başkanı Kınık: Kızılay'ın sivil savunma mekanizması FETÖ tarafından çökertildi," Sendika (14 Feb. 2023), https://sendika.org/2023/02/kizilay-baskani-kinik-kizilayin-sivil-savunma-mekanizmasi-feto-tarafindan-cokertildi-677145 ["Red Crescent President Kınık: Red Crescent's civil defense mechanism was destroyed by FETÖ"].

20 "Melih Gökçek: FETÖ insanları üç harflilerle etki altına alıyor," BİRGün (24.07.2016), https://www.birgun.net/haber/melih-gokcek-feto-insanlari-uc-harflilerle-etki-altina-aliyor-121294, ["Melih Gökçek: FETÖ influences people with three letters"].

21 "Metro Turizm'de namaz krizi," Arti Gerçek (12 June 2017), https://artigercek.com/guncel/otobuste-namaz-tartismasi-22661h ["Prayer crisis in Metro Tourism"].

22 "Kazaların sık yaşandığı yere 'FETÖ' tabelası," Haber7 (17.08.2016), https://www.haber7.com/guncel/haber/2081358-kazalarin-sik-yasandigi-yere-feto-tabelasi ["'FETO' sign at place where accidents occur frequently"]. *See also* "Sakarya 'çıtayı yükseltti': Sık kaza yapılan noktalara 'Dikkat FETÖ çıkabilir' levhası," Diken (17/08/2016), https://www.diken.com.tr/sakarya-citayi-yukseltti-sik-kaza-yapilan-noktalara-dikkat-feto-cikabilir-levhasi/ ["Sakarya 'raised the bar': 'Attention FETÖ may appear' sign at points where accidents occur frequently"].

23 "Turkish government destroys more than 300,000 books," Gaurdian (Aug. 6, 2019), https://www.theguardian.com/books/2019/aug/06/turkish-government-destroys-more-than-300000-books.

Chapter 15

Inflicting Hate on the Gülen Family

Sometimes, the depth to which Erdoğan will go to ruin the lives of others is confounding. The stories are legion and tragic. But one of the most unfathomable was the attack on Fethullah Gülen's family, especially the elder members. Scores of relatives, regardless of age or gender, became victims of hate and discrimination. There is no way to understand this but as part of the regime's politicide project.

A fundamental human quality is the natural bond of kinship established within the family into which one is born or of which one becomes a member. A basic right is to expect another's respect for the ties of kinship. Article 20 of Türkiye's Constitution states, "Everyone has the right to demand respect for his or her private and family life." It is a fixed tenet of a democratic society that no individual should face judgment or marginalization due to family ties. There is no guilt by association.

Condemning, belittling, or isolating someone solely based on family connections infringes upon that person's rights and freedoms. Hate speech can, and often does, target people because of their familial ties. They can become subjects of divisive, demeaning, and hate-fueled rhetoric—and even hate crime. This happened to the family of Fethullah Gülen in various despicable ways.

After the fizzled coup, the regime unleashed a more concerted hate speech project against Fethullah Gülen's relatives than before. The hate campaign, undulating to the beating rhythm of pro-government media, aimed at ostracizing and isolating the family, casting aside the family's dignity, honor, and integrity. Accusing them of "terrorism" rendered them vulnerable within the larger society and hindered their ability to defend themselves and undercut their familial solidarity.

What follows are some of the tribulations that the government malevolently inflicted on the Gülen family.

Salih Gülen, Fethullah Gülen's brother, following the July 15 coup mess, learned of an arrest warrant against him, solely based on his relation to his brother and without evidence. The government had already shut down his small printing press in Erzurum and seized all his assets. By July 15, Salih Gülen had begun cancer treatment and suffered from other ailments.

At nearly age seventy, fearing further deterioration of his health from likely imprisonment, he chose not to surrender to authorities and went into hiding with acquaintances. This disrupted his cancer treatment, and his health declined. He passed away in March 2019, alone in the house where he had found refuge to escape injustice. His family, unaware of his whereabouts, could not attend his funeral.

Kutbettin Gülen, another brother of Fethullah Gülen, had worked at the Çağlayan printing press in Izmir for years. Prior to July 15, 2016, the government had appointed a trustee over the press and terminated his employment contract. After July 15, an arrest warrant was issued against him as a "Member of a Terrorist Organization," without any evidence, and the government detained him. Without any reason other than being Fethullah Gülen's brother, he was sentenced to ten years and six months in prison.[1] Besides his age, he has several health infirmities (heart problems, high blood pressure, and a herniated disc). After undergoing serious surgery in early 2022, he was returned to prison within twenty-four hours, although in no condition to care for himself. Authorities rejected health-related requests for his release.

Kutbettin Gülen's son, Ahmet Ramiz Gülen, having recently graduated from university after the coup attempt, was arrested without any legal evidence, imprisoned, and sentenced to twelve years in prison. During the trial proceedings, the presiding judge asked him if he considered his uncle Fethullah Gülen to be the "head of a terrorist organization." No one would argue that the trial was based on evidence or that the verdict was not propelled by incrimination, reprisals, and discrimination because of family ties.

Asiye Gülen, Kutbettin Gülen's daughter, was detained in June 2023 in her home. News of her detention, relayed by pro-government media, reflected the coordinated hate-driven approach against the family. She was formally arrested four days later, and the media again broadcast hate-filled narratives. The indictment against her itemizes mundane and legal activities like having a social security record at a company associated with Hizmet, holding an account at Bank Asya, being a member of a union before its closure by decree, and working as a book editor—all cited as evidence of membership in a terrorist organization. Her formal accusation cites her for referring to her uncle respectfully as "Hoca Efendi" and "Hocam" ("Honorable Teacher") as proof of terrorist organization membership.

Kazım Avcı, son of Fethullah Gülen's aunt, Dürdane Avcı, served as a branch manager in the Ministry of National Education for years and retired from his post as an advisor to Türkiye's parliament. He was arrested in December 2015 for being part of the "parallel state," one of Erdoğan's disparaging umbrella attack terms for Hizmet. Even though he was already in prison on July 15, 2016, because of his Gülen relationship, he was sentenced to life imprisonment for "attempting to violate the Constitution," with his relation to Fethullah Gülen as a reason. Because of his role as founder of the Mehmet Akif Cultural Association, which was closed by decree, the regime relegated him to prison for seventeen years and four months.

Avcı lost his left leg at age twelve in a train accident. He uses a prosthetic limb and cannot walk without assistance. During his trial, the prosecutor gratuitously belittled him with the term "lame," while emphasizing his relation to Fethullah Gülen. He suffers from heart ailments, diabetes, high blood pressure, and is at risk of prostate cancer. Despite these infirmities, his advanced age, and a 68% disability rating, he was locked in solitary confinement as a "dangerous" inmate for years. In February 2022, he suffered a heart attack. Health diagnosis reports were clear that staying in prison posed a life-threatening risk because he was unable to attend to his basic needs. Nevertheless, requests for release on health grounds were unreasonably and inhumanely denied.

Selahaddin Gülen is the son of Seyfullah (Sıbgatullah) Gülen, Fethullah Gülen's brother. While working as a teacher in the United States, he went to Kenya to marry but got caught up in legal rendition proceedings initiated there by Türkiye. On May 3, 2021, Türkiye's National Intelligence Agency (MİT) unlawfully abducted him.[2]

Sixteen days later, Erdoğan bragged, "We will soon reveal a significant figure from the FETÖ team; we have him right now." On the last of May, news of his arrest was released to the media and information that his interrogation would commence the next day, but with no explanation as to why he was held incognito for a month. During his trial in the following November, he testified that, "I was subjected to insults merely due to my Gülen surname until the day MİT handed me over after capturing me."[3]

The formal accusation or indictment against him detailed mundane activities, but all Hizmet-related, such as meeting his Uncle Fethullah, attending a preparatory school, meeting individuals, holding an account at Bank Asya, and working as a teacher in the United States as evidence of "Membership in a Terrorist Organization." These legally legitimate activities were typical "proof of guilt" for Hizmet people.

Following trial, the Ankara 27th High Criminal Court sentenced him to three years and four months in prison. The reason his heavy sentence deviated from the lower possible sentencing limit was because of his family ties to his uncle. His request for probation was rejected, and the Court of Cassation finalized the verdict against him on appeal.

Kemal Kevser Gülen, also a son of Seyfullah Gülen, and his wife Hale Gülen faced adversity following the coup attempt. He had been a newscaster on Hizmet-related TV channels (such as Samanyolu Haber Television and Samanyolu TV). After July 15, an arrest warrant was issued for him; his assets were seized because of his association with his uncle. He was forced to leave the country clandestinely and seek asylum in another nation.

His wife, Hale Gülen, attempted to legally exit Türkiye to Georgia via the Sarp (Sarpi) Border Gate in July 2017. Although there were no warrants or investigations against her, she was detained and later arrested at the border due to a query regarding her husband's Interpol arrest warrant, an abuse of Interpol discussed earlier.

Her indictment proof included her marriage to Kemal Gülen, possessing one U.S. dollar bill, being a member of a foundation, sending her children to educational institutions, being a newspaper subscriber, and having a Bank Asya account—all Hizmet-related. Despite being acquitted in trial court, an appellate court overturned the ruling because of a routine banking transaction with her account at Bank Asya and sentenced her to one year and thirteen months in prison for "aiding a terrorist organization." A Catch-22 in the making: even if you win your trial, the appeals court may still convict you. The state gets two chances at it.

Seyfullah Gülen, Fethullah Gülen's brother, passed away in 2014. Seyfullah's wife Mükafat Gülen passed away in 2022. The Edremit Directorate of Religious Affairs instructed all mosque staff not to perform the funeral prayer. Despite family attempts at two different mosques, no one would perform the funeral prayer. Relatives had to conduct the prayer at the cemetery.

Mehmet Mezher Gülen, nephew of Fethullah Gülen, had a long, distinguished career as a teacher and school administrator. He was detained in May 2015 and subsequently arrested. The indictment (formal accusation) against him highlighted his relation to his uncle, alleging involvement in "meetings," having a Bank Asya account, and "overseeing all schools affiliated with the organization."

In April 2018, the Izmir 13th Heavy Penal Court sentenced him to twenty-one years in prison without mitigating circumstances, deviating from the lower sentencing limit because of his surname and his teaching and administrative roles at a Hizmet school. He lost his appeal.

Judge Alev Özcan, who had previously ordered Mehmet Gülen's detention, participated in the appellate review of the case, even though Türkiye's Code of Criminal Procedure Article 23, Section 2, prohibits this dual role. Disregarding such a clear legal mandate not only violates the right to a fair trial but also signifies bias and a gross lack of impartiality. Mehmet Gülen, who dedicated his life to educating the country's future citizens and admittedly had no involvement in violent actions, received a twenty-one-year prison term.

The police executed an arrest warrant at the residence of Sümeyra Gülen, wife of Mehmet Gülen, for her father, Yusuf Bekmezci. She was also detained and later released under judicial control. The discovery of a Bank Asya cheque at her residence and the fact that her children attended Hizmet educational institutions were evidence against her.

Despite fully complying with judicial control obligations, she was arrested following her first hearing in November 2018 when the court deemed judicial control insufficient, claiming she could flee, as did some of her relatives (but not her husband). The court sentenced her to one year and thirteen months in prison for the Bank Asya account.

Mehmet and Sümeyra Gülen's son, Fethullah, ranked third in Türkiye's 2014 university entrance examination for branches TM 1 and TM 2. His name and family ties, however, prevented him from studying in Türkiye. He had to pursue his education abroad.

The government detained Selman Gülen, nephew of Fethullah Gülen, in August 2016, held in custody for twenty-three days, and then formally arrested him. Following trial, the court sentenced to eight years and nine months in prison for membership in an armed terrorist organization.[4] Pro-government media reported on his detention, arrest, and imprisonment under the headline "Gülen's nephew." Additionally, his photos were shared publicly, portraying him as guilty solely because of his surname.

Selman Gülen was kept in solitary confinement for a prolonged period while in prison. He also shared a prison cell with journalist and writer Ahmet Altan, who, after his release from prison, drafted an article, "Paper Flute," in which he mentioned Selman.[5]

Altan described how Selman had no visitors in prison and played a flute that he himself made, giving recitals in the prison courtyard. Altan also reflected on how, despite both being innocent, they were singularly unable to convey their innocence to the judges in court, who did not listen to them.

Selman completed his entire prison sentence and was released in June 2022. However, in July 2023, a year later, he was re-arrested along with his wife and her parents when the Istanbul police and MİT detained Selman Gülen, his wife, and in-laws and seized $14,000 from them and their passports.[6] Subsequent news reports, which indicated a centralized source, described his father-in-law's home as a "cell house" and emphasized the familial connection to Fethullah Gülen.[7] The media reports framed the re-arrest as part of the movement's "restructuring," without mentioning the previous imprisonment and the completed sentence.

In the second case, realleging the same charges as before, the court sentenced Selman to six more years and three months in prison for being in a terrorist organization. He was granted conditional release under judicial control, including a ban on traveling abroad.[8] A second trial for the same offense was not uncommon for Hizmet people and showed how the regime manipulated the legal process and trod on the constitutional principle against double jeopardy.

Another family harassment of note occurred in June 2023, when Istanbul security forces arrested Gülen's niece Asiye Gülen and her husband in Istanbul and seized what the police said were organizational items (a computer, cell phones, and the like).[9] The arrests came a year after Turkish forces apprehended another niece attempting to flee to Greece.

There are other instances of Fethullah Gülen's relatives, close and distant, and even acquaintances from the same village being subjected to hate speech and discrimination.

Reports from independent and international institutions have documented much of this hate-driven oppression. For instance, an August 2023 comprehensive report by the Netherlands' Ministry of Foreign Affairs about the situation in Türkiye devoted a separate section to the situation of Fethullah Gülen's relatives.[10]

Final Comment

Erdoğan's willingness to ruin the lives of others is as unfathomable as it is unconscionable. He knows no restraint for his hatred, even if unreasonable and over the top. The attack on Fethullah Gülen's family, especially the elder members, was vindictive and directed at personally hurting Gülen, which it did greatly. Their only "crime" was being his relative. Nor did it matter to Erdoğan that international law and Türkiye's national law forbade family or kin punishment, such was his spite and his intent to achieve his politicide project.

Endnotes

1 "Brother of Fethullah Gülen detained by Turkish police," Guardian (Oct. 02, 2016), https://www.theguardian.com/world/2016/oct/02/brother-of-fethullah-gulen-detained-by-turkish-police.

2 "Nephew of Fethullah Gulen seized and brought back to Turkey," BBC (31 May 2021), https://www.bbc.com/news/world-europe-57304094.

3 "Turkish Agents Capture Nephew of US-Based Cleric Overseas," VOA News (May 31, 2021), https://www.voanews.com/a/europe_turkish-agents-capture-nephew-us-based-cleric-overseas/6206441.html.

4 "Teröristbaşı Gülen'in yeğeni yakalandı," Yeni Şafak (17/08/2016), https://www.yenisafak.com/gundem/teroristbasi-gulenin-yegeni-yakalandi-2513182 ["Terrorist Chief Gülen's nephew was captured"].

5 Ahmet Altan, "Kâğıttan flüt," T24 (09 Nov. 2019), https://t24.com.tr/k24/yazi/kagit-flut,2455 ["Paper flute"].

6 "Turkey detains yet another family member of Islamic scholar Gülen," Turkish Minute {July 14, 2023), https://www.turkishminute.com/2023/07/14/turkey-detains-yet-another-family-member-of-islamic-scholar-gulen/.

7 "FETÖ elebaşı Fetullah Gülen'in yeğeni Selman Gülen yakalandı," Sabah (14.7.2023), https://www.sabah.com.tr/gundem/2023/07/13/feto-elebasi-fetullah-gulenin-yegeni-selman-gulen-yakalandi ["Selman Gülen, nephew of FETÖ leader Fetullah Gülen, captured"].

8 "Fethullah Gülen'in yeğeni Selman Gülen tahliye edildi," Kronos (13 May 2024), https://kronos37.news/fethullah-gulenin-yegeni-selman-gulen-tahliye-edildi/ ["Fethullah Gülen's nephew Selman Gülen released"].

9 "Türkiye police arrest Gulen's niece," Middle East Monitor (June 25, 2023), https://www.middleeastmonitor.com/20230625-turkiye-police-arrest-gulens-niece/.

10 "General Country of Origin Information Report on Türkiye (August 2023)" Government of the Netherlands (31-08-2023), https://www.government.nl/documents/reports/2023/08/31/general-country-of-origin-information-report-on-turkiye-august-2023, pp.45-46.

Chapter 16

Hate Speech and Politicide

This book has attempted to sketch the painful contours of the politicide that Erdoğan and his group have long unleashed against the Gülen Movement. The different strategies and events laid out in earlier chapters are only an overview of this scheme, which would fill volumes if documented in detail.

The hate speech at play binds all the actions together. It tips Erdoğan's hand that this is not just a question of consolidating totalitarian power that is at play, but a concerted campaign to eradicate Hizmet from Turkish society in the process, civil death, because its vision of civil society is at odds with the desires of Erdoğan and his allies and inimical to their autocratic agenda.

Erdoğan's hate speech campaign knits together the various components of his politicide drive, separate pieces that together have inflicted untold misery upon hundreds of thousands of innocent people. The overarching hate speech panoply, which this chapter lays out, helps paint the backdrop of liability for crimes against humanity and responsibility for politicide.

This chapter and the following consider international law violations in Erdoğan's war on Hizmet and the extent to which the international forum should hold him and Türkiye accountable. The international community is supportive of doing so, but the governments are reluctant.

The next and final chapter examines international law liability. To hold Türkiye responsible under international law means finding an overarching crime against humanity, in this case, against Hizmet. And another question. Is Erdoğan guilty of criminal conduct to the extent it would invoke the Rome Statute, the International Criminal Court?

Propping Up Discrimination and Undermining Equality

The European Court on Human Rights (ECtHR) has been clear, as it wrote in *Erbakan v. Türkiye*, that "tolerance and respect for the equal dignity of all human beings constitute the foundations of a democratic, pluralistic society. That being so, it may be necessary in certain democratic societies to sanction or even prevent forms of expression which spread, incite, promote, or justify hatred based on intolerance."[1]

Hate speech by design is exclusionary. It is targeting, derogatory, prejudiced, bias-inducing, and intolerant. Vulnerable minorities, disadvantaged groups, or dissenting factions of society tend to be its primary recipients. Just to recap, manifestations of hate speech are myriad and include:

- Systematic discrimination, marginalization, othering, isolation, alienation, or targeted hatred against individuals or groups specifically based on race or ethnic origin, religion, creed, disability, age, nationality, veteran status, sexual orientation, gender, sexual identity, immigrant status, politics, beliefs, or related characteristics ("Politics" and "beliefs" are the applicable categories regarding Hizmet)
- Claiming that a group is subhuman, inferior, or deserving of hatred (e.g., portraying a group as malicious, corrupt, diabolical, and the like), explicitly or implicitly
- Slanders, stereotypes, false statements, untrue theories about a specific group, explicit or implicit, or declarations that the group poses a threat
- Content and actions centered around symbols representing or targeting groups, such as flags or emblems (e.g., showcasing Nazi flags to target Jews or burning the Quran)[2]

The first three listings are all operative regarding Erdoğan's and Türkiye's war on the Gülen Movement.

Hate speech conflicts with the fundamental rights and liberties of the person or group being targeted and, depending on the circumstances, can take it outside the scope of the speaker's freedom of expression and subject that hate speech to limitations and even punish it.

Even when statements within the ambit of free expression do not entail an imminent threat, hate speech can intensify hostility and alienation toward those targeted, even posing a tangible risk to them. The line between protected speech and unprotected speech is sometimes hard to discern and may appear blurry. It can be quite context-dependent.

In an ECtHR Turkish case, for example, the court denied Article 10 free speech protection under the European Convention on Human Rights Article 10 to Müslüm Gündüz, an Islamist figure who published a direct hate speech attack in print on a public intellectual.[3] He attacked the victim for his moderate Islamic beliefs.

In another case, the court gave Gündüz Article 10 protection for uttering similar, but more generalized, Islamist remarks as part of a late-night televised political panel discussion.[4] The court focused on the political nature of the panel discussion where the hateful comments occurred, noting that they were not focused on anyone specifically or directly. Context mattered. Erdoğan would not meet the *Gündüz* test for free speech.

Perpetrators of hate speech can be ordinary citizens, writers, artists, politicians, or public officials. The spectrum is unlimited. Those with a greater capacity to influence public opinion, such as journalists or public figures, can cause far more detrimental consequences than ordinary citizens. Their hate speech leads to quicker and more profound consequences.

There is a vast difference between a random, unrelated individual utterance one-on-one and a sustained media or government campaign. Drawing a continuum from a single interpersonal utterance to a years-long intensive campaign puts Erdoğan and Türkiye almost as far to the other end of the continuum as possible.

Distinguishing Hate Speech v. Free Speech

Criticism of another's thoughts, beliefs, or behaviors, within the bounds of universal legal norms, is an option and, sometimes a necessity, in democratic society. What is crucial is that such criticism should not escalate to inciting unlawful activity or crime against the person.

Freedom of expression, a fundamental liberty, embodies various definitions but essentially constitutes the right to convey, explain, disseminate, and persuade others of one's thoughts, beliefs, opinions, attitudes, or sentiments by peaceful means through speech, writing, or other means and to receive the same from another. Free expression is a two-way street. It is part of another's free expression that community members should have the opportunity to listen to it if they wish. In a democratic society vigorous, even raucous, free speech is at play, but not its suppression.

The right of free expression, as articulated in European Convention on Human Rights (ECHR) Article 10, permits only narrow restrictions such as necessary in democratic society, for example, safeguarding national security, territorial integrity, public safety, crime prevention, health or morals, protecting the rights and reputations of others, preventing the spread of confidential information, and ensuring the authority and impartiality of the judiciary. Article 10 allows for limitations on speech that incites violence, hatred, or discrimination.

These limitations must be foreseen by law (that is, not *ad hoc*), aim for legitimate purposes, and be proportionate to the prescribed aim without conflicting with democratic principles. Despite being a cornerstone of democratic order and a fundamental human right of hierarchical proportions, freedom of expression loses its protection when it invites or exhibits violence against another's fundamental rights..

It is a delicate fence that separates freedom of expression from hate speech, which United Nations Secretary-General António Guterres has tried to articulate:

> Addressing hate speech does not mean limiting or prohibiting freedom of speech. It means keeping hate speech from escalating into something more dangerous, particularly incitement to discrimination, hostility, and violence, which is prohibited under international law.[5]

Erdoğan and his people long ago crashed through that fence, as this book has amply demonstrated with verbatim quotations of words, phrases, speeches in person and in the media and escalated into hate-driven crimes.

Hate Crimes and Violence, Physical and Non-Physical

Hate crimes cross that fence boundary, over which Erdoğan and colleagues have themselves vaulted. Hate crimes and hate speech, while intricately connected, are distinct legal concepts. Hate speech involves the expression of hatred toward an individual or group based on various characteristics but does not necessarily progress to physical actions or violence beyond the realm of speech, although hate crimes often find their roots in hate speech. Outward manifestations of intolerance and bigotry may set the stage for criminal actions.

Generally, hate speech aims to inflict or incite violence of some kind, whether physical, psychological, economic, or demeaning harm. Verbal assaults and hostility can encompass mocking, degrading name-calling, destructive criticisms, false accusations, coercion, and threats. Psychological violence may entail threatening, pressuring, intimidating, ignoring, or ostracizing an individual. Hate crimes might also target the victim's individual property. Often, they are vigilante crimes. They may also involve public property or community property (mosque, synagogue, church, for example). The list is long.

It is important not to keep the phenomena of hate crimes narrow, as sometimes seems the tendency. Although hate crimes often involve physical violence, they may include non-physical psychological violence and other insidious activity, such as discrimination, which may be as harmful as physical injury or even more harmful.

This latter genre of violence directly affects designated groups or individuals associated with a group sharing similar characteristics, beliefs, and activities. Stripping away fundamental rights (free expression, due process, the rights to travel, for example) and discharging people from their jobs, for example, are forms of violence.

Considering the potential volatile progression of hate speech into a rights violation, zero tolerance toward hate speech should be the goal. This is particularly crucial given historical instances, such as Türkiye's, where systematic and planned hate speech has escalated into mass actions targeting a specific population. The potential for hate speech to evolve into societal cancer is ever-present. For this reason, hate crimes should be appropriately and quickly punished.

Hate speech can lay the societal groundwork for violence. As hate speech becomes normalized and eventually mainstreamed, the state is perceived to have the right to perpetrate acts against individuals or groups, veiling certain crimes under the umbrella of state violence rather than individual violence.

Systematic and policy-driven hate speech has driven recent grotesque crimes against humanity, such as in Bosnia, Rwanda, Uganda, and Myanmar, to cite tragic examples quite apart from the twentieth-century genocides that preceded them. The Political Instability Task Force, sponsored by the U.S. government, estimated that forty-three genocides occurred between 1956 and 2016, resulting in fifty million deaths, within a sixty-year span.[6] Add to that the six million Jewish victims of the Holocaust and millions of others, and the numbers point to the capacity of hate crimes to inflict enormous casualties on humankind. That is why hate speech is so dangerous and contrary to international law.

As noted earlier, the task force distinguishes between genocides and politicides. In genocides, the victimized groups are defined primarily in terms of communal characteristics (i.e., ethnicity, religion, or nationality). In politicides, the victim groups are defined primarily in terms of their societal hierarchical position or political opposition to the regime and dominant groups. Nazi Germany was a practitioner of both. Türkiye is a practitioner of politicide regarding Hizmet.

Türkiye's Experience

As previously noted, Türkiye is no stranger to hate crimes, historically or contemporarily, on large and smaller scales toward groups and people within the country.

Although a legal framework in Turkish national legislation exists that could be somewhat effective against hate crimes, the approach of the judiciary toward hate speech and hate crimes is quite problematic. Judicial authorities, instead of primarily protecting targeted individuals or groups, tend to adopt a statist interpretation of the law, allowing hate speech by public officials against private individuals but not the other way around. Insulting the president or government, whatever "insulting" means, is a crime that may land one in prison.

According to the Human Rights Association in Türkiye (İnsan Hakları Derneği, İHD), since 2010, fifteen people have been killed and 1,097 have been injured in 280 racist attacks.[7] It is presumed that the actual figures regarding hate crimes surpass the data accessible to the Human Rights Association, particularly since law enforcement keeps no records specific to hate crimes. Hate speech and hate crimes, often vigilante action, are part of everyday Turkish life beyond the documented statistics.

Nor does the data reflect government-perpetrated or government-encouraged hate crimes.

International Approaches

International legal opinion is quite robust against hate speech and its practitioners, whether individuals or the state.

Countries have formulated hate crimes differently in their criminal systems. Twenty-three member states of the Organization for Security and Co-operation in Europe (OSCE) recognize hate motivation as an aggravating factor in all offenses. Twenty-five other OSCE countries specifically regulate hate speech as certain offenses. Some countries, like England and the Czechia, for instance, treat it as an independent offense, while, in others, it is among factors that enhance punishment. Türkiye's approach is much more limited.

OSCE is a regional security-oriented intergovernmental organization comprising fifty-seven member states in Europe, North America, and Asia. Its mandate includes issues like arms control, the promotion of human rights, freedom of the press, and free and fair elections.

Since 1997, various other European entities have focused on the problem of hate speech. This includes the Council of Europe's Committee of Ministers,[8] the European Commission against Racism and Intolerance (ECRI),[9] the Parliamentary Assembly of the Council of Europe,[10] and the European Agency for Fundamental Rights (FRA). The United Nations developed a 2020 United Nations Strategy and Action Plan on Hate.[11]

The issue is problematic enough as an international concern that the UN General Assembly declared June 18 as the "International Day for Countering Hate Speech" with the aim of "promoting inter-religious and intercultural dialogue" against hate speech.[12] This day was first commemorated in 2022.

Other international organizations have involved themselves as well—including the UN Human Rights Committee (OHCHR) and the Committee on the Elimination of Racial Discrimination (CERD). They employ different methods to combat hate speech and crimes, such as collecting data, publishing annual reports, and urging offending countries to take remedial measures.

OSCE, which comprises fifty-seven countries (including Türkiye), views a hate crime as one committed with a motive of hate, that is, a specific intent of prejudice toward the victim.[13] Türkiye, although it submits other OSCE annual data, is one of the countries where law enforcement does not register hate crime cases.

The European Court of Human Rights' Perspective on Hate Speech

The philosophy behind the European Convention on Human Rights (ECHR) is an institutional framework based on democratic values to prevent extremism, which, historically, eventually emerges to suppress democratic values. In sync with this objective, the European Court of Human Rights (ECtHR) has issued significant rulings, finding various forms of aggressive expression contrary to the Convention, such as racism, xenophobia, anti-Semitism, hardline nationalism, and discrimination against minorities and immigrants.

The court attempts a balanced perspective between extremist incitement on one hand and, on the other, individuals' rights to freely express their opinions and "provoke, shock, or disturb" others, particularly journalists and politicians.

In the absence of a precise, universally accepted definition of hate speech, the court has outlined two different approaches to address hate speech to bring it out from under ECHR Article 10's protection of freedom of expression and to establish it as an abuse of such protection:

(a) If the expressions in question amount to hate speech and deny fundamental ECHR values, the ECtHR applies ECHR Article 17 (prohibition of rights abuse);

(b) If the expressions qualify as hate speech but lack the capacity to destroy fundamental ECHR values, the court excludes them from protection under Article 10, by applying the restrictions articulated in that article, and Article 11 (national security or public safety, prevention of disorder or crime, protection of health or morals, or the protection of the rights and freedoms of others).[14]

Türkiye runs afoul of both approaches.

Erbakan v. Türkiye in July 2006 was a key decision on these points, emphasizing tolerance and respect for the equal dignity of all individuals, and providing guidance on the obligations of states concerning hatred and discrimination. The ECtHR, with a broad perspective on hate speech and crimes and their resulting human rights violations, evaluates incidents that could constitute hate crimes along with the fundamental rights associated with the incident under the ban on discrimination.

Unlawful discrimination arises when a person or group cannot equally enjoy their fundamental rights or other legal rights compared to others in a similar position based on factors such as language, ethnic origin, race, gender, age, sexual orientation, or disability. Although international treaties prohibit discrimination, they do not provide a specific definition. Therefore, the ECtHR prohibits discrimination broadly for Article 14 equal protection purposes.

The ECtHR's criminal law jurisprudence regarding hate crimes recognizes the need for a response proportionate to the harm caused. Likewise, the court imposes duties on states. In the *Šečić v. Croatia* decision concerning a skinhead's' attack on a Romani person, the court highlighted a country's duty to take all reasonable additional measures to uncover racist motives in violent incidents.[15]

In this context, the court imposes four affirmative obligations on states:

1. Linking ECHR Article 14 (prohibiting discrimination) with Article 2 (protecting the right to life), Article 3 (prohibiting torture and inhuman treatment), and Article 8 (protecting the right to private life) to fashion or discern a hate crime.
2. Acknowledging that an offense can be committed both by the state and by private individuals regarding the same incident or separate incidents.
3. Expanding hate crimes beyond racial bias to include religious hatred, homophobia, disability, political opinions, and gender-based discrimination.[16]
4. Broadening positive obligations to include associative discrimination, where a person faces discrimination due to association with another individual.[17]

In the case of *Norwood v. United Kingdom*, an individual was punished for displaying a hate-inciting poster against a religious group, Muslims. The ECtHR considered a request for relief under ECHR Article 17, the prohibition of abuse of rights and concluded that the applicant did not have protection under ECHR Article 10, guaranteeing freedom of expression, because his hate crime was outside the scope of the rights assured by Article 10.[18]

Similarly, in *Balsytė-Lideikienė v. Lithuania,* the court rejected the petition of a person distributing and publishing the "Lithuania calendar 2000," inciting ethnic hatred. The court noted the applicant's expressions of aggressive nationalism and ethnic centrism that incited hatred against Jews and Poles and emphasized the necessity for measures against the individual because of an urgent societal need, within the limits of local courts' discretion.[19]

Former decisions of the Turkish Constitutional Court have noted the absence of a universally accepted definition of hate speech. In a 2015 decision involving Fethullah Gülen,[20] the court agreed that hate speech might underlie statements that may seem rational or normal and indicated that criteria distinguishing hate speech from other speech can be determined by ECtHR case law and international texts.[21]

However, after a year of legal maneuvering, the court dismissed the case, not wanting to upset the government. The Gülen litigation was against an internet posting of a hostile interview by a television station under government sway.

The ECtHR is clear that it declines to protect speech that directly fosters intolerance or propagates hatred, considering it to be outside the realm of ECHR Article 10 free expression protection, emphasizing the significance of tolerance and respect for human dignity as the bedrock of a democratic and pluralistic society. On the other hand, the court is careful to construe the facts of a case in favor of Article 10 when possible.[22] The balancing can be quite difficult.

Erdoğan Government Violates the Penal Code Prohibition of Politicide

In this context, Article 76 of the Turkish Penal Code (under the "International Crimes" section, "Genocide and Crimes Against

Humanity") defines genocide as: "...the commission of one of the following [five] acts as part of a plan with the intent to destroy, in whole or in part, a national, ethnic, racial, or religious group...."

Similarly, Article 77 of the Penal Code ("Crimes Against Humanity") proscribes eight different crimes against humanity if they encompass the "systematic performance [of] an act, against a part of society and in accord with a plan with a political, philosophical, racial, or religious motive. The crimes described include intentional killing, injury, torture, inhuman treatment, or depriving one of liberty.

It is noteworthy that Article 77 follows upon the genocide prohibition and, in a sense, broadens the concept to include "a political, philosophical, racial or religious motive," expanding the definition of hate crime. In comparing Articles 76 and 77, one main difference would be the gravity of punishment. Otherwise, the legal impetus is the same. In other words, Article 77 describes and proscribes politicide and would apply to Hizmet's persecution.

While Article 77 does not proscribe hate speech in and of itself, hate speech certainly is the key to establishing the motivation behind the "systematic performance" of a "plan." The next chapter delineates further how the Erdoğan regime is engaged in politicide and thus crimes against humanity under Turkish law and international law.

Although no specific Turkish statute addresses hate crimes at length, Article 122 of the Penal Code does proscribe four general classes of crime committed with a hate motive. A person who obstructs the sale, transfer, lease of movable or immovable property, the utilization of certain services, employment recruitment, or ordinary economic activities of an individual due to hatred based on language, race, nationality, color, sex, disability, political opinion, philosophical belief, religion, or sect, faces imprisonment from one to three years.[23]

Turkish government officials and private citizens have been in stark violation of this law from the beginning; neither they nor the courts have felt obligated to abide by Article 122.

Both in law and practice, the state has positive and negative obligations in this context. If the state engages in policies and actions that are contrary to the principle of equality and the prohibition against discrimination, it creates *ipso facto* a discriminatory regime. Türkiye has done that.

Likewise, a state pursuing a policy of hatred toward a person or group would lead to implementing discriminatory practices because the state would view them as not entitled to equal rights or any basic rights and freedoms, for that matter. If the state engages in discriminatory practices, society is likely to reflect similar attitudes and behaviors toward targeted individuals and groups, especially if couched in hate rhetoric. Such is the case with Türkiye.

The hate policies propounded by Turkish government officials turned into direct action, often resulting in serious hate crimes, which the judges condoned. The impunity granted by judicial authorities was widespread and became firmly entrenched in Türkiye's legal system.

This hate speech not only showed its ruthlessness and inhumaneness within state and private institutions but also within Turkish society at large. Public entities did not refrain from inflicting the most severe forms of discrimination on individuals accused of Hizmet affiliation, with disastrous consequences in their lives.

Because of these hate policies, public officials, who, despite being obliged to treat everyone equally under the law, committed crimes involving discrimination and hate crimes based on "political view" or "philosophical belief," prohibited by Article 122 of the Turkish Penal Code.

It is interesting that, in March 2024, the title of Article 122 was amended from "Discrimination" to "Hatred and Discrimination." The Hizmet hatred was so ingrained by then that the incongruity or irony went right past everyone. Not that it mattered much. Türkiye and Erdoğan were already well down the path of trampling on the country's own law and on international law to which it had promised to adhere.

Transition from Hate Crimes to Crimes Against Humanity

The no-holds-barred hate speech perpetrated by the Erdoğan regime against Hizmet people as a class or association or those associated with the movement has paved the way for systemic hate crimes to firm up what would qualify as crimes against humanity and provide the backbone thereof.

Türkiye has been consistently violating its own law, namely Article 77 (crimes against humanity) and Article 122 (hate crimes and discrimination). In multiple ways, as described through this book, the government and Erdoğan have also breached the ECHR and the International Covenant on Civil and Political Rights (ICCPR), both of which are binding on Türkiye, as part and parcel of their forceful politicide operation. They have used their unapologetic hate speech campaign to cloak and propel their annihilation project.

United Nations independent expert Alfred de Zayas has provided a perceptive insight that the attacks on Hizmet fit a "genocidal pattern of human-rights abuses." This mirrors the politicide pattern. Adapting scholar Gregory Stanton's ten stages of genocide analysis analogously to politicide, the Erdoğan regime has gone through eight of the stages (classification, symbolization, discrimination, dehumanization, organization, polarization, preparation, and persecution).[24] The remaining two stages are extermination and denial

Türkiye and its government have long known from the start that they are in violation of their own national law and international norms. They cannot claim otherwise.

The final question, taken up by the next chapter, is framing the case for politicide and crimes against humanity and Erdoğan's and Türkiye's liability therefor.

Endnotes

1 *Erbakan c. Turquie* (No. 59405/00), European Court of Human Rights (6 July 2006), https://hudoc.echr.coe.int/eng#{%22itemid%22:[%22001-76232%22]}.

2 *See* "Panelists discuss strategies for addressing hate speech at OSCE conference," Turkish Minute (Oct. 11, 2024), https://turkishminute.com/2024/10/11/panelists-discussed-strategies-for-addressing-hate-speech-at-osce-conference/.

3 *Gündüz v. Turkey* (No. 59745/00), European Court of Human Rights (13.11.2003), https://hudoc.echr.coe.int/eng?i=002-4631. *See also Gündüz v. Turkey* (No. 59745/00), European Court of Human Rights, https://hudoc.echr.coe.int/eng?i=001-23973.

4 *Id. And see Gündüz* v *Turkey* (No. 35071/97), European Court of Human Rights (14 June 2004) https://hudoc.echr.coe.int/eng?i=001-61522.

5 "The UN Strategy and Plan of Action," United Nations, https://www.un.org/en/hate-speech/un-strategy-and-plan-of-action-on-hate-speech.

6 Charles H. Anderton, Jurgen Brauer, *Economic Aspects of Genocides, Other Mass Atrocities, and Their Prevention* (Oxford University Press: New York, 2016). *See also* Daniel C. Esty, et al., "State Failure Task Force Report: Phase II Findings," Wilson Center (1999), https://www.wilsoncenter.org/sites/default/files/media/documents/event/Phase2.pdf.

7 "Special Report on Hate Crimes and Recent Racist Attacks in Turkey," İnsan Hakları Derneği (Human Rights Association) (22 Sept. 2020) https://ihd.org.tr/en/wp-content/uploads/2020/09/sr20200922_Hate-Crimes-and-Racist-Attacks-Report_Sept-2020.pdf.

8 "Recommendation No. R (97) 20 of the Committee of Ministers to Member States on 'Hate Speech,'" Council of Europe (30 October 1997), https://rm.coe.int/1680505d5b, (Appendix, p.107).

9 General Policy Recommendation No. 15 on Combating Hate Speech, CRI (2016)15 (8 Dec. 2015), http://www.coe.int/t/dghl/monitoring/ecri/activities/GPR/EN/Recommendation_N15/ REC-15-2016-015-ENG.pdf.

10 "ECRI General Policy Recommendation No. 15 on Combating Hate Speech," Council of Europe, European Commission against Racism and Intolerance (8 Dec. 2015), https://rm.coe.int/ecri-general-policy-recommendation-no-15-on-combating-hate-speech/16808b5b01. *See also* "Resolution 2275 (2019) The Role and Responsibilities of Political Leaders in Combating Hate Speech and Intolerance," Parliamentary Assembly of the Council of Europe, https://pace.coe.int/en/files/27636. *See also* "Resolution 1510 (2006) Freedom of Expression and Respect For Religious Beliefs," Parliamentary Assembly of the Council of Europe, https://pace.coe.int/en/files/17457/html.

11 "United Nations Strategy and Plan of Action on Hate Speech: Detailed Guidance on Implementation for United Nations Field Presences," United Nations (September 2020), https://www.un.org/en/genocideprevention/documents/UN%20Strategy%20and%20PoA%20on%20Hate%20Speech_Guidance%20on%20Addressing%20in%20field.pdf.

12 "International Day for Countering Hate Speech, 18 June," United Nations, https://www.un.org/en/observances/countering-hate-speech.

13 Organization for Security and Co-operation in Europe, *Hate Crime Laws: A Practical Guide* (Warsaw: OSCE Office for Democratic Institutions and Human Rights, 2009), https://www.osce.org/files/f/documents/3/e/36426.pdf.

14 *Erbakan, supra.* n.1.

15 *Šečić v. Croatia*, No. 40116/02, European Court of Human Rights (31 May 2007),

https://hudoc.echr.coe.int/eng#{%22itemid%22:[%22002-2695%22]}.

16 *Milanovic v. Serbia* (No: 44614/07), European Court of Human Rights (14 Dec. 2010), https://hudoc.echr.coe.int/eng?i=001-102252. *See also* "Croatian authorities did not protect a mentally and physically disabled man from repeated harassment," European Court of Human Rights (24 July 2012), https://hudoc.echr.coe.int/app/conversion/pdf/?library=ECHR&id=003-4029516-4701786&filename=Chamber%20judgment%20Dordevic%20v.%20Croatia%2024.07.12.pdf. *See also Đorđević v. Croatia* (No. 41526/10), European Court of Human Rights (24 July 2012), https://hudoc.echr.coe.int/eng?i=001-112322. *See also Virabyan v. Armenia* (No: 40094/05), European Court of Human Rights (2 Oct. 2012), https://hudoc.echr.coe.int/tur?i=001-113302. *See also M.C. and A.C. v. Romania* (No. 12060/12), European Court of Human Rights (12 April 2016), https://hudoc.echr.coe.int/eng?i=002-10990.

17 *Škorjanec v. Croatia* (No: 25536/14), European Court of Human Rights (28 March 2017), https://hudoc.echr.coe.int/eng?i=001-172327.

18 *Norwood v. United Kingdom* (No. 23131/03), European Court of Human Rights (16 Nov. 2004), https://hudoc.echr.coe.int/eng?i=001-67632.

19 *Balsytė-Lideikienė v. Lithuania* (No. 72596/01), European Court of Human Rights (4 Nov. 2008), https://hudoc.echr.coe.int/eng?i=001-89307.

20 *Fethullah Gülen Başvurusu* (No. 2014/12225) T.C. Anayasa Mahkemesi (The Constitutional Court of the Republic of Turkey) (14/07/2015), https://kararlarbilgibankasi.anayasa.gov.tr/BB/2014/12225, (para.38) (The Constitutional Court decided not to accept a case against an internet posting of a hostile interview by a television station under the government's sway).

21 Şeyma Kuş, "Avrupa İnsan Hakları Mahkemesi Ve Anayasa Mahkemesi Kararlarında Nefret Söylemi," Yüksek Lisans Tezi, Sosyal Bilimler Enstitüsü, İstanbul Üniversitesi, (İstanbul 2020), s.106 [Şeyma Kuş, "Hate Speech in the Decisions of the European Court of Human Rights and the Constitutional Court," Master's Thesis, Institute of Social Sciences, Istanbul University (Istanbul, 2020), p.106]..

22 "Erbakan v. Turkey," Columbia Global Freedom of Expression, https://globalfreedomofexpression.columbia.edu/cases/erbakan-v-turkey/.

23 Article 122, Turkish Penal Code (Law No. 5237), revised by Law No. 6529 (2 March 2014).

24 Alfred de Zayas, "Crimes Against Humanity in Erdoğan's Turkey," RealClear Religion (Feb. 26, 2021), https://www.realclearreligion.org/articles/2021/02/26/crimes_against_humanity_in_Erdoğans_turkey_661936.html. *See also* "Opinions adopted by the Working Group on Arbitrary Detention at its eighty-eighth session, 24–28 August 2020," Human Rights Council (18 Sept. 2020), https://www.ohchr.org/sites/default/files/Documents/Issues/Detention/Opinions/Session88/A_HRC_WGAD_2020_51_Advance_Edited_Version.pdf. *See also* "Opinions adopted by the Working Group on Arbitrary Detention at its eighty-eighth session, 24–28 August 2020," Human Rights Council (25 Sept. 2020), https://www.ohchr.org/sites/default/files/Documents/Issues/Detention/Opinions/Session88/A_HRC_WGAD_2020_47_Advance_Edited_Version.pdf.

Chapter 17

International Law: Crimes Against Humanity

This concluding chapter considers the international possibilities for holding Erdoğan and Türkiye liable for the violations of fundamental human rights and crimes against humanity inflicted the Gülen Movement for almost a decade and a half.

One cannot write a single summary paragraph outlining the Erdoğan regime's persecution of Hizmet because of its breadth and depth, unremittingly sustained since before 2013 and still ongoing.

This text and all the assembled reports it has cited (and others not cited) show the systemic, state-driven violations of fundamental human rights, and efforts to eradicate the movement for political reasons and thus perpetrate politicide against the movement and those associated with it or sympathetic to it.

Just unilaterally applying self-styled "terrorist" nomenclature like a *deus ex machina* does not absolve Erdoğan and Türkiye of their relentless wrongdoing or of their politicide against Hizmet..

The litany of human rights violations against Hizmet is long and well-catalogued:

- Torture
- Discriminatory regime practices, facilitated by the emergency decrees, against Hizmet members, detrimentally impacting all aspects of their lives.
- Physical and sexual abuse, neglect, inhuman and degrading treatment, and punishment in detention facilities and prisons
- Denial of medical care and inhumane conditions in detention facilities and prisons

- Massive summary employment terminations without just cause or due process
- Denying people the right to pursue their professions (professional annihilation)
- Incarceration for possession of books and literature written or published by people affiliated with Hizmet (all previously approved by the government) or participating in "Hizmet meetings"
- Denying exit from Türkiye, preventing people from seeking asylum in other countries
- Capturing, kidnapping, and rendition of persons from foreign countries
- Forcing families to vacate state-provided housing
- Cancelation of passports
- "Branding" passports, school documents, and other official documents
- Stripping citizenship of Hizmet-related Turks abroad who do not return to Türkiye upon government mandate
- Seizure of institutions and property worth billions of dollars without due process or compensation
- Summary shutdown of all Hizmet-related media outlets and publishing houses contrary to free press rights
- Seizure of Hizmet nonprofit eleemosynary facilities, programs, and institutions worth billions of dollars without due process, judicial hearing, or compensation
- Complete lack of due process in civil and criminal settings, including lack of effective appeal, and rewriting laws to accomplish this
- Changing the country's criminal law procedural protections to make proceedings more onerous and problematic for Hizmet defendants during the two-year state of emergency
- Imposing family or kin punishment
- Imprisonment for supplying food to Hizmet-connected families adversely affected by government action
- Incarceration for providing informal educational tutoring for children
- Arresting young people for using secret "Hizmet-coded" words and gestures, as defined by the authorities *ad hoc*

- Denying religious funeral services
- Harassment and jailing of attorneys and human rights advocates, who represent Hizmet people or who dissent from and protest against government tactics and practices
- Deliberate non-compliance with binding rulings of the European Court of Human Rights
- Sustained, extensive, and comprehensive government-endorsed and perpetrated hate speech campaign by regime and surrogates, riddled with insults, lies, and fabrications
- Public branding as "terrorist" and "treasonous" criminals without appropriate judicial process
- Penalizing and denying the exercise of fundamental freedoms (such as free speech and association)
- Summary confiscation of individuals' property and assets without due process, judicial review, or compensation
- Inflicting severe psychological stress and causing suicides
- Denial of access to financial institutions and benefits (such as credit cards and loans)
- Depriving retirees of their economic, financial, and social rights
- Restricting retirees from using their former titles, and effectively blocking them from establishing, or working, for private security companies
- Canceling permits to bear arms needed for private security employment
- Stripping away medals people had earned for exceptional achievements or valiant heroism for their country
- Harassing and assaulting Hizmet people in foreign countries and using hate speech there against them
- Preventing people from exercising their right to earn a livelihood (occupational annihilation)
- Denying pension payments to former public employees and officials
- Granting immunity to officials and others who commit any of the foregoing actions

These hate-motivated and government-engineered violations are not about individual acts of discrimination against some people, but rather perpetrated against an entire group of people for the sole reason of their association and beliefs as Hizmet members and sympathizers. This is a systemic regime campaign aimed at "civil death" or "social annihilation," without distinction, whether young or old, child or adult, women or men.

As part of the government's hate-driven goal of marginalization and politicide, all individuals associated with Hizmet were falsely maligned as traitors, terrorists, and coup plotters, stripped of economic and employment rights, deprived of their property, and essentially left with their families to a slow civil death.

A necessary hate policy component was to manage societal perceptions and align society with the official narrative that Hizmet members were inimical to Türkiye. The policy is intended to cause harm, even violence, to innocent people and manipulate the populace, neighbor against neighbor, family member against family member. Erdoğan against Hizmet.

There are two possible legal options to end and rectify the oppression: one is through the criminal process (the International Criminal Court, "ICC"). The other is through the civil, non-criminal process (the European Court of Human Rights, "ECtHR").

Report of the United Nations High Commissioner for Human Rights

In March 2018, the UN High Commissioner on Human Rights issued an incisive critique of Türkiye's first eighteen months of the state of emergency. The report helps navigate either the ICC or ECtHR legal alternative.

The title of the press release introducing the report summarized it well: "Turkey: UN report details extensive human rights violations during the protracted state of emergency."[1] The following paragraphs outline its salient findings.[2] Nothing is new from what the book has already laid out, but the High Commissioner's critique adds validation and some additional facts.

The initial contextual observation is that routine extensions of the state of emergency led to profound human rights violations against hundreds of thousands of people--from arbitrary deprivation of the right to work and to freedom of movement, to torture and other ill-treatment, arbitrary detentions, and infringements of the rights to freedom of association and expression.

The state of emergency facilitated the deterioration of the human rights situation and the erosion of the rule of law in Türkiye and may "have long-lasting implications on the institutional and socio-economic fabric of Turkey." The sheer number, frequency, and lack of connection of several [emergency] decrees to any national threat ... point to the use of emergency powers to stifle any form of criticism or dissent vis-à-vis the Government."

"The numbers are just staggering: nearly 160,000 people arrested during an 18-month state of emergency; 152,000 civil servants dismissed, many arbitrarily; teachers, judges, and lawyers dismissed or prosecuted; journalists arrested, media outlets shut down and websites blocked – clearly the successive states of emergency declared in Turkey have been used to severely and arbitrarily curtail the human rights of a very large number of people," UN High Commissioner Zeid Ra'ad Al Hussein said.

One of the most alarming findings of the report," he added, "is how Turkish authorities reportedly detained some one hundred women who were pregnant or had just given birth, mostly on the grounds that they were 'associates' of their husbands, who are suspected of being connected to terrorist organizations. Some were detained with their children and others violently separated from them. This is simply outrageous, utterly cruel, and surely cannot have anything whatsoever to do with making the country safer."

The report cites the April 2017 referendum that extended Erdoğan's executive powers into both the legislature and the judiciary as "seriously problematic," resulting in interference with the judiciary and curtailment of parliamentary oversight over the executive branch. Twenty-four emergency decrees were promulgated by the end of 2017, with many regulating matters unrelated to the state of emergency and used to limit legitimate activities by civil society actors. The decrees also fostered impunity, affording immunity to administrative authorities acting within the framework of the decrees.

The critique contains accounts from individuals dismissed from their jobs for perceived Hizmet links for using specific messaging applications or through analysis of their social media contacts. "The decrees broadly refer to 'link or connection' with 'terrorist organizations' without describing the nature of such links, giving large discretion of interpretation to the authorities," the report states, adding there were serious due process violations. "Many individuals arrested … were not provided with specific evidence against them and were unaware of investigations against them."

The report also documents torture and ill-treatment in custody, including severe beatings, threats of sexual assault and actual sexual assault, electric shock, and waterboarding by police, gendarmerie, military police, and security forces.

Those dismissed from their jobs lost their income, social benefits, medical insurance, and even their homes, as various decrees stipulated that public servants, "shall be evicted from publicly-owned houses or houses owned by a foundation in which they live within fifteen days."

"Since the stated purpose of the emergency regime was to restore the normal functioning of the democratic institutions, it is unclear how measures such as the eviction of families of civil servants from publicly-owned housing may contribute to this goal," the report states.

About three hundred journalists were arrested because their publications contained "apologist sentiments regarding terrorism" or other "verbal act offenses" or for "membership" in terrorist organizations. More than 100,000 websites were blocked in 2017, including a high number of pro-Kurdish websites and satellite TV channels.

The report recommended that Türkiye restore the normal functioning of its institutions and revise and repeal all legislation that is not compliant with Türkiye's international human rights obligations. It also stressed the need to ensure independent, individualized reviews and compensation for victims of arbitrary detentions and dismissals.

The report disclaimed being an exhaustive account of the human rights situation in Türkiye but illustrative of patterns of human rights violations rampant in the country.

We now turn to the potential of bringing criminal and civil judicial actions against Erdoğan and Türkiye

The Rome Statute: An Argument for the Charge of Crimes Against Humanity

As to the criminal component enforcement, the International Criminal Court (ICC) created by the Rome statute in 1998 makes any person in political power liable for crimes against humanity. It was adopted at a diplomatic conference in Rome in July 1998 and took effect on 1 July 2002. As of February 2024, 124 states are parties to the statute. Türkiye is not.

The Rome Statute established four core international crimes: genocide, crimes against humanity, war crimes, and the crime of aggression. There is no statute of limitations for those crimes, which means charges can be filed at any time. There is no cut-off date.

Under the Rome Statute, the ICC can only investigate and prosecute the four core crimes in situations where states are "unable" or "unwilling" to do so themselves. The court has jurisdiction over crimes only if committed in the territory of a state party (Türkiye is not a state party) or are committed by a national of a state party. An exception to this rule is that the ICC has jurisdiction whenever authorized by the United Nations Security Council.

The relevant parts of Article 7 of the Rome Statute ("Crimes against humanity") provide:

1. For the purpose of this Statute, "crime against humanity" means any of the following acts when committed as part of a widespread or systematic attack directed against any civilian population, with knowledge of the attack:

   .....

   (e) Imprisonment or other severe deprivation of physical liberty in violation of fundamental rules of international law;

   (f) Torture;

   (h) Persecution against any identifiable group or collectivity on political, racial, national, ethnic, cultural, religious, gender as defined in paragraph 3, or other grounds that are universally recognized as impermissible under international law, in connection with any act referred to in this paragraph or any crime within the jurisdiction of the Court;

(i) Enforced disappearance of persons;

.....

(k) Other inhumane acts of a similar character intentionally causing great suffering, or serious injury to body or to mental or physical health.

2. For the purpose of paragraph 1:

.....

(e) "Torture" means the intentional infliction of severe pain or suffering, whether physical or mental, upon a person in the custody or under the control of the accused; except that torture shall not include pain or suffering arising only from, inherent in or incidental to, lawful sanctions;

.....

(g) "Persecution" means the intentional and severe deprivation of fundamental rights contrary to international law by reason of the identity of the group or collectivity;

.....

(i) "Enforced disappearance of persons" means the arrest, detention or abduction of persons by, or with the authorization, support or acquiescence of, a State or a political organization, followed by a refusal to acknowledge that deprivation of freedom or to give information on the fate or whereabouts of those persons, with the intention of removing them from the protection of the law for a prolonged period of time.

As this book has painstakingly laid out, Erdoğan has unquestionably and repeatedly engaged in and met all the foregoing elements of the Rome Statute to qualify him for indictment and trial for crimes against humanity. For more than a decade, he has rigorously persecuted the Gülen Movement through the intentional and severe deprivation of fundamental rights contrary to international law by reason of the group's identity or collectivity.

Whether Erdoğan can be brought to the bar of the ICC is highly problematic, given that Türkiye is not a signatory to the Rome Statute and does not accept ICC jurisdiction. That does not prevent indictment by the UN Security Council, particularly given the damning reports of the UN High Commissioner for Human Rights; but it makes enforcement of the indictment improbable.

There are heavy political considerations that militate contrariwise. One is Türkiye's being a NATO member and a sometimes ally of Europe. Another is its geopolitical significance, which has increased in recent years. Yet another is Erdoğan's mercurial solipsistic personality, which can be unpredictable. There are other significant consequential factors, as well.

Even if the likelihood of enforcing the Rome Statute is close to zero in possibility, it is instructive to look at this analogously for an approach with the European Court of Human Rights. In other words, if the ICC had jurisdiction and Erdoğan were in the docket, what would the verdict be? Guilty or not? And what weight would that carry for the court?

The European Court of Human Rights Option: a Claim of Crimes Against Humanity and a Charge of Politicide

A second avenue is a civil, non-criminal prosecution in the European Court of Human Rights against Türkiye for crimes against humanity amounting to politicide. Certainly, the facts presented in this book and the facts recognized by ECtHR decisions, the United Nations, and other entities argue strongly, if not irrefutably, that Türkiye has systematically engaged in crimes against humanity and gross violations of fundamental human rights and continues to do so. Hate speech and crimes have been the wrapping around the goal of politicide.

These actions are intended to, and do, deny fundamental rights and freedoms to every individual associated with Hizmet, such as the right to life, personal freedom, and security, due process in criminal and civil cases (including a fair trial and the presumption of innocence, the right to work, and property rights). The actions are directed against a specific class of people with the intent to discriminate against them and deny them equal protection.

Describing these activities as "discrimination" is insufficiently mild and belies the inhumane and unlawful atrocities inflicted systematically and intentionally as policy upon a group of innocent people. The gross violations of fundamental human rights against Hizmet people and those associated with them are more than substantial enough to justify a claim of crimes against humanity and a charge of politicide on the part of Erdoğan and Türkiye.

The Undergirding Pillars of Democratic Civil Society: Equality and Non-Discrimination

The cornerstone of a democracy is that it protects individuals' and groups' basic rights and freedoms and their exercise. Those fundamental rights include a person's freedom of thought, expression, association, equal treatment, livelihood, protection against discrimination, and the right to be free from violence and persecution.

Civil society rests upon respect for one's fundamental rights and lifestyle choices, regarding which people should not be marginalized, even if others or the majority disagree. The only constraint is that they cause no serious harm to self or another and, even then, the restraint must be as minimal as possible. Otherwise, discrimination is forbidden.

An individual or group that faces discrimination because of religious, philosophical, political beliefs, or lifestyle choices, which leads to their societal exclusion and exposure to vitriol, suffers a violation of human dignity. This also undermines the flourishing of society from which all benefit and to which minority people and groups contribute. In this case, civil society and democracy, all the people of Türkiye, suffer from the government's attempted annihilation of Hizmet.

Under international human rights law, the principle of equality and the prohibition of discrimination safeguard citizens against both hate speech and discriminatory actions by the state, other entities, or individuals. Rooted in the concept of human dignity, the principles of equality and the prohibition of discrimination are often used interchangeably to encompass treating individuals equally in the same or similar situations, while permitting differential treatment to those not in identical circumstances only when necessary and, even then, as narrowly or minimally as possible.

The International Covenant on Civil and Political Rights, the International Covenant on Economic, Social and Cultural Rights, and the European Convention on Human Rights, to which Türkiye has subscribed, all prohibit systematic and planned discrimination.[3] Signatory party states to these treaties are obligated to ensure the rights recognized in these agreements to all individuals within their jurisdiction without regard to … political or other opinion … or other status. Similarly, the principle of equality and the prohibition of discrimination are outlined in the Constitution of Türkiye,[4] although not adhered to or honored by the government.

The European Court of Human Rights has interpreted this to mean that, if there is no reasonable and objective justification for disparate treatment or, if the means to achieve a legitimate aim are disproportionate to that aim, unlawful discrimination is presumed to be afoot.

The prohibition of discrimination and the principle of equality are positive and negative facets of each other, two sides of the same coin. Together, they are foundational to equality before the law. The European Convention on Human Rights (ECHR), Article 14 ("Prohibition of Discrimination"), expresses it concisely and elegantly:

> The enjoyment of the rights and freedoms set forth in this Convention shall be secured without discrimination on any ground such as sex, race, color, language, religion, political or other opinion, national or social origin, association with a national minority, property, birth, or other status.

The European Court of Human Rights, in interpreting Article 14, defines discrimination as treating individuals differently in the absence of an objective and reasonable cause. In cases of differential treatment, the ECtHR carefully evaluates the proportionate relationship between the intended legitimate objective and the means used. The exception may not eat up the rule.

Article 14 affirms that Hizmet's rights and freedoms recognized in the Convention must be "secured without discrimination on any ground such as … political or other opinion … or any other status." Türkiye's systemic denial of Hizmet's fundamental rights and freedoms for political or other opinion and of those associated with Hizmet can and has become an attempt at politicide.

Systemic Discrimination and Denial of Equal Protection

Human rights in Türkiye are governed by its domestic law and international law treaties, including the ECHR, the International Covenant on Civil and Political Rights (ICCPR), and the International Covenant on Economic, Social and Cultural Rights (ICESCR), to all which Türkiye is a signatory. They take precedence over Turkish legislation according to Article 90 of the Turkish Constitution and as required by those international covenants. Türkiye became a party to the ECHR in 1954 and recognized the ECtHR's compulsory jurisdiction in 1990.

All those covenants prohibit discrimination for "political or other opinion," as do the United Nations Declaration of Rights and the Constitution of Türkiye. They apply with vigor to the pervasive and ongoing persecution of Hizmet people as a class and those associated with them.

The ICCPR has no enforcement mechanism as does the ECHR through the ECtHR. A Human Rights Committee (HRC) "enforces" ICCPR by explaining the meaning and scope of ICCPR provisions, but these conclusions and observations are not legally binding. However, states are expected to act in good faith, consistent with the HRC's views. Those views or positions are helpful in interpreting other conventions, such as the ECHR.

Likewise, the Universal Declaration of Human Rights, adopted by the United Nations in 1948, is not legally binding like the other charters and therefore cannot be directly enforced. However, it serves as a guiding framework and has influenced international and regional human rights treaties, which are legally binding on the countries that have ratified them, like Türkiye. Türkiye has signed the Universal Declaration of Human Rights.

Similarly, as a member of the Organization for Security and Co-operation in Europe (OSCE), Türkiye agreed in Copenhagen in 1990 that participating states should "guarantee to all persons equal and effective protection against discrimination on any ground."[5] Moreover, the revised version of the European Social Charter in Section 5, Paragraph (E) ensures the exercise of rights without discrimination based on reasons such as .... political or other opinions ... or other status.

One manifestation of systemic discriminatory and hate-based regime policies during this period has been its application of the state of emergency decrees to Hizmet people as a class in such a way that they implicitly annul the Constitution and laws of Türkiye and explicitly contradict international law and conventions.

During this process, the Anti-Terror Law, re-interpreted far from the intention of prior Turkish parliaments and past precedents of the country's Constitutional Court, became the fundamental apparatus for threatening Hizmet-associated people and subjecting them to a discriminatory, hate-based politicide. The regime contorted universal legal criteria concerning terrorist organizations and membership therein, contrary to international law as well as previous decisions of the Constitutional Court, to serve the cause of Hizmet's annihilation.

Qualifying as a Crime Against Humanity Within Framework of International Documents

The term discrimination, in the context in which Erdoğan and his functionaries have perpetrated it for more than a decade, is a weak description of the brutal reality of the politicide, civil death, against those associated with the Gülen Movement, with whose political ideas they are in profound conflict. Politicide is the most consequential and deadly form of discrimination. This epitome of discrimination is precisely what the international charters seek to prevent.

What ties together all the fundamental rights violations described in this book is the panorama of politicide with its unrelenting and undaunting machinations against Hizmet people, as a group, and those associated with them, cloaked with piercing hate speech. It is discrimination in its ultimate and grossest form, rising to the level of systemically inflicted civil death.

There is no question that the avowed purpose is the elimination of Hizmet as an association. The motive is not hidden but loudly proclaimed from the rooftops and over the media. The only question is whether the Erdoğan regime has engaged in, and continues to engage in, crimes against humanity that amount to politicide. The answer can only be affirmative.

The campaign against people because of their association with Hizmet encompass the systemic collective violations of the following panoply of fundamental rights, which are part of the severe discriminatory treatment inflicted by the regime upon the Gülen Movement because of its exercise of fundamental rights.

Appendix A contains the full texts of the respective provisions cited in the subsequent enumeration of rights violations. The respective comparable Turkish provisos are included, although the Erdoğan government breaches them with abandon and the courts' acquiescence; but they show the country's recognition of the fundamental human rights that it flouts.

Prohibition of Torture

- ECHR Article 3
- ICCPR Article 7
- Article 5 of the Universal Declaration of Human Rights (UDHR)
- Turkish Constitution Article 17

Equal Protection and Non-Discrimination

- ECHR Article 14
- ICCPR Articles 2, 19
- ICESCR Article 2
- UDHR Articles 2, 26
- Turkish Constitution Article 10

Freedom from Cruel, Inhuman, or Degrading Treatment or Punishment

- ECHR Article 3
- ICCPR Articles 7
- UDHR Article 5
- Turkish Constitution Article 17

Freedom of Expression

- ECHR Article 10
- ICCPR Article 19

- UDHR Article 19
- Turkish Constitution Article 26

Freedom of Assembly and Association

- ECHR Article 11
- ICCPR Article 21
- UDHR Article 20
- Turkish Constitution Article 34

Freedom of Thought and Conscience

- ECHR Article 9
- ICCPR Article 18
- UDHR Article 18
- Turkish Constitution Article 25

Freedom from Retroactive Criminal Prosecution and Enhanced Punishment

- ECHR Article 7
- ICCPR Article 15
- UDHR Article 11(2)
- Turkish Constitution Article 38

Right to a Fair Trial

- ECHR Article 6
- ICCPR Article 14
- UDHR Article 10

Right to Effective Remedy for Violation of Rights and Freedoms

- ECHR Article 13
- ICCPR Article 2.3
- UDHR Article 8

Right to a Natural Judge

- ICCPR Article 2.3(b)
- UDHR Article 10

Right to Freedom of Movement Within One's Country and to Leave It

- ECHR Article 2, Protocol 4
- ICCPR Article 12
- UDHR Article 13

Prohibition on Arbitrarily Depriving People of Their Nationality

- UDHR Article 15

Right to Seek Asylum in Another Country

- UDHR Article 14
- Turkish Constitution Article 37

Privacy, Family, Home, and Correspondence

- ECHR Article 8
- ICCPR Article 17 (adding honor and reputation)
- UDHR Article 12 (adding honor and reputation)

Right to Work and Due Process in Employment Termination

- ICESCR Article 6.1
- 77 ILO Convention Articles 4, 7, and 8

International Labour Organisation (ILO) Convention 158 to which Türkiye is a signatory party protects against arbitrary dismissals without due process.

Right to Adequate Standard of Living

- ICESCR Article 11.1
- UDHR Article 25

Unlawful Derogation of Fundamental Rights During State of Emergency

- ECHR Article 15
- ICCPR Article 4
- ICESCR Article 5.2
- Turkish Constitution Article 15

Professional Annihilation: Multi-Purposed

One critical foundation of the discrimination and annihilation edifice that Erdoğan built against Hizmet is the two-step combination attack on the employment of Hizmet professionals: first, the mass dismissals; and then restrictions on securing other similar employment thereafter. For example, dismissed jurists could not practice as lawyers. Teachers discharged from Hizmet institutions could not teach elsewhere. Other measures accompanying their dismissals subjected them to a broad spectrum of violations of human rights guaranteed by international instruments.

State-sanctioned dismissals based on perceived or actual political or other affiliation violate the fundamental rights to freedom of expression, association, thought, concerted activity, free assembly, and due process ensured by the international covenants to which Türkiye is a party. They result from the overarching breach of the right to non-discrimination and equal protection, if selectively perpetrated, as indeed Erdoğan and Türkiye did.

Besides purely punitive personal measures, another strong impetus behind the regime's professional annihilation effort is to deny Hizmet the ability to financially support itself and its works as a movement or association since that depends on the largesse of its supporters, especially professionals with greater resources. That, too, is the motivation behind the regime's summary seizure of billions of dollars of Hizmet-related assets without compensation, to dispossess it of financial backing and remove its support structure—part of the politicide project.

No doubt the European Court of Human Rights should find Türkiye culpable of crimes against humanity, demand the cessation, and require just compensation and restoration of rights for all those who suffered from the politicide, individuals and institutions.

Final Comments

In 2020, the Working Group on Arbitrary Detention of the United Nations Human Rights Council noted a significant increase in the number of cases brought to it over a three-year period concerning the extraterritorial abductions and arbitrary detentions in Türkiye of Hizmet-affiliated victims.

The UN group emphasized that, under certain circumstances, widespread or systematic imprisonment or other severe deprivation of liberty in violation of international law may constitute "crimes against humanity."[6] The Erdoğan regime crossed that bridge years ago and continues its persecution unabated.

The list of ECtHR decisions against Türkiye is long; and, as its *Yalçınkaya* case underscored,[7] the list of non-compliance is likewise long.[8] Given the Turkish courts' refusal to apply relief to claimants, enforcement of ECtHR decisions and ICCPR compliance will have to fall to the Council of Europe, which has the matter under consideration. Solution will be no easy matter, given Erdoğan's recalcitrance.[9] The Council of Europe must take seriously Türkiye's snubbing of the European Court of Human Rights and put teeth into sanctions.

In violation of the strictures of international law and its own internal law, Türkiye has created an overarching edifice of illegal discrimination that denies equal protection to those associated with Hizmet. It has shored up that edifice with a sustained hate speech campaign and deliberate violation of an array of fundamental human rights, which has purposely inflicted undue harm, pain, and even death on those associated with the Gülen Movement with the goal of the movement's civil death and annihilation—politicide. The facts are incontrovertible. Nor do Erdoğan and his government disavow the goal; they embrace it.

Addressing and ending the Hizmet politicide crisis is paramount. It has adversely affected hundreds of hundreds of thousands of innocent victims and continues to do so. It can be a matter of life and death. Not taking up the task will open the door to other budding totalitarian and autocratic rulers, bent on power and wealth. One cannot overstate the risk to democracy. The international community has correctly assessed the situation, but governments are pulling their punches, no doubt for fear of offending Türkiye because of its increasing geopolitical significance.

The United Nations High Commissioner for Human Rights outlined the two-step process forward. One is that Türkiye restore the normal functioning of its institutions, revise and repeal all legislation that is not compliant with Türkiye's international human rights obligations. Second is to ensure independent, individualized reviews and compensation for victims of arbitrary detentions and dismissals. Structural reform and remedial relief for those who suffered unjustly.

Failure to deal appropriately and effectively with Erdoğan flashed a message of impunity to others lurking in the shadows with authoritarian tendencies to replicate.

The time to reverse the course of Erdoğan and Türkiye is now and in the most appropriate and strongest measures possible, not only for the people of Türkiye and Hizmet but also for the international community that hopes and aspires for wider democracy and civil society.

Endnotes

1 "Turkey: UN report details extensive human rights violations during protracted state of emergency," Office of the High Commissioner for Human Rights (20 March 2018), Turkey: UN report details extensive human rights violations during protracted state of emergency | OHCHR.

2 "Report on the impact of the state of emergency on human rights in Turkey, including an update on the South-East, January – December 2017," Office of the United Nations High Commissioner for Human Rights (March 2018), https://www.ohchr.org/sites/default/files/Documents/Countries/TR/2018-03-19_Second_OHCHR_Turkey_Report.pdf.

3 Article 2, International Covenant on Civil and Political Rights; Article 2, International Covenant on Economic, Social and Cultural Rights; and Article 14, European Convention on Human Rights.

4 Part One, Article 10 of the Constitution of Türkiye.

5 "Hate crime against other groups," OSCE, https://hatecrime.osce.org/hate-crime-against-other-groups.

6 "Opinions adopted by the Working Group on Arbitrary Detention at its eighty-eighth session, 24–28 August 2020," Human Rights Council (18 September 2020), https://www.ohchr.org/sites/default/files/Documents/Issues/Detention/Opinions/Session88/A_HRC_WGAD_2020_51_Advance_Edited_Version.pdf. *See also* "Opinions adopted by the Working Group on Arbitrary Detention at its eighty-eighth session, 24–28 August 2020," Human Rights Council (25 September 2020), https://www.ohchr.org/sites/default/files/Documents/Issues/Detention/Opinions/Session88/A_HRC_WGAD_2020_47_Advance_Edited_Version.pdf.

7 *Yüksel Yalçinkaya v. Türkiye* (No. 15669/20), ECtHR (26 Sept. 2023), ECHR (courthousenews.com). *See also* Emre Turkut, "'Article 7' Shockwaves, ByLock and Beyond: Unpacking the Grand Chamber's Yalçinkaya Judgment," Strasbourg Observers (Oct. 13, 2013), https://strasbourgobservers.com/2023/10/13/article-7-shockwaves-bylock-and-beyond-unpacking-the-grand-chambers-yalcinkaya-judgment/.

8 "Turkey Flouts European Court Judgments," Human Rights Watch (June 4, 2021), https://www.hrw.org/news/2021/06/04/turkey-flouts-european-court-judgments. *See also* "Turkey: Council of Europe Votes for Infringement Process," Human Rights Watch (Feb. 2, 2022), https://www.hrw.org/news/2022/02/02/turkey-council-europe-votes-infringement-process. *See also* "After July 15, Violation Judgements Against Turkey by the ECtHR," Justice Square, https://justicesquare.org/after-15-july-violation-judgements-against-turkey-by-the-ecthr/. (Summary overview of ECtHR judgements against Türkiye through April 2023). *See also* United Nations Resolutions and Reports Concerning Türkiye (Appendix D).

9 "Joint Application by Six Civil Society Organisations for the Initiation of the Implementation Process of Yalçınkaya Decision," Justice Square (July 8, 2024), https://justicesquare.org/joint-call-by-6-ngos/.

Conclusion

Overall, at this time in history, the autocrats and totalitarians are ascendant. We must recognize that reality and push back forcefully. Hopefully, this book contributes to that effort and, in some fashion, will help hold Türkiye accountable for all the acts of injustice that it has perpetrated against the people of Hizmet and their supporters for far more than a decade. History teaches disastrous consequences if we do not repulse powermongers and protect democratic institutions.

Hizmet was a major roadblock in Türkiye to Erdoğan's march to authoritarianism. Hizmet stood for building civil society in the country. The movement was strikingly successful, but its values and moral integrity clashed with Erdoğan and his group who preferred to aggrandize power and wealth for themselves at the expense of building a democratic nation. Their response to Hizmet was politicide.

The regime's politicide agenda gradually evolved from the hate policies targeting Hizmet after the December 2013 corruption scandal, which rocked Erdoğan's world. The bizarre abortive 2016 coup attempt became the pretext for a no-holds-barred attack on Hizmet as official state policy. Systemic crimes against humanity undergirded the government's assault.

Civil death, annihilation, politicide, is the goal. Erdoğan pulled no punches in proclaiming that provocative hate-filled agenda, often publicly. The war on Hizmet also provided the smokescreen the regime needed to dramatically alter the levers of power, concentrating dominance in one person and group and eviscerating the separation of powers structure needed for a democracy to survive and thrive.

The state nailed down a discriminatory government while galvanizing society through hate speech. The regime captured the institutions of government and conscripted them into the politicide project. The media decided to play the game and become partners. Opposition sectors, influenced by—or taking unprincipled advantage of—the atmosphere of hate, let themselves be drawn into the politicide orbit.

Instead of raising their voices against rampant injustice, sizeable segments of Turkish society acquiesced in, and even applauded, the crimes against Hizmet and the overarching structure of discrimination and denial of equal protection. They unwittingly made others—and perhaps themselves—future victims of state-crafted "witch hunts," oppression, and crimes against humanity.

The civil death project launched against Hizmet became the vehicle to regularize arbitrary detentions, arrests, dismissals from employment, seizure of assets, closure of institutions, and curtailment of freedoms. The government strove to create a veneer of legitimacy for these unconscionable actions through hate speech fueled by prejudice, misinformation, conspiracy theories, and propaganda—all untethered to truth. The unabashed intent was, and is, to condemn Hizmet members, supporters, and associates to civil death.

The politicide program, couched in divisive, hate-provoking, and violence-inciting speech of the vilest kind, also served the Erdoğan regime to camouflage and excuse its failures, corruption, and descent from a nascent democratic republic to autocratic rule. The relentless drumbeat of hate speech from official and unofficial government organs, interlaced with false nationalism, and the parlaying of a cascade of false facts succeeded in diminishing Hizmet's societal support.

Implemented as a policy, this annihilation scheme extended its tentacles into prisons, in the courts, on the streets, in neighborhoods, and across all social, economic, and cultural spheres. In the process of being relegated to civil death, people became victims of crimes against humanity, not in isolated incidents, but as casualties of a cohesive, overarching plan, not because of what they had done but because of who they were and because of their and Hizmet's democratic political views and their passion for civil society..

The people of Türkiye are also victims of Hizmet's suppression in myriad ways. The country has suffered and will continue to suffer. The government has deprived the Turkish people of an ally in Hizmet and has pushed them off their path to a more democratic civil society.

Hizmet has a respected history of devoting efforts to education, dialogue, and tolerance. It categorically rejects injustice, crime, radicalism, violence, and terrorism. Despite being subjected to the regime's hate policies, discriminatory practices, and efforts at politicide, it maintains its existence within the framework of universal humanitarianism and compassionate Islamic values. Its work continues as strong as ever across the globe, although not in Türkiye.

Politicide, a crime against humanity, annihilation, is Erdoğan's despotic endgame. The international community recognizes this and has supported the Gülen Movement in its struggle against the regime's overreach and the untold suffering it has wantonly inflicted.

Erdoğan's incremental march toward authoritarian rule reflects an alarming movement around the world, including in the United States and Europe, to bend and coopt civil society institutions to serve an autocrat's agenda. Erdoğan gives us a lesson from the playbook of despotic governance that we dare not ignore, not only for the sake of Hizmet but also for the future of democracy.

The time has come—and is long overdue—for international democratic governments to acknowledge the situation more firmly for what it is and take appropriate steps, steps they have thus far shown themselves reluctant to take. Everyone has responsibility in this effort.

Justice and the integrity of the international human rights movement are at stake.

Timeline

2000-2010	Türkiye moves firmly toward European Union accession and introduces democratic reforms, including of the judiciary
2010	Constitutional referendum (expanding human rights protections and reforming judiciary, in part through restructuring and expanding HSYK)
2013	Gezi Park protests (May 28 to August 20)
	Government corruption scandal unfolds (December 17)
2014	Presidential palace is built Criminal Judgeships of Peace infrastructure goes into operation
2016	Turkish National Security Council (MGK) designates FETÖ as a terrorist (January 8). Another MGK declaration and five months categorize Hizmet as a parallel state structure and a terrorist organization posing a national security threat.
	Parliament restructures HSYK, established by the 1982 Constitution and restructured by 2010 constitutional referendum
	Coup attempt (July 15)
	Purges begin (July 16)
	State of Emergency declared (July 20)

2017 Constitutional referendum (undoing judiciary reforms of 2010 referendum, reconfiguring HYSK as KYK, and adopting a strong presidential governance model) (April 16)

Reza Zarrab pleads guilty in New York for his role in the December 2017 corruption scandal (October 26)

2018 Türkiye transitions from a parliamentary system to a presidential system, abolishing the office of Prime Minister and giving the president both head of state and head of government roles.

State of Emergency ends (July 18)

Courts and the Like

Türkiye

Constitutional Court

The Constitutional Court of Türkiye is the highest legal body for constitutional review. It reviews the constitutionality, in both form and substance, of laws, decrees having the force of law, and the parliament's rules of procedure. If necessary, it also functions as the Supreme Criminal Court to hear any cases raised about the president, vice president, members of the cabinet, or judges of the high courts. In addition, it examines individual applications on the grounds that one of the fundamental rights and freedoms of European Convention on Human Rights, which are guaranteed by the constitution, has been violated by public authorities.

Council of State

The Council of State is the country's highest administrative court. It hears appeals from lower administrative courts and matters over which law has given it direct and primary jurisdiction. It also hears cases between government entities.

Court of Cassation

The Court of Cassation, officially called the Supreme Court of Appeals, is the last instance for reviewing verdicts of courts of criminal and civil justice in Türkiye.

Trial Level Civil and Criminal Courts ("First Instance")

Specialized Courts (such as family, commercial, labor, and the like)

Europe

Council of Europe

The Council of Europe is an international organization with the goal of promoting human rights, democracy, and the rule of law in Europe and beyond. Türkiye is one of the forty-six member states, which altogether encompass 700 million people.

Venice Commission

The Venice Commission (officially, European Commission for Democracy through Law) is an advisory body of the Council of Europe, comprised of independent experts in constitutional law from sixty-one countries.

European Convention On Human Rights

The European Convention on Human Rights is a supranational convention to protect human rights and political freedoms in Europe. Drafted in 1950 by the newly formed Council of Europe, the convention entered into force in 1953.

European Court of Human Rights

The European Court of Human Rights enforces the European Convention on Human Rights Türkiye is one of the forty-six countries that have obligated themselves to abide by the convention and voluntarily honor and enforce judgments of the court. Aggrieved residents of a country can appeal to the court if their country has violated their rights under the convention. The Council of Europe's Parliamentary Assembly elects the ECtHR judges.

Afterword

In *Erdoğan's Civil Death Project: Persecution of the Hizmet Movement in Türkiye*, James C. Harrington and Coşkun Yorulmaz provide a harrowing and meticulously documented analysis of President Erdoğan's campaign to eradicate the Hizmet movement. Through mass purges, emergency decrees, the bending of the judiciary, torture, hate speech, and the criminalization of dissent, they reveal how an entire segment of Turkish civil society was driven toward "civil death."

This book details not only the persecution of Hizmet but also the broader collapse of the rule of law in Türkiye — a collapse with consequences that reverberate far beyond its borders. It is a case study in how democracies can unravel when state institutions are weaponized against their own people.

Having represented victims of Türkiye's repression before the European Court of Human Rights and the bodies of the United Nations, we recognize in these pages both the lived experiences of our clients and the wider dismantling of fundamental freedoms.

This is important since the persecution of the Hizmet Movement is not an isolated tragedy. Today it is Hizmet, yesterday it was the Kurds, and tomorrow it will be the Kemalists — for authoritarian regimes ultimately spare no one but themselves.

The book clearly reveals how hate speech, emergency decrees, and the instrumentalization of the judiciary can converge to strip citizens of their most basic protections. The stories we encounter in our litigation — of judges dismissed overnight, families torn apart, and individuals branded as terrorists for acts as simple as education or association — echo the patterns so carefully documented by the authors.

This book reminds us that authoritarianism rarely announces itself with a single event. It creeps in through legal exceptions that become the rule, through language that normalizes exclusion, and through courts that abandon their duty to protect. The case of Türkiye underscores the responsibility of the international community, and particularly of European institutions, to uphold the standards they have pledged to defend.

It is therefore our hope that these pages will resonate not only with legal practitioners, but with all who believe that the protection of rights is the cornerstone of a free society.

Johan Heymans*, Managing Partner at Van Steenbrugge Advocaten*
Johan Vande Lanotte*, Former Deputy Prime Minister in federal governments in Belgium*

Appendix A

Relevant International Human Rights Provisions

European Convention on Human Rights (ECHR)

Article 2 - Right to life

1. Everyone's right to life shall be protected by law. No one shall be deprived of his life intentionally save in the execution of a sentence of a court following his conviction of a crime for which this penalty is provided by law.

2. Deprivation of life shall not be regarded as inflicted in contravention of this Article when it results from the use of force which is no more than:

(a) in defence of any person from unlawful violence;

(b) in order to effect a lawful arrest or to prevent the escape of a person lawfully detained;

(c) in action lawfully taken for the purpose of quelling a riot or insurrection.

Article 2, Protocol No. 4

1. Everyone lawfully within the territory of a State shall, within that territory, have the right to liberty of movement and freedom to choose his residence. 2. Everyone shall be free to leave any country, including his own.

3. No restrictions shall be placed on the exercise of these rights other than such as are in accordance with law and are necessary in a democratic society in the interests of national security or public safety, for the maintenance of ordre public, for the prevention of crime, for the protection of health or morals, or for the protection of the rights and freedoms of others.

4. The rights set forth in paragraph 1 may also be subject, in particular areas, to restrictions imposed in accordance with law and justified by the public interest in a democratic society.

Article 3 - Prohibition of torture

No one shall be subjected to torture or to inhuman or degrading treatment or punishment.

Article 6 – Right to a fair trial

1. In the determination of his civil rights and obligations or of any criminal charge against him, everyone is entitled to a fair and public hearing within a reasonable time by an independent and impartial tribunal established by law. Judgment shall be pronounced publicly but the press and public may be excluded from all or part of the trial in the interests of morals, public order or national security in a democratic society, where the interests of juveniles or the protection of the private life of the parties so require, or to the extent strictly necessary in the opinion of the court in special circumstances where publicity would prejudice the interests of justice.

2. Everyone charged with a criminal offence shall be presumed innocent until proved guilty according to law.

3. Everyone charged with a criminal offence has the following minimum rights:

(a) to be informed promptly, in a language which he understands and in detail, of the nature and cause of the accusation against him;

(b) to have adequate time and facilities for the preparation of his defence;

(c) to defend himself in person or through legal assistance of his own choosing or, if he has not sufficient means to pay for legal assistance, to be given it free when the interests of justice so require;

(d) to examine or have examined witnesses against him and to obtain the attendance and examination of witnesses on his behalf under the same conditions as witnesses against him;

(e) to have the free assistance of an interpreter if he cannot understand or speak the language used in court.

Article 7 - No punishment without law

1. No one shall be held guilty of any criminal offence on account of

any act or omission which did not constitute a criminal offence under national or international law at the time when it was committed. Nor shall a heavier penalty be imposed than the one that was applicable at the time the criminal offence was committed.

2. This Article shall not prejudice the trial and punishment of any person for any act or omission which, at the time when it was committed, was criminal according to the general principles of law recognised by civilised nations.

Article 8 – Right to respect for private and family life

1. Everyone has the right to respect for his private and family life, his home and his correspondence.

2. There shall be no interference by a public authority with the exercise of this right except such as is in accordance with the law and is necessary in a democratic society in the interests of national security, public safety or the economic well-being of the country, for the prevention of disorder or crime, for the protection of health or morals, or for the protection of the rights and freedoms of others.

Article 9 - Freedom of thought, conscience and religion

1. Everyone has the right to freedom of thought, conscience and religion; this right includes freedom to change his religion or belief and freedom, either alone or in community with others and in public or private, to manifest his religion or belief, in worship, teaching practice and observance.

2. Freedom to manifest one's religion or beliefs shall be subject only to such limitations as are prescribed by law and are necessary in a democratic society in the interests of public safety, for the protection of public order, health or morals, or for the protection of the rights and freedoms of others.

Article 10 – Freedom of expression

1. Everyone has the right to freedom of expression. This right shall include freedom to hold opinions and to receive and impart information and ideas without interference by public authority and regardless of frontiers. This article shall not prevent States from requiring the licensing of broadcasting, television or cinema enterprises.

2. The exercise of these freedoms, since it carries with it duties and responsibilities, may be subject to such formalities, conditions, restric-

tions or penalties as are prescribed by law and are necessary in a democratic society, in the interests of national security, territorial integrity or public safety, for the prevention of disorder or crime, for the protection of health or morals, for the protection of the reputation or rights of others, for preventing the disclosure of information received in confidence, or for maintaining the authority and impartiality of the judiciary.

Article 11 – Freedom of assembly and association

1. Everyone has the right to freedom of peaceful assembly and to freedom of association with others, including the right to form and to join trade unions for the protection of his interests.

2. No restrictions shall be placed on the exercise of these rights other than such as are prescribed by law and are necessary in a democratic society in the interests of national security or public safety, for the prevention of disorder or crime, for the protection of health or morals or for the protection of the rights and freedoms of others. This article shall not prevent the imposition of lawful restrictions on the exercise of these rights by members of the armed forces, of the police or of the administration of the State.

Article 13 - Right to an effective remedy

Everyone whose rights and freedoms as set forth in this Convention are violated shall have an effective remedy before a national authority notwithstanding that the violation has been committed by persons acting in an official capacity.

Article 14 - Prohibition of discrimination

The enjoyment of the rights and freedoms set forth in this Convention shall be secured without discrimination on any ground such as sex, race, colour, language, religion, political or other opinion, national or social origin, association with a national minority, property, birth or other status.

Article 15 – Derogation in time of emergency

1. In time of war or other public emergency threatening the life of the nation any High Contracting Party may take measures derogating from its obligations under this Convention to the extent strictly required by the exigencies of the situation, provided that such measures are not inconsistent with its other obligations under international law.

2. No derogation from Article 2, except in respect of deaths resulting

from lawful acts of war, or from Articles 3, 4 (paragraph 1) and 7 shall be made under this provision.

3. Any High Contracting Party availing itself of this right of derogation shall keep the Secretary General of the Council of Europe fully informed of the measures which it has taken and the reasons therefor. It shall also inform the Secretary General of the Council of Europe when such measures have ceased to operate and the provisions of the Convention are again being fully executed.

Article 17 - **Prohibition of abuse of rights**

Nothing in this Convention may be interpreted as implying for any State, group or person any right to engage in any activity or perform any act aimed at the destruction of any of the rights and freedoms set forth herein or at their limitation to a greater extent than is provided for in the Convention.

International Covenant on Civil and Political Rights (ICCPR)

Article 1

1. All peoples have the right of self-determination. By virtue of that right they freely determine their political status and freely pursue their economic, social and cultural development.

Article 2

1. Each State Party to the present Covenant undertakes to respect and to ensure to all individuals within its territory and subject to its jurisdiction the rights recognized in the present Covenant, without distinction of any kind, such as race, colour, sex, language, religion, political or other opinion, national or social origin, property, birth or other status.
2. Where not already provided for by existing legislative or other measures, each State Party to the present Covenant undertakes to take the necessary steps, in accordance with its constitutional processes and with the provisions of the present Covenant, to adopt such laws or other measures as may be necessary to give effect to the rights recognized in the present Covenant.
3. Each State Party to the present Covenant undertakes:

(a) To ensure that any person whose rights or freedoms as herein recognized are violated shall have an effective remedy, notwithstanding that the violation has been committed by persons acting in an official capacity;

(b) To ensure that any person claiming such a remedy shall have his right thereto determined by competent judicial, administrative or legislative authorities, or by any other competent authority provided for by the legal system of the State, and to develop the possibilities of judicial remedy;

(c) To ensure that the competent authorities shall enforce such remedies when granted.

Article 4

1. In time of public emergency which threatens the life of the nation and the existence of which is officially proclaimed, the States Parties to the present Covenant may take measures derogating from their obligations under the present Covenant to the extent strictly required by the exigencies of the situation, provided that such measures are not

inconsistent with their other obligations under international law and do not involve discrimination solely on the ground of race, colour, sex, language, religion or social origin.
2. No derogation from articles 6, 7, 8 (paragraphs I and 2), 11, 15, 16 and 18 may be made under this provision....
3. Any State Party to the present Covenant availing itself of the right of derogation shall immediately inform the other States Parties to the present Covenant, through the intermediary of the Secretary-General of the United Nations, of the provisions from which it has derogated and of the reasons by which it was actuated. A further communication shall be made, through the same intermediary, on the date on which it terminates such derogation.

Article 7

No one shall be subjected to torture or to cruel, inhuman or degrading treatment or punishment. In particular, no one shall be subjected without his free consent to medical or scientific experimentation.

Article 12

1. Everyone lawfully within the territory of a State shall, within that territory, have the right to liberty of movement and freedom to choose his residence.
2. Everyone shall be free to leave any country, including his own.
3. The above-mentioned rights shall not be subject to any restrictions except those which are provided by law, are necessary to protect national security, public order (ordre public), public health or morals or the rights and freedoms of others, and are consistent with the other rights recognized in the present Covenant.
4. No one shall be arbitrarily deprived of the right to enter his own country.

Article 14

1. All persons shall be equal before the courts and tribunals. In the determination of any criminal charge against him, or of his rights and obligations in a suit at law, everyone shall be entitled to a fair and public hearing by a competent, independent and impartial tribunal established by law. The press and the public may be excluded from all or part of a trial for reasons of morals, public order (ordre public) or national security in a democratic society, or when the interest of the private lives of

the parties so requires, or to the extent strictly necessary in the opinion of the court in special circumstances where publicity would prejudice the interests of justice; but any judgement rendered in a criminal case or in a suit at law shall be made public except where the interest of juvenile persons otherwise requires or the proceedings concern matrimonial disputes or the guardianship of children.

2. Everyone charged with a criminal offence shall have the right to be presumed innocent until proved guilty according to law.

3. In the determination of any criminal charge against him, everyone shall be entitled to the following minimum guarantees, in full equality:

- (a) To be informed promptly and in detail in a language which he understands of the nature and cause of the charge against him;
- (b) To have adequate time and facilities for the preparation of his defence and to communicate with counsel of his own choosing;
- (c) To be tried without undue delay;
- (d) To be tried in his presence, and to defend himself in person or through legal assistance of his own choosing; to be informed, if he does not have legal assistance, of this right; and to have legal assistance assigned to him, in any case where the interests of justice so require, and without payment by him in any such case if he does not have sufficient means to pay for it;
- (e) To examine, or have examined, the witnesses against him and to obtain the attendance and examination of witnesses on his behalf under the same conditions as witnesses against him;
- (f) To have the free assistance of an interpreter if he cannot understand or speak the language used in court;
- (g) Not to be compelled to testify against himself or to confess guilt.

4. In the case of juvenile persons, the procedure shall be such as will take account of their age and the desirability of promoting their rehabilitation.

5. Everyone convicted of a crime shall have the right to his conviction and sentence being reviewed by a higher tribunal according to law.

6. When a person has by a final decision been convicted of a criminal offence and when subsequently his conviction has been reversed or he has been pardoned on the ground that a new or newly discovered fact shows conclusively that there has been a miscarriage of justice, the person who has suffered punishment as a result of such conviction shall be compensated according to law, unless it is proved that the non-disclosure of the unknown fact in time is wholly or partly attributable to him.
7. No one shall be liable to be tried or punished again for an offence for which he has already been finally convicted or acquitted in accordance with the law and penal procedure of each country.

Article 15

1. No one shall be held guilty of any criminal offence on account of any act or omission which did not constitute a criminal offence, under national or international law, at the time when it was committed. Nor shall a heavier penalty be imposed than the one that was applicable at the time when the criminal offence was committed. If, subsequent to the commission of the offence, provision is made by law for the imposition of the lighter penalty, the offender shall benefit thereby.
2. Nothing in this article shall prejudice the trial and punishment of any person for any act or omission which, at the time when it was committed, was criminal according to the general principles of law recognized by the community of nations.

Article 17

1. No one shall be subjected to arbitrary or unlawful interference with his privacy, family, home or correspondence, nor to unlawful attacks on his honor and reputation.
2. Everyone has the right to the protection of the law against such interference or attacks.

Article 18

1. Everyone shall have the right to freedom of thought, conscience and religion. This right shall include freedom to have or to adopt a religion or belief of his choice, and freedom, either individually or in community with others and in public or private, to manifest his religion or belief in worship, observance, practice and teaching.
2. No one shall be subject to coercion which would impair his freedom to have or to adopt a religion or belief of his choice.

3. Freedom to manifest one's religion or beliefs may be subject only to such limitations as are prescribed by law and are necessary to protect public safety, order, health, or morals or the fundamental rights and freedoms of others....

Article 19

1. Everyone shall have the right to hold opinions without interference.
2. Everyone shall have the right to freedom of expression; this right shall include freedom to seek, receive and impart information and ideas of all kinds, regardless of frontiers, either orally, in writing or in print, in the form of art, or through any other media of his choice.
3. The exercise of the rights provided for in paragraph 2 of this article carries with it special duties and responsibilities. It may therefore be subject to certain restrictions, but these shall only be such as are provided by law and are necessary:

   (a) For respect of the rights or reputations of others;

   (b) For the protection of national security or of public order (ordre public), or of public health or morals.

Article 20

1. Any propaganda for war shall be prohibited by law.
2. Any advocacy of national, racial or religious hatred that constitutes incitement to discrimination, hostility or violence shall be prohibited by law.

Article 21

The right of peaceful assembly shall be recognized. No restrictions may be placed on the exercise of this right other than those imposed in conformity with the law and which are necessary in a democratic society in the interests of national security or public safety, public order (ordre public), the protection of public health or morals or the protection of the rights and freedoms of others.

Article 22

1. Everyone shall have the right to freedom of association with others, including the right to form and join trade unions for the protection of his interests.
2. No restrictions may be placed on the exercise of this right other than those which are prescribed by law and which are necessary in a democratic society in the interests of national security or public safety, public

order (ordre public), the protection of public health or morals or the protection of the rights and freedoms of others....

Article 23

1. The family is the natural and fundamental group unit of society and is entitled to protection by society and the State....

Article 26

All persons are equal before the law and are entitled without any discrimination to the equal protection of the law. In this respect, the law shall prohibit any discrimination and guarantee to all persons equal and effective protection against discrimination on any ground such as race, colour, sex, language, religion, political or other opinion, national or social origin, property, birth or other status.

International Covenant on Economic, Social and Cultural Rights (ICESCR)

Article 5

1. Nothing in the present Covenant may be interpreted as implying for any State, group or person any right to engage in any activity or to perform any act aimed at the destruction of any of the rights or freedoms recognized herein, or at their limitation to a greater extent than is provided for in the present Covenant.
2. No restriction upon or derogation from any of the fundamental human rights recognized or existing in any country in virtue of law, conventions, regulations or custom shall be admitted on the pretext that the present Covenant does not recognize such rights or that it recognizes them to a lesser extent.

Article 2.2

2. The States Parties to the present Covenant undertake to guarantee that the rights enunciated in the present Covenant will be exercised without discrimination of any kind as to race, colour, sex, language, religion, political or other opinion, national or social origin, property, birth or other status.

Article 6.1

The States Parties to the present Covenant recognize the right to work, which includes the right of everyone to the opportunity to gain his living by work which he freely chooses or accepts, and will take appropriate steps to safeguard this right.

Article 11.1

The States Parties to the present Covenant recognize the right of everyone to an adequate standard of living for himself and his family, including adequate food, clothing and housing, and to the continuous improvement of living conditions. The States Parties will take appropriate steps to ensure the realization of this right, recognizing to this effect the essential importance of international co-operation based on free consent.

International Labour Organisation Convention

C158 - Termination of Employment Convention, 1982 (No. 158)

Part II. Standards of General Application

Division A. Justification for Termination

Article 4

The employment of a worker shall not be terminated unless there is a valid reason for such termination connected with the capacity or conduct of the worker or based on the operational requirements of the undertaking, establishment or service.

Division B. Procedure Prior To Or at the Time of Termination

Article 7

The employment of a worker shall not be terminated for reasons related to the worker's conduct or performance before he is provided an opportunity to defend himself against the allegations made, unless the employer cannot reasonably be expected to provide this opportunity.

Division C. Procedure of Appeal Against Termination

Article 8

1. A worker who considers that his employment has been unjustifiably terminated shall be entitled to appeal against that termination to an impartial body, such as a court, labour tribunal, arbitration committee or arbitrator.
2. Where termination has been authorised by a competent authority the application of paragraph 1 of this Article may be varied according to national law and practice.

Universal Declaration of Human Rights

Article 2

Everyone is entitled to all the rights and freedoms set forth in this Declaration, without distinction of any kind, such as race, colour, sex, language, religion, political or other opinion, national or social origin, property, birth or other status.

Article 5

No one shall be subjected to torture or to cruel, inhuman or degrading treatment or punishment.

Article 7

All are equal before the law and are entitled without any discrimination to equal protection of the law. All are entitled to equal protection against any discrimination in violation of this Declaration and against any incitement to such discrimination.

Article 8

Everyone has the right to an effective remedy by the competent national tribunals for acts violating the fundamental rights granted him by the constitution or by law.

Article 9

No one shall be subjected to arbitrary arrest, detention or exile.

Article 10

Everyone is entitled in full equality to a fair and public hearing by an independent and impartial tribunal, in the determination of his rights and obligations and of any criminal charge against him.

Article 12

No one shall be subjected to arbitrary interference with his privacy, family, home or correspondence, nor to attacks upon his honor and reputation. Everyone has the right to the protection of the law against such interference or attacks.

Article 13

Everyone has the right to freedom of movement and residence within the borders of each state.

Everyone has the right to leave any country, including his own, and to return to his country.

Article 14

Everyone has the right to seek and to enjoy in other countries asylum from persecution.

This right may not be invoked in the case of prosecutions genuinely arising from non-political crimes or from acts contrary to the purposes and principles of the United Nations.

Article 15

Everyone has the right to a nationality.

No one shall be arbitrarily deprived of his nationality nor denied the right to change his nationality.

Article 18

Everyone has the right to freedom of thought, conscience and religion; this right includes freedom to change his religion or belief, and freedom, either alone or in community with others and in public or private, to manifest his religion or belief in teaching, practice, worship and observance.

Article 19

Everyone has the right to freedom of opinion and expression; this right includes freedom to hold opinions without interference and to seek, receive and impart information and ideas through any media and regardless of frontiers.

Article 20

Everyone has the right to freedom of peaceful assembly and association.

No one may be compelled to belong to an association.

Article 23

Everyone has the right to work, to free choice of employment, to just and favourable conditions of work and to protection against unemployment. Everyone, without any discrimination, has the right to equal pay for equal work.

Rome Statute of the International Criminal Court

Part 2 - Jurisdiction, admissibility and applicable law

Article 5: Crimes within the jurisdiction of the Court

1. The jurisdiction of the Court shall be limited to the most serious crimes of concern to the international community as a whole. The Court has jurisdiction in accordance with this Statute with respect to the following crimes:

(a) The crime of genocide;

(b) Crimes against humanity;

(c) War crimes;

(d) The crime of aggression.

.....

Article 6: Genocide

For the purpose of this Statute, "genocide" means any of the following acts committed with intent to destroy, in whole or in part, a national, ethnical, racial or religious group, as such:

(a) Killing members of the group;

(b) Causing serious bodily or mental harm to members of the group;

(c) Deliberately inflicting on the group conditions of life calculated to bring about its physical destruction in whole or in part;

.....

Article 7: Crimes against humanity

1. For the purpose of this Statute, "crime against humanity" means any of the following acts when committed as part of a widespread or systematic attack directed against any civilian population, with knowledge of the attack:

.....

(e) Imprisonment or other severe deprivation of physical liberty in violation of fundamental rules of international law;

(f) Torture;

.....

(h) Persecution against any identifiable group or collectivity on political, racial, national, ethnic, cultural, religious, gender … or other grounds that are universally recognized as impermissible under international law, in connection with any act referred to in this paragraph or any crime within the jurisdiction of the Court;

(i) Enforced disappearance of persons;

.....

(k) Other inhumane acts of a similar character intentionally causing great suffering, or serious injury to body or to mental or physical health.

2. For the purpose of paragraph 1:

.....

(e) "Torture" means the intentional infliction of severe pain or suffering, whether physical or mental, upon a person in the custody or under the control of the accused; except that torture shall not include pain or suffering arising only from, inherent in or incidental to, lawful sanctions;

.....

(g) "Persecution" means the intentional and severe deprivation of fundamental rights contrary to international law by reason of the identity of the group or collectivity;

.....

(i) "Enforced disappearance of persons" means the arrest, detention or abduction of persons by, or with the authorization, support or acquiescence of, a State or a political organization, followed by a refusal to acknowledge that deprivation of freedom or to give information on the fate or whereabouts of those persons, with the intention of removing them from the protection of the law for a prolonged period of time.

.....

Note: Türkiye's Relations with the International Criminal Court (ICC)

Even though Türkiye is not a state party to The Rome Statute, the activities of the ICC are closely followed and the annual meetings of the Assembly of States Parties, which take place in The Hague or New York, are attended by our officials. (Noted in Turkish Ministry of Foreign Affairs website: https://www.mfa.gov.tr/turkiye_s-relations-with-the-international-criminal-court-_icc)

Appendix B

Constitution and Laws of Türkiye

Constitution of the Republic of Türkiye

CHAPTER ONE
General Provisions

I. Nature of fundamental rights and freedoms
The fundamental rights and freedoms also comprise the duties and responsibilities of the individual to the society, his/her family, and other individuals....
II. Restriction of fundamental rights and freedoms
Article 13- (As amended on October 3, 2001; Act No. 4709)
Fundamental rights and freedoms may be restricted only by law and in conformity with the reasons mentioned in the relevant articles of the Constitution without infringing upon their essence. These restrictions shall not be contrary to the letter and spirit of the Constitution and the requirements of the democratic order of the society and the secular republic and the principle of proportionality.
III. Prohibition of abuse of fundamental rights and freedoms
Article 14- (As amended on October 3, 2001; Act No. 4709)
None of the rights and freedoms embodied in the Constitution shall be exercised in the form of activities aiming to violate the indivisible integrity of the State with its territory and nation, and to endanger the existence of the democratic and secular order of the Republic based on human rights.

No provision of this Constitution shall be interpreted in a manner that enables the State or individuals to destroy the fundamental rights and freedoms recognized by the Constitution or to stage an activity with the aim of restricting them more extensively than stated in the Constitution.

The sanctions to be applied against those who perpetrate activities contrary to these provisions shall be determined by law.

IV. Suspension of the exercise of fundamental rights and freedoms

Article 15- (As amended on April 16, 2017; Act No. 6771)

In times of war, mobilization, a state of emergency, the exercise of fundamental rights and freedoms may be partially or entirely suspended, or measures derogating the guarantees embodied in the Constitution may be taken to the extent required by the exigencies of the situation, as long as obligations under international law are not violated.

(As amended on May 7, 2004; Act No. 5170) Even under the circumstances indicated in the first paragraph, the individual's right to life, the integrity of his/her corporeal and spiritual existence shall be inviolable except where death occurs through acts in conformity with law of war; no one shall be compelled to reveal his/her religion, conscience, thought or opinion, nor be accused on account of them; offences and penalties shall not be made retroactive; nor shall anyone be held guilty until so proven by a court ruling.

PART ONE

General Principles

X. Equality before the law

Article 10-

Everyone is equal before the law without distinction as to language, race, colour, sex, political opinion, philosophical belief, religion, sect, and similar grounds.

PART TWO

Fundamental Rights and Duties

IV. Suspension of the exercise of fundamental rights and freedoms.

Article 15- (As amended on April 16, 2017; Act No. 6771, but not substantially changed)

In times of war, mobilization, a state of emergency, the exercise of fundamental rights and freedoms may be partially or entirely suspended, or measures derogating the guarantees embodied in the Constitution may be taken to the extent required by the exigencies of the situation, as long as obligations under international law are not violated.

Even under the circumstances indicated in the first paragraph, the individual's right to life, the integrity of his/her corporeal and spiritual existence shall be inviolable except where death occurs through acts in conformity with law of war; no one shall be compelled to reveal his/her religion, conscience, thought or opinion, nor be accused on account of them; offences and penalties shall not be made retroactive; nor shall anyone be held guilty until so proven by a court ruling.

CHAPTER TWO
Rights and Duties of the Individual

I. Personal inviolability, corporeal and spiritual existence of the individual

Article 17- Everyone has the right to life and the right to protect and improve his/her corporeal and spiritual existence.

The corporeal integrity of the individual shall not be violated except under medical necessity and in cases prescribed by law; and shall not be subjected to scientific or medical experiments without his/her consent. No one shall be subjected to torture or mal-treatment; no one shall be subjected to penalties or treatment incompatible with human dignity.

(As amended on May 7, 2004; Act No. 5170, April 16, 2017; Act No. 6771) The act of killing in case of self-defense and, when permitted by law as a compelling measure to use a weapon, during the execution of warrants of capture and arrest, the prevention of the escape of lawfully arrested or convicted persons, the quelling of riot or insurrection, or carrying out the orders of authorized bodies during state of emergency, do not fall within the scope of the provision of the first paragraph....

III. Personal liberty and security

Article 19 – Everyone has the right to personal liberty and security.
No one shall be deprived of his/her liberty except in the following cases where procedure and conditions are prescribed by law:

Execution of sentences restricting liberty and the implementation of security measures decided by courts; arrest or detention of an individual in line with a court ruling or an obligation upon him designated by law.... Individuals against whom there is strong evidence of having committed an offence may be arrested by decision of a judge solely for the purposes of preventing escape, or preventing the destruction or alteration of evidence, as well as in other circumstances prescribed by law and necessitating detention. Arrest of a person without a decision by a judge may be executed only when a person is caught in flagrante delicto or in cases where delay is likely to thwart the course of justice; the conditions for such acts shall be defined by law.

Individuals arrested or detained shall be promptly notified, in all cases in writing, or orally when the former is not possible, of the grounds for their arrest or detention and the charges against them; in cases of offences committed collectively this notification shall be made, at the latest, before the individual is brought before a judge.

(As amended on April 16, 2017; Act No. 6771) The person arrested or detained shall be brought before a judge within at latest forty-eight hours and in case of offences committed collectively within at most four days, excluding the time required to send the individual to the court nearest to the place of arrest. No one can be deprived of his/her liberty without the decision of a judge after the expiry of the above specified periods. These periods may be extended during a state of emergency or in time of war.

(As amended on October 3, 2001; Act No. 4709) The next of kin shall be notified immediately when a person has been arrested or detained.

Persons under detention shall have the right to request trial within a reasonable time and to be released during investigation or prosecution. Release may be conditioned by a guarantee as to ensure the presence of the person at the trial proceedings or the execution of the court sentence.

Persons whose liberties are restricted for any reason are entitled to apply to the competent judicial authority for speedy conclusion of proceedings regarding their situation and for their immediate release if the restriction imposed upon them is not lawful.

(As amended on October 3, 2001; Act No. 4709) Damage suffered by persons subjected to treatment other than these provisions shall be compensated by the State in accordance with the general principles of the compensation law.

IV. Privacy and protection of private life

A. Privacy of private life

Article 20- Everyone has the right to demand respect for his/her private and family life. Privacy of private or family life shall not be violated. (Sentence repealed on May 3, 2001; Act No. 4709)

Unless there exists a decision duly given by a judge on one or several of the grounds of national security, public order, prevention of crime, protection of public health and public morals, or protection of the rights and freedoms of others, or unless there exists a written order of an agency authorized by law, in cases where delay is prejudicial, again on the above-mentioned grounds, neither the person, nor the private papers, nor belongings of an individual shall be searched nor shall they be seized. The decision of the competent authority shall be submitted for the approval of the judge having jurisdiction within twenty-four hours. The judge shall announce his decision within forty-eight hours from the time of seizure; otherwise, seizure shall automatically be lifted. (As amended on October 3, 2001; Act No. 4709)

Everyone has the right to request the protection of his/her personal data. This right includes being informed of, having access to and requesting the correction and deletion of his/ her personal data, and to be informed whether these are used in consistency with envisaged objectives. Personal data can be processed only in cases envisaged by law or by the person's explicit consent. The principles and procedures regarding the protection of personal data shall be laid down in law. (Paragraph added on September 12, 2010; Act No. 5982)

VII. Freedom of thought and opinion

Article 25- Everyone has the freedom of thought and opinion. No one shall be compelled to reveal his/her thoughts and opinions for any reason or purpose; nor shall anyone be blamed or accused because of his/ her thoughts and opinions.

VIII. Freedom of expression and dissemination of thought

Article 26- Everyone has the right to express and disseminate his/her thoughts and opinions by speech, in writing or in pictures or through other media, individually or collectively. This freedom includes the liberty of receiving or imparting information or ideas without interference by official authorities. This provision shall not preclude subjecting transmission by radio, television, cinema, or similar means to a system of licensing.

(As amended on October 3, 2001; Act No. 4709) The exercise of these freedoms may be restricted for the purposes of national security, public order, public safety, safeguarding the basic characteristics of the Republic and the indivisible integrity of the State with its territory and nation, preventing crime, punishing offenders, withholding information duly classified as a state secret, protecting the reputation or rights and private and family life of others, or protecting professional secrets as prescribed by law, or ensuring the proper functioning of the judiciary....

XI. Rights and freedoms of assembly

Freedom of association

Article 33- Everyone has the right to form associations, or become a member of an association, or withdraw from membership without prior permission.

No one shall be compelled to become or remain a member of an association.

Freedom of association may be restricted only by law on the grounds of national security, public order, prevention of commission of crime, public morals, public health and protecting the freedoms of other individuals.

The formalities, conditions, and procedures to be applied in the exercise of freedom of association shall be prescribed by law. Associations may be dissolved or suspended from activity by the decision of a judge in cases prescribed by law. However, where it is required for, and a delay constitutes a prejudice to, national security, public order, prevention of commission or continuation of a crime, or an arrest, an authority may be vested with power by law to suspend the association from activity. The decision of this authority shall be submitted for the approval of the judge having jurisdiction within twenty-four hours. The judge shall announce his/her decision within forty-eight hours; otherwise, this administrative decision shall be annulled automatically.

Provisions of the first paragraph shall not prevent imposition of restrictions on the rights of armed forces and security forces officials and civil servants to the extent that the duties of civil servants so require.

The provisions of this article shall also apply to foundations. (As amended on October 3, 2001; Act No. 4709)

A. Right to hold meetings and demonstration marches

Article 34- Everyone has the right to hold unarmed and peaceful meetings and demonstration marches without prior permission.

The right to hold meetings and demonstration marches shall be restricted only by law on the grounds of national security, public order, prevention of commission of crime, protection of public health and public morals or the rights and freedoms of others.

The formalities, conditions, and procedures to be applied in the exercise of the right to hold meetings and demonstration marches shall be prescribed by law. (As amended on October 3, 2001; Act No. 4709)

XIII. Provisions on the protection of rights

A. Freedom to claim rights

Article 36- Everyone has the right of litigation either as plaintiff or defendant and the right to a fair trial before the courts through legitimate means and procedures.

No court shall refuse to hear a case within its jurisdiction. (As amended on October 3, 2001; Act No. 4709).

A. Principle of natural judge

Article 37- No one may be tried by any judicial authority other than the legally designated court.

Extraordinary tribunals with jurisdiction that would in effect remove a person from the jurisdiction of his legally designated court shall not be established.

B. Principles relating to offences and penalties

Article 38- No one shall be punished for any act which does not constitute a criminal offence under the law in force at the time committed; no one shall be given a heavier penalty for an offence other than the penalty applicable at the time when the offence was committed.

The provisions of the above paragraph shall also apply to the statute of limitations on offences and penalties and on the results of conviction.

Penalties, and security measures in lieu of penalties, shall be prescribed only by law.

No one shall be considered guilty until proven guilty in a court of law. No one shall be compelled to make a statement that would incriminate himself/herself or his/her legal next of kin, or to present such incriminating evidence.

Findings obtained through illegal methods shall not be considered evidence. (Paragraph added on October 3, 2001; Act No. 4709)

Criminal responsibility shall be personal.

No one shall be deprived of his/her liberty merely on the ground of inability to fulfil a contractual obligation. (Paragraph added on October 3, 2001; Act No. 4709, and repealed on May 7, 2004; Act No. 5170)

Neither death penalty nor general confiscation shall be imposed as punishment. (As amended on May 7, 2004; Act No. 5170)

The administration shall not impose any sanction resulting in restriction of personal liberty. Exceptions to this provision may be introduced by law regarding the internal order of the armed forces.

No citizen shall be extradited to a foreign country because of an offence, except under obligations resulting from being a party to the International Criminal Court. (As amended on May 7, 2004; Act No. 5170).

Penal Code of Türkiye

SECOND VOLUME

Special Provisions

FIRST CHAPTER

International Offences

FIRST SECTION

Genocide and Offenses against Humanity

Genocide

Article 76

(1) Execution of any one of the following acts under a plan against members of national, racial or religious groups with the intention of destroying the complete or part of the group, creates the legal consequence of an offence defined as genocide.

a) Voluntary manslaughter

b) To act with the intension of giving severe corporal or spiritual injury,

c) To impose conditions that make survival of complete or part of the group members impossible,

d) To impose that prevent births in the group,

e) To transfer minors of a group to another group,

(2) A person who commits the offense of genocide is sentenced to heavy imprisonment.

(3) The court may adjudicate imposition of security precautions upon the legal entities due to such offenses,

(4) These offenses are not subject to statute of limitation

Offences Against Humanity

Article 77

(1) The systematic performance an act, described below, against a part of society and in accordance with a plan with a political, philosophical, racial or religious motive shall constitute a crime against humanity:

a) Intentional killing;

b) Intentional injury;

c) Torture or inhuman treatment or slavery;

d) Depriving one from his/her liberty;

e) The subjecting of persons to biological experiments;

f) Sexual assault; sexual abuse of children;

g) Impregnation by force;

h) Forced prostitution.

(2) Where the act described in paragraph one subparagraph (a) is committed the offender shall be sentenced to a penalty of aggravated life imprisonment. Where an act described in any other paragraph is committed then a penalty of imprisonment for a term of not less than eight years shall be imposed. However, for the acts of intentional killing and intentional injury defined in paragraph one, subparagraph (a) and (b) respectively there shall be an actual aggregation of the offences, in accordance with the number of victims identified.

(3) Legal entities shall be subject to security measures in respect of these offences.

(4) There shall be no limitation period in respect of these offences.

Offences Against Liberty

Hatred and Discrimination[1]

Article 122

(1) Any person who

(a) Prevents the sale, transfer or rental of a movable or immovable property offered to the public,

(b) Prevents a person from enjoying services offered to the public,

(c) Prevents a person from being recruited for a job,

(d) Prevents a person from undertaking an ordinary economic activity on the ground of hatred based on differences of language, race, nationality, colour, gender, disability, political view, philosophical belief, religion or sect shall be sentenced to a penalty of imprisonment for a term of one year to three years. (Amended on 2 March 2014 – By Article 15 of the Law no. 6529)

----

[1] By Article 15 of Law No. 6529, dated 2 March 2014, the title of "Discrimination" was amended as "Hatred and Discrimination."

Appendix C

State of Emergency Provisions: Türkiye Constitution

The Turkish government declared a state of emergency on 20 July 2016 under Article 120 of the Constitution, which at the time provided:

> In the event of the emergence of serious indications of widespread acts of violence aimed at the destruction of the free democratic order established by the Constitution or of fundamental rights and freedoms, or serious deterioration of public order because of acts of violence, the Council of Ministers, meeting under the chairmanship of the President of the Republic, after consultation with the National Security Council, may declare a state of emergency in one or more regions or throughout the country for a period not exceeding six months.

Article 121 of the Constitution sets out the rules governing a state of emergency:

> In the event of a declaration of a state of emergency under the provisions of Articles 119 and 120 of the Constitution this decision … shall be submitted immediately to the Turkish Grand National Assembly [parliament] for approval…. The Assembly may alter the duration of the state of emergency, extend the period for a maximum of four months each time at the request of the Council of Ministers, or may lift the state of emergency.
>
> The financial, material, and labour obligations which are to be imposed on citizens in the event of the declaration of state of emergency

> under Article 119, and, applicable according to the nature of each kind of state of emergency, the procedures as to how fundamental rights and freedoms shall be restricted or suspended in line with the principles of Article 15, how and by what means the measures necessitated by the situation shall be taken, what sort of powers shall be conferred on public servants, what kind of changes shall be made in the status of officials, and the procedure governing emergency rule shall be regulated by the Law on State of Emergency.
>
> During the state of emergency, the Council of Ministers, meeting under the chairmanship of the President of the Republic, may issue decrees having force of law on matters necessitated by the state of emergency. These decrees shall be … submitted to the … Assembly on the same day for approval; the time limit and procedure for their approval by the Assembly shall be indicated in the Rules of Procedure.

Türkiye is a signatory party to the European Convention of Human Rights and the International Covenant on Civil and Political Rights, and thus has obligations thereunder.

A constitutional referendum on 16 April 2017, among other things, adopted amended Constitution Article 119, replacing Articles 120 and 121, that greatly strengthened the president's hand to issue state of emergency decrees without approval of the cabinet.

Turkish Constitution III. Administration of State of Emergency

Article 119- (As amended on April 16, 2017; Act No. 6771)

> In the event of war, the emergence of a situation necessitating war, mobilization, an uprising, strong rebellious actions against the motherland and the Republic, widespread acts of violence of internal or external origin threatening the indivisibility of the country and the nation, emergence of widespread acts of violence aimed at the destruction of the Constitutional order or of fundamental rights and freedoms, serious deterioration of public order because of acts of violence, occurrence of natural disasters, outbreak of dangerous epidemic diseases or emergence of a serious economic crisis; the Pre-

sident of the Republic may declare state of emergency in one region or nationwide for a period not exceeding six months.

The decision to declare state of emergency shall be ... submitted for approval to the ... Assembly of Türkiye on the same day.... The Assembly may reduce or extend the period of, or lift, the state of emergency.

[The Assembly] may extend the period for a maximum of four months each time at the request of the President of the Republic...

The financial, material and labour obligations to be imposed on citizens, the manner of restriction and temporary suspension of fundamental rights and freedoms in line with the principles of the Article 15, and the provisions to be applied and actions to be carried out in the event of state of emergency shall be regulated by law. In the event of state of emergency, the President of the Republic may issue presidential decrees on matters necessitated by the state of emergency, notwithstanding the limitations set forth in the second sentence of the seventeenth paragraph of the Article 104 [which provides "The fundamental rights, individual rights and duties included in the first and second chapters and the political rights and duties listed in the fourth chapter of the second part of the Constitution shall not be regulated by a presidential decree]. Such decrees which have the force of law ... and shall be submitted for approval to the [Assembly] on the same day.

... [P]residential decrees issued during the state of emergency shall be debated and decided in the [Assembly] within three months. Otherwise, presidential decrees issued during the state of emergency shall be annulled automatically.

Appendix D

Various United Nations Resolutions and Reports Concerning Türkiye

Human Rights Council, Working Group on Arbitrary Detention, Opinions

(in chronological order)
Cihangir Çenteli, A/HRC/WGAD/2023/66;
Ali Ünal, A/HRC/WGAD/2023/3;
Muhammet Şentürk, A/HRC/WGAD/2023/29;
Alettin Duman, Tamer Tibik, A/HRC/WGAD/2022/8 ;
Osman Karaca, A/HRC/WGAD/2020/84;
Ahmet Dinçer Sakaoğlu, A/HRC/WGAD/2020/67;
Levent Kart, A/HRC/WGAD/2020/66;
Nermin Yasar, A/HRC/WGAD/2020/74;
Arif Komiş, Ülkü Komiş and four minors, A/HRC/WGAD/2020/51;
Kahraman Demirez, Mustafa Erdem, Hasan Hüseyin Günakan, Yusuf Karabina, Osman Karakaya and Cihan Özkan, A/HRC/WGAD/2020/47;
Faruk Serdar Köse, A/HRC/WGAD/2020/30;
Akif Oruc, A/HRC/WGAD/2020/29;
Abdulmatip Kurt, A/HRC/WGAD/2020/2;
Ercan Demir, A/HRC/WGAD/2019/79;
Melike Göksan, Mehmet Fatih Göksan, A/HRC/WGAD/2019/53;
Mustafa Ceyhan, A/HRC/WGAD/2019/10;
Hamza Yaman, A/HRC/WGAD/2018/78;
Muharrem Gençtürk, A/HRC/WGAD/2018/44;

Ahmet Caliskan, A/HRC/WGAD/2018/43;
Mestan Yayman, A/HRC/WGAD/2018/42;
Mesut Kaçmaz, Meral Kaçmaz and two minors, A/HRC/WGAD/2018/11;
10 individuals associated with the newspaper *Cumhuriyet*, A/HRC/WGAD/2017/41;
Kursat Çevik, A/HRC/WGAD/2017/38; and,
Rebii Metin Görgeç, A/HRC/WGAD/2017/1.

Committee against Torture, Concluding Observations
Convention against Torture and Other Cruel, Inhuman or Degrading Treatment or Punishment, CAT/C/TUR/CO/5 (14 Aug. 2024)

Human Rights Committee
International Covenant on Civil and Political Rights, Concluding Observations CCPR/C/TUR/CO/2 (28 Nov. 2024)
Case of Mukadder Alakuş Right to life; torture and ill-treatment; arbitrary arrest and detention; conditions of detention; right to a fair trial) (CCPR 3736/2020) (1 March 2023) and
Case of Mümüne Açikkollu (Right to life; torture and ill-treatment; arbitrary arrest and detention; right to a fair trial) (CCPR/C/136/D/3730/2020) (20 Feb. 2023)

Committee on the Elimination of Discrimination against Women, Concluding Observations
Convention on the Elimination of All Forms of Discrimination against Women CEDAW/C/TUR/CO/8 (12 July 2022)

Committee on the Rights of the Child, Concluding Observations
Convention on the Rights of the Child, CRC/C/TUR/CO/4-5 (21 June 2023)

Appendix E

Comparison Scale of Erdoğan's Actions Between Türkiye and United States

"The Scale of Türkiye's Purge Is Nearly Unprecedented"
By Josh Keller, Iaryna Mykhyalyshyn, and Safak Timur
New York Times (Aug. 2, 2016)

Only rarely in modern history has a leader detained and fired as many perceived adversaries as President Recep Tayyip Erdoğan of Turkey has since a failed coup attempt last month. Here is how Mr. Erdoğan's vast purge would look if Americans were targeted at a similar scale.

ALMOST 9,000 POLICE OFFICERS FIRED

Equivalent to firing every police officer in Philadelphia, Dallas, Detroit, Boston, and Baltimore.

The Interior Ministry fired the police officers, some of whom government officials said had supported the coup attempt. Turkish officials have acknowledged that the number of people targeted in the purge is probably much greater than the number of conspirators.

21,000 PRIVATE SCHOOL TEACHERS SUSPENDED

Like revoking the licenses of every third teacher in private elementary and high schools across the United States.

In addition to the teachers suspended, the government intends to close more than 1,000 private schools it linked to Fethullah Gülen, a cleric who the government said was the mastermind of the coup attempt. (Mr. Gülen has denied this.). Education officials said they planned to convert the schools into public schools and hire 40,000 new teachers.

10,012 SOLDIERS DETAINED

Equivalent to taking nearly every fourth officer in the U.S. Army into custody.

The military, which has long been a unifying force for the country, is now deeply divided, diminished and discredited. A rebel faction of the military initiated the coup attempt. Since then, nearly half of the top generals and admirals have been jailed or dismissed and more than 5,000 army officials have been sent to pretrial detention.

2,745 MEMBERS OF THE JUDICIARY SUSPENDED

Like suspending every state judge in California, Texas, New York, and Georgia.

The future has been uncertain for the judges and judicial staff members suspected of being followers of Mr. Gülen — including two members of Türkiye's highest court — since a board of judges and prosecutors suspended them a day after the coup attempt. Government officials said they intended to hire 5,000 new judges and prosecutors by the end of August. Mr. Erdoğan also announced a three-month state of emergency that enables his ministers to pass decrees that have the force of law with the approval of Parliament.

21,700 MINISTRY OF EDUCATION OFFICIALS FIRED

Equivalent to firing nearly every third employee of the U.S. Department of Education.

The officials terminated from the Education Ministry had responsibilities that included appointing teachers and preparing curriculum. The evidence against them is unclear. Ministry officials said the school year would begin in September as planned, but a variety of exams, including distance learning and public officer exams, have already been delayed.

1,500 UNIVERSITY DEANS FORCED TO RESIGN

Like forcing all American university deans to resign.

Every university dean in Türkiye was forced to resign without an explanation of who would replace them or whether they would be allowed to reapply for their jobs. "Who is going to run the universities? They will open in six or seven weeks," Steven A. Cook, a Türkiye expert at the Council on Foreign Relations, said in the week after the coup attempt. Some academics who signed a petition this year protesting the government's war against Kurdish militants were also suspended from their jobs.

MORE THAN 100 MEDIA OUTLETS SHUT DOWN

Equivalent to issuing arrest warrants for conservative journalists, closing television and radio stations and censoring dozens of news-related websites.

More than 100 broadcast, newspaper, magazine and other media companies have been shut down, and at least 28 journalists and media workers were detained, according to the Committee to Protect Journalists. Many of them were pro-Hizmet. "The scale of this rout of the media is staggering," Nina Ognianova, the committee's Europe and Central Asia Program coordinator, said in a statement. Türkiye has long been criticized for its press restrictions. In the past, critical journalists have faced legal investigations and, in some cases, long prison sentences.

MORE THAN 1,500 MINISTRY OF FINANCE OFFICIALS SUSPENDED

Like suspending nearly everybody at the U.S. Treasury who regulates banks and designs and prints money.

The government suspended more than 1,500 finance officials within the first two days after the attempted coup. Prime Minister Binali Yıldırım said the episode would not have a major effect on the country's economy. "We have such a strong economy that we overcome this coup with small scratches," Mr. Yıldırım said.

Sources: World Bank (U.S. and Turkish Armies), Eurostat (Türkiye's police and judges), Bureau of Justice Statistics (U.S. police), Federal Judicial Center (U.S. judges), U.S. Department of Education, U.S. Department of the Treasury, National Center for Education Statistics, Turkish Ministry of National Education, Turkish Ministry of Finance. http://www.nytimes.com/interactive/2016/08/02/world/europe/turkey-purge-Erdoğan-scale.html.

INDEX

D

E

F

G

N

O

P

R

S

T

U

V

W

X

Y

Z